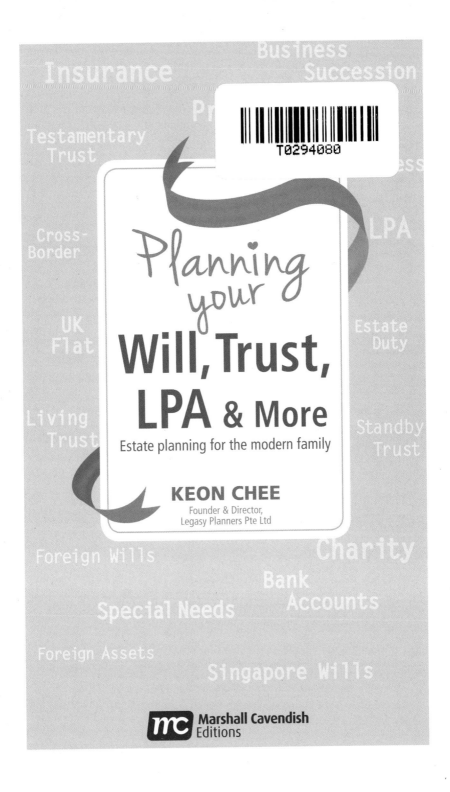

Reprinted 2021

Published by Marshall Cavendish Editions
An imprint of Marshall Cavendish International

A member of the
Times Publishing Group

Other Marshall Cavendish Offices:
Marshall Cavendish Corporation, 800 Westchester Ave, Suite N-641, Rye Brook,
NY 10573, USA • Marshall Cavendish International (Thailand) Co Ltd, 253 Asoke,
16th Floor, Sukhumvit 21 Road, Klongtoey Nua, Wattana, Bangkok 10110, Thailand •
Marshall Cavendish (Malaysia) Sdn Bhd, Times Subang, Lot 46, Subang Hi-Tech
Industrial Park, Batu Tiga, 40000 Shah Alam, Selangor Darul Ehsan, Malaysia

Marshall Cavendish is a registered trademark of Times Publishing Limited

National Library Board, Singapore Cataloguing-in-Publication Data

Names: Chee, Keon.
Title: Planning your will, trust, LPA & more : estate planning for the modern
    family / Keon Chee.
Description: Singapore : Marshall Cavendish Editions, [2020]
Identifiers: OCN 1190521517 | ISBN 978-981-47-9459-6 (paperback)
Subjects: LCSH: Estate planning--Singapore. | Finance, Personal--Singapore.
Classification: DDC 332.024016--dc23

Printed in Singapore

Source of maps on pages 240 (Malaysia), 246 (Indonesia), 254 (Thailand), 262 (The
Philippines), 275 (Vietnam), 282 (China), 290 (Australia), 299 (UK) and 306 (US):
The World Factbook 2020. Washington, DC: Central Intelligence Agency, 2020.

To my mother –
my dearest friend and hero

CONTENTS

Preface

With one instruction in a Will, a person can impact his family for decades. Such is the power of estate planning – it can either set children up to lead happy and successful lives or, with poor planning, cause close-knit families to fight and fritter away their wealth.

These days, people often give to others beyond their immediate family. A person who makes a gift to charity leaves a legacy of kindness to the community as well as to his family. Estate planning at its core spreads benevolence all around. A family's estate planner holds a position of privilege and shoulders hefty responsibility.

Estate planning can, however, be a very complex subject, full of technical language and unending flexibility. I find myself constantly simplifying and using analogies to convey my points to the persons I am planning for and to the students who attend my classes.

For example, I would explain to a mother of two young children that a Trust is like a protected piggy bank: someone called the trustee will look after her monies when she passes away, and will make payments to her children over a period of time. Of course, I would have the technical definitions at the back of my mind to substantiate my insights and to clarify the finer details.

Albert Einstein said, "If you can't explain it to a six-year-old, you don't understand it yourself." I live very closely by this quote.

WHY I WROTE THIS BOOK

To write about estate planning in simple language is one of the main reasons I embarked on this book project. I want to provide a simple explanation of how things work in this area while being authoritative in the accuracy of what is being written. I believe that if I am able to make things simple to understand, readers would be more likely to take action on their estate plans, and that would be the most desired outcome.

To help me in the latter objective of being authoritative, I brought together nearly 30 practitioners from a dozen countries to contribute by adding depth and breadth to the information relating to their respective countries and specialist area. Each of them was told to provide the reader with planning insights and if advice or more information is needed, the reader could contact them directly. I am immensely grateful for their tremendous contributions, expertise and friendship. Their brief profiles are found at the back of the book.

Second, people don't naturally wake up in the morning and proclaim, "What a great day it is to plan for my future death!" In order to encourage families to take action sooner rather than later, I invited several of my accomplished financial adviser friends to share their experiences on how to "close the deal". Closing the deal means the transfer of benefits. Not closing the deal means yet another day or week would pass without an estate plan in place for the individual in question.

Third, I want very much to dispel the common belief that Trusts are expensive and complicated, and only for the wealthy. The fact is that anyone who has young children or elderly parents would need a Trust to stagger the distribution of monies over time. A Will that makes immediate payments only could be a defective plan for many families. For example, a lump sum gift of several million dollars to a young beneficiary could rob the initiative out of him to lead a productive life. Trusts can, of course, be more costly and complex given a family's unique situation, but there are basic Trusts that can be set up affordably and quite simply to meet the needs of many families.

MODERN ESTATE PLANNING

Do any of the following qualities describe you?

- You have a long life – you may run out of retirement funds and could lose mental capacity one day due to old age.

- You are wealthy – or if you are not, you have the ability to create wealth with insurance and investments.
- You love to travel and you may not be born in Singapore – you own foreign properties and bank accounts. Or your spouse could be a foreigner – one in every three marriages in Singapore is between a Singapore citizen and a foreigner.
- You may be divorced – you are also concerned about the possible divorce of your children.
- You may have married into a blended family, where there are children from other marriages and relationships.
- You are likely to start or own a business, or be self-employed.
- You want to leave something to charity.

Modern estate planning requires a broad knowledge of many areas for the modern Singaporean. I started to acquire this broad knowledge five years ago.

Where I didn't know enough of an area, such as divorce or estate administration, I would take a course or volunteer to co-teach with an experienced practitioner. Where expertise was not readily available in Singapore, I would take an overseas trip to meet foreign lawyers and practitioners in order to learn about how estate planning is done in their countries.

I am not an expert in estate planning or in any particular area of estate planning. I started as a Trust practitioner nine years ago, and today I work as a Trust and Estate Planning Consultant at Kensington Trust Singapore Limited. I can easily count at least a hundred people in Singapore who have more experience and knowledge in Trusts and estate planning than I do. My strength, however, lies in being able to simplify and teach estate planning in a way that can be easily understood.

We live in a world where the road has many forks and can take us on many amazing journeys. It is often difficult to know the final destination of these journeys. In estate planning, I believe I have found what is not only the final destination, but the final journey. This book is a major milestone in that journey.

ACKNOWLEDGEMENTS

I wish to acknowledge several people who have helped me along the way.

To Lee Chiwi, CEO of Precepts Trustee (previously known as Rockwills Trustee), who hired me in September 2011 and threw me into the fire by getting me to teach Trustee Duties in a STEP Certificate class the following April. I am immensely grateful for the opportunities to learn under his charge.

To Guy Burnett, my UK and New Zealand lawyer friend who encouraged me to study law and who frequently explained key legal concepts to me (which often took time to sink in). It took me six years but I finally graduated at the age of 53.

To Ernest Wong, who has encouraged and advised me from the very start of my entrepreneurial journey. Ernest is a rare gentleman who has intellect, humour and good old naughtiness.

To the website SingaporeLegalAdvice.com, founded by Chan Yuk Lun, which has a trove of articles that give simple and authoritative explanations of the laws in Singapore. Their articles have been invaluable in helping me and many others to understand the different aspects of the law.

To America, the land of opportunity, where I excelled in school for the first time in my life after failing the A Levels three times in Singapore. I arrived in Illinois in 1981 and graduated from an Ivy League university 13 years later.

And to my parents, the best parents in the world, to whom I owe everything.

Introduction

This is a take-action book to get your estate planning done.

Each chapter contains insights from experienced practitioners who are sharing their expertise on "this is how it's done."

If you read this book and do not take action, then I would have failed in my mission. Take action – whether it is to create an estate plan or to review a plan that you have already done.

This book is divided into four parts and contains 37 chapters. To benefit from this book, I would suggest that you:

- read the six chapters in Part 1 – there are six essential documents that every person should consider in their estate plan and the information in this part is crucial;
- after reading Part 1, you may cherry pick your way through the rest of the book – if you want to know more about Trusts, go through chapters 7, 8 and 9; if you want to know about Christian and Muslim estate planning, read chapters 17 and 18; if you run a private business, Part 3 would be relevant to you, and if you own foreign assets or are a foreigner in Singapore, Part 4 would be useful.

Here are a few important points about the book:
- Simple language is used. Technical and legal terms are minimised. Legislation has been moved to the footnotes as much as possible.
- Unless indicated otherwise, the reference to "he" includes "she", "him" includes "her" and so on, as we find the use of "he/she" and "him/her" awkward.
- Many acronyms are not explained because one can easily Google the terms to find out what they mean and it would a long-drawn process to explain every acronym when most of them are commonly known. CPF, COVID-19 and MOM

are in common use, while ChFC and LLB can be easily
Googled.

While great effort has been made to provide the most up-to-
date and accurate content, there will invariably be errors, and
if you spot any, please write to us at info@legasyplanners.com.
We will be compiling corrections and other notices at www.
legasyplanners.com/epbook. If you have suggestions, questions or
compliments, we would love to hear from you, too.

Thank you for choosing this book and I hope you enjoy it.

Part 1

The Six Essential Estate Planning Documents

It used to be that a Will was all you needed. Listing your assets, naming the beneficiaries who would receive your assets, and that was about it.

Not anymore. Our increased wealth means that most of us, when we pass away, will have hundreds of thousands or even millions of dollars in our estates. If you have young children or elderly parents, you would need to consider a Trust to stagger payments to them rather than giving them their entire gifts immediately.

The Lasting Power of Attorney (LPA) is an essential document that is activated if we lose mental capacity. Our increased longevity means that we have a higher chance of losing our mental capacity in our later years.

The Will, Trust and LPA together are what constitutes must-have documents for most of us.

The Advanced Medical Directive (AMD) and advanced care plan (ACP) are normally thought of as later-life planning documents. However, you are never too young to set them up and you will want to learn about how they relate to your Will, Trust and LPA.

The sixth essential document is the Grant of Probate. The Grant is a court document that is applied for on a person's death to validate the Will and to legally appoint the person (personal representative) who can call in the assets and make distributions to the beneficiaries. The document itself is not our focus because obtaining the Grant is rather procedural. Instead, we will focus on the planning steps we need to take today to give our families as few problems as possible when we pass away.

Once you have considered these essential documents, we will look at special situations that require more detailed planning. These special situations can revolve around the family, business owners and the ownership of assets in a foreign country. We cover these special situations in Parts 2, 3 and 4.

Chapter 1

Will

by **Keon Chee**
with **Patrick Chang & Samuel Tan**

*"Everybody wants to go to heaven,
but nobody wants to die."*
– Unknown

You have one week to live. Would you write your Will if you have not done so? The answer with little exception is yes.

Don't be one of the 80% of working adults in Singapore who have not written a Will. You may have lots of reasons for not having a Will, including:

- I don't want to think about death.
- I'm not rich.
- I cannot afford a Will.
- I don't have time now.

You may think of other reasons but none of them would really be valid for putting off setting up one of the most important documents in your life.

DO I NEED A WILL?

Every adult needs a Will, if for no other reason than to officially close up your affairs and to make sure that whatever assets you have will go where you want them to go.

Despite the importance of writing a Will, most people pass away without one, like in the case of Mr Tan.

Mr Tan felt he was "too poor" to write a Will

Mr Tan passed away without a Will. He was a widower and lived in his solely owned HDB flat with Mary, his only daughter. Mary, aged 30 and single, contributed to the monthly mortgage and expected to inherit the home. When Mr Tan passed away, his three children, including Mary, became entitled to a one-third share each of the flat. Mary wanted to keep the flat for herself while her two brothers wanted the flat sold for cash. The children fought amongst themselves over this matter. With a Will, Mr Tan could have made his wishes clear and helped to avoid such a dispute.

WHAT IS A WILL?

A Will is a legal document that sets out your wishes for the distribution of your assets after your death. Being a legal document, it means that the instructions are enforceable in a court of law.

You need a Will for the following:

- To have your property distributed according to your wishes after your death (these are your *Gifts*).
- To specify who should receive your assets after your death (these are your *Beneficiaries*).
- To specify who should carry out the terms of your Will (this is your *Executor*).
- To name someone to care for minor children if both parents pass away (this is the *Guardian*).

Here is what a Will looks like. The paragraphs below are numbered for easier reference. Note that this simplified example is *not* a legally binding Will.

1. Introduction

The first paragraph identifies who is writing the Will. He is

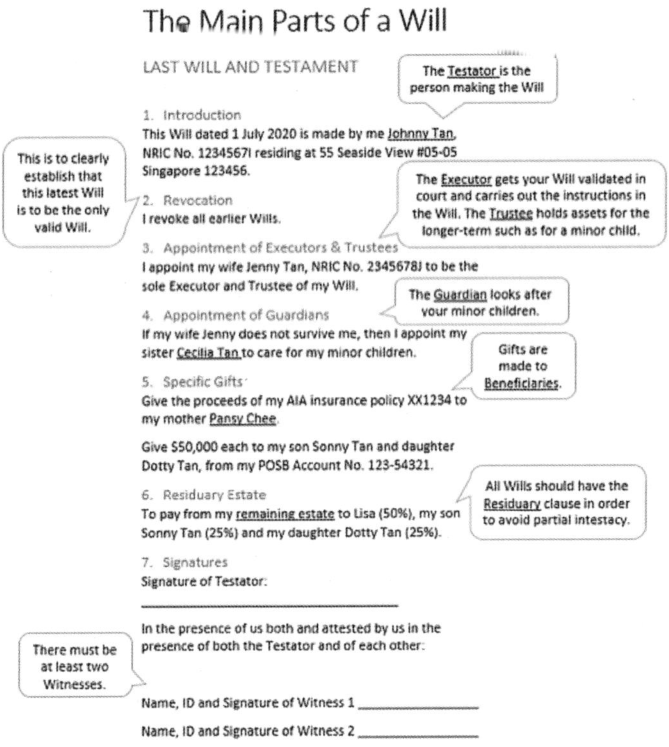

The Main Parts of a Will

LAST WILL AND TESTAMENT

> The Testator is the person making the Will

1. Introduction
This Will dated 1 July 2020 is made by me Johnny Tan, NRIC No. 1234567I residing at 55 Seaside View #05-05 Singapore 123456.

> This is to clearly establish that this latest Will is to be the only valid Will.

2. Revocation
I revoke all earlier Wills.

> The Executor gets your Will validated in court and carries out the instructions in the Will. The Trustee holds assets for the longer-term such as for a minor child.

3. Appointment of Executors & Trustees
I appoint my wife Jenny Tan, NRIC No. 2345678J to be the sole Executor and Trustee of my Will.

> The Guardian looks after your minor children.

4. Appointment of Guardians
If my wife Jenny does not survive me, then I appoint my sister Cecilia Tan to care for my minor children.

> Gifts are made to Beneficiaries.

5. Specific Gifts
Give the proceeds of my AIA insurance policy XX1234 to my mother Pansy Chee.

Give $50,000 each to my son Sonny Tan and daughter Dotty Tan, from my POSB Account No. 123-54321.

6. Residuary Estate
To pay from my remaining estate to Lisa (50%), my son Sonny Tan (25%) and my daughter Dotty Tan (25%).

> All Wills should have the Residuary clause in order to avoid partial intestacy.

7. Signatures
Signature of Testator:
_____

In the presence of us both and attested by us in the presence of both the Testator and of each other:

> There must be at least two Witnesses.

Name, ID and Signature of Witness 1 _____

Name, ID and Signature of Witness 2 _____

Figure 1.1 – The Main Parts of a Will

called the testator. The testator's NRIC or passport number is normally used to identify the person. His address is another piece of information confirming the identity of the testator.

2. Revocation
The revocation clause revokes Wills that the testator may have made in the past. Revoking your earlier Wills helps to ensure that the earlier Wills no longer have any legal effect.

Even if you have never made a Will before, you should include this clause as it helps to remove any doubt that this is your latest Will.

3. Appointment of executors and trustees

The executor is responsible for carrying out the wishes of the deceased as spelt out in his Will. The tasks that the executor performs include making funeral arrangements, locating the assets of the deceased, paying debts owed by the deceased, and distributing the assets to the beneficiaries under the Will.

With that kind of responsibility, it's a good idea to pick someone you can trust, who is organised and who is able to deal with the stress of the job.

Immediate gifts such as "Give $100,000 to Ivy," are handled by the executor. When there is a delayed gift such as "Give $10,000 a year to Halley for ten years," the executor passes $100,000 to someone called the trustee for safekeeping. (Note: The executor and trustee can be the same person.) The trustee holds the $100,000 for ten years and distributes $10,000 to Halley once a year.

Such an instruction creates a Trust for the benefit of Halley. We will look at Trusts in detail in chapters 2, 7, 8 and 9.

4. Appointment of guardians

The biological parents are the legal guardians of minor children below age 21. If one of them passes on, the surviving biological parent becomes the sole guardian of the minor child. The guardian provides care and concern whereas the trustee safeguards the assets.

If both parents pass on, another guardian (called the testamentary guardian) can be appointed in the Will. It is suggested that the parents appoint the same person. Sometimes, however, the parents may want to appoint different people. For example, the father wants to appoint his brother while the mother wants to appoint her sister. When this happens, both separately named guardians can act jointly in the future.

5. Specific gifts

Beneficiaries are the people who will receive your assets.

When making a specific gift, the asset must be accurately described. For example, "I give the cash in my OCBC savings account number X1234Y to my son."

6. Residuary Estate

Your residuary estate is what remains after specific gifts have been made, and debts and taxes have been paid. You can specify a percentage of your net estate to be given to your beneficiaries. For example, Johnny wishes to give his residuary estate to Lisa (50%), Sonny (25%) and Dotty (25%).

7. Signatures

The testator must be at least 21 years old. The testator must sign the Will at the foot of the document. The testator's signature must be witnessed by two or more witnesses, who must sign the Will in his presence.

The witnesses do not need to know the contents of the Will. The witnesses must know that the document is intended to be that person's Will. Beneficiaries of the Will, or spouses of beneficiaries, should not witness the Will; otherwise the gifts to them become void, although the Will would still be valid.

CONCLUSION

Writing a Will is not expensive or complicated. It is a powerful document because it contains your wishes on what happens to your property after your death and how your family would be looked after.

FREQUENTLY ASKED QUESTIONS
1. What if I pass away without a Will?

If you pass away without a Will, your assets will be distributed according to the default law called the Intestate Succession Act. According to the Act:

Table 1.1 – Passing Away without a Will[1]

SURVIVOR	ABSENT	WHO GETS WHAT
Spouse	Children, parents	Spouse gets everything
Spouse, children		Spouse gets half, children gets the other half in equal portions
Children	Spouse	Children get everything in equal portions. Grandchildren can claim their parent's share in equal portions if their parent is dead.
Spouse, parents	Children	Spouse gets half, parents get half in equal portions.
Parents	Spouse, children	Parents get everything in equal portions.
Brothers and sisters (or children of the deceased brother or sister)	Spouse, children, parents	Brothers and sisters get equal portions. Their children can claim their share for them in equal portions if they are deceased.
Grandparents	Spouse, children, parents, brothers and sisters or children of such brothers and sisters	Grandparents take the estate in equal portions.
Uncles and aunts	Spouse, children, parents, brothers and sisters or children of such brothers and sisters, grandparents	Uncles and aunts take the estate in equal portions.
None	Everyone	Government takes everything

Source: https://singaporelegaladvice.com/law-articles/in-the-absence-of-a-will-how-is-the-deceased-estate-distributed/

Do not ponder too much about who gets what when you do not have a Will. Plan on getting your Will done and when you do, the bewildering set of rules above need not concern you anymore.

---

1   "What Happens If You Die Without a Will in Singapore?" Singapore Legal Advice, 15 April 2019 <https://singaporelegaladvice.com/>.

2. Can I write my own Will?

Yes, you can. You do not need a Will writer or lawyer to write a Will for you. For a Will to be valid:

- The Will has to be in writing.
- The testator must be at least 21 years old.
- The testator must sign the Will at the foot of the document.
- The testator's signature must be witnessed by two or more witnesses, who must also sign the Will in his presence.
- The testator is of sound mind.

If you are thinking of a cheap or DIY Will, please think again. Your Will is probably the most important document you will write. Speak to a professional Will writer or lawyer who will take the time to ask questions to understand your family situation in order to write a Will that provides the best care for your family.

3. Is it possible to have two Wills?

Yes, it is and it is not uncommon. Suppose Michelle is Singaporean and she has a bank account and a condo in Singapore and in Thailand. It is recommended that she has a Thai Will to deal with her Thai assets and a Singapore Will to deal with her Singapore assets. Her Thai Will should revoke only previous Thai Wills that deal with her Thai assets, while her Singapore Will revokes only previous Singapore Wills that deal with her Singapore assets.

4. Is it possible to have two Singapore Wills?

We once had a client who invested in a private property (a condominium) with a friend and did not want her family members to know of the existence of both her friend and the property. She had one Will written to handle the private property which was to be gifted to her friend, and she had a second Will written to deal with her other assets in order to avoid any potential f amily conflict.

5. Who can I appoint as Executor?

It is quite natural to appoint a beneficiary to be the executor of the Will, because the beneficiary has a vested interest in the estate. If there is more than one beneficiary, consider appointing the beneficiary with the biggest stake in the estate. If the beneficiaries have equal shares in the estate, consider appointing the one who is capable, willing and trustworthy.

Sometimes, there are situations that warrant the appointment of two executors to act jointly. For example, Mary wants her husband to be executor but she feels that he is not good with financial details. She can appoint her sister who is an accountant to act jointly with her husband.

It comes as no surprise that the executor will probably be doing the job for the first time. We recommend that a checklist of duties is prepared for the executor to follow, making it less stressful for the executor and for the family.

Some testators prefer a neutral person to act as a professional executor, such as a corporate entity. In Singapore, licensed trust companies can be appointed to act as executors in Wills.

6. Who can I appoint as trustee?

In some cases, we need another person to hold the assets bequeathed to a beneficiary as the beneficiary is incapable of managing the gift. Such beneficiaries include young children, elderly relatives, mentally or physically challenged individuals, as well as individuals who have negative habits like gambling and heavy spending.

When appointing an individual trustee, do consider the person's integrity, age, health condition and whether the person has the beneficiaries' welfare at heart.

Alternatively, you may appoint a licensed trust company. Such companies hold a trust business licence to conduct trust business under the law and are supervised by the Monetary Authority of Singapore (MAS).

7. How can I give away my CPF savings?

CPF savings cannot be given away through the Will. Instead, you can make a CPF nomination to specify who will receive your CPF savings, and what percentage each nominee should receive, when you pass on. If a CPF nomination is not made, the deceased member's CPF savings are distributed to family members under the Intestate Succession Act, or an Inheritance Certificate (for Muslims).

8. How can I give away the cash in my bank account?

If your bank account is held in your sole name, you can specify in your Will that you wish the cash in your bank account be given to whoever you wish.

If you have a joint bank account with another individual, on the passing of one account holder, the surviving account holder will be entitled to the entire balance in the joint account.

While this suggests that you need not mention the joint bank account in your Will, we suggest that you still do so. One reason is that your joint account holder may pass away before you do, leaving you the sole account holder at your passing. In this case, the bank account is a sole account that you can deal with directly.

A second reason is to clarify in your Will that you intend for the surviving joint account holder to receive the sole ownership of the joint bank account if you pass away first. While this seems redundant, there have been cases where the cash in a joint bank account was transferred into the estate of the deceased rather than to the surviving joint account holder. This occurred when the intention of the account holder who passed away, in particular such as a parent who contributed most or solely to the account balance, was not for the surviving account holder who is his child to benefit fully from the account. It is also common for joint accounts to be set up by spouses where one spouse may contribute solely to the account.

9. How can I give away my HDB flat?

Like bank accounts, HDB homes can be solely owned by you or jointly owned by two or more persons as joint tenants. In general, they can be treated like bank accounts as far as gifting is concerned. However, whether your beneficiaries can receive your gift rests on HDB ownership eligibility rules. For example, the surviving joint tenant has to be at least 21 and be a Singapore Citizen or Permanent Resident.

HDB homes can also be held jointly under a tenancy-in-common scheme, where the deceased owner's share in the flat can be distributed according to his wishes. This means his share in the property can be passed on according to the terms of his Will. If there is no will, the share is distributed according to intestacy rules.

10. How can I give away my private property?

Like HDB homes, private property can be solely or jointly owned (in joint tenancy or tenancy-in-common). Unlike HDB homes, private property is subject to fewer restrictions as far as ownership is concerned. For example, foreigners can own private property whereas they cannot own landed residential property[2] or HDB homes directly.

If you own a property that is of high value or it is sentimental because it is the family home, you may consider transferring the property to a trustee to hold for a period of time. Putting the property into a trust means that your beneficiaries would be able to enjoy the property while not being able to sell the property to spend the proceeds. You can specify, for example, that the property be transferred to your child when he reaches the age of 35.

11. I have made an insurance nomination. Can I still deal with the proceeds of insurance in the Will?

Like CPF savings, the proceeds of insurance policies will go to the

---

2   Foreigners have restrictions on what they can own – www.sla.gov.sg/property-boundary-n-ownership/foreign-ownership-of-property.

beneficiaries nominated in the insurance policies and are not dealt with in the Will[3].

Insurance policies these days can have very large pay-outs. A female non-smoker aged 40, for instance, can purchase a 25-year $1 million term insurance policy for about $90 per month that covers death and TPD (total permanent disability). We have come across policies with pay-outs of over $10 million, $50 million and more!

The great challenge today is how such large amounts should be distributed. We have seen teenagers become millionaires at age 18 because that is the age at which nominated policies are paid to beneficiaries in one lump sum.

In chapter 2, we discuss how the proceeds of an insurance policy can be held back in a Trust to be distributed over a period of time and with conditions included.

12. What happens to assets not specifically distributed under the Will?

Any assets owned by the deceased that has not been specifically gifted under a Will is called the residuary estate and is dealt with by the residuary clause in the Will. If there is no residuary clause then the residuary estate will be distributed according to intestacy rules, which is likely not what the deceased wanted.

We will never know how much exactly we are going to leave behind upon our passing. Having a catch-all clause to include all other assets not specifically given away is a prudent step to take.

13. Where should I keep my Will?

Your Will should be available when it is needed most at your passing, and therefore its safekeeping is absolutely important.

Some individuals keep their Will at home in a locked drawer together with other important documents. One concern is fire. Putting it in a home safe deposit box is a safer bet. While safer in the event of fire, your home safe deposit box could still be

---

3   There is an exception where a revocable insurance nomination can be revoked through the Will. It is a seldom used exception and we will not discuss this in any detail.

accessed by someone with the access code. Another option is to use a professional Will custody service that stores your Will in a secured facility with protection from tampering, destruction, fire and water damage.

It is not recommended to keep your Will in a bank safe deposit box. The safe deposit box is probably too safe. The bank will ask for the Grant of Probate before allowing a family member to access the safe deposit box, but the executor needs the Will inside the box to apply for the Grant of Probate!

14. Do I need to maintain a Schedule of Assets during my lifetime?

Most of us would like to keep our list of assets private and confidential. The question is: would it make it easier for our executor to find out what we have if we do not list our assets when we are still able to do so?

Your family members face the immense task of finding out what assets you own and where they are located, to assessing their market value. A Schedule of Assets is required by the court before the orderly distribution of your assets can take place.

In our experience, more than 90% of applications for the Grant of Probate (or Letters of Administration if the deceased passed away without a will) are delayed because the deceased did not compile a Schedule of Assets prior to his passing.

Your Schedule of Assets can be updated informally whenever assets are acquired and sold. The values of the assets can be an estimate and may need updating only when the values have changed significantly. The schedule lists what you own and owe, and that would be of great help when the Grant of Probate is being applied for.

Another reason for its importance is that financial institutions will only pay out the items listed in the Schedule of Assets and nothing more. For example, if the deceased has three accounts with a bank and only two accounts are listed in the Schedule of Assets, the bank will require the executor to have the Schedule of Assets amended to include the missing account before proceeding to release the money in the missing account.

15. Can I disinherit my family member in my Will and can they challenge my Will?

If you are Singaporean and non-Muslim, you have the freedom to give to whoever you wish. You can give 100% of your assets to a friend or charity even if you are married with children.

If your immediate family feels that they have not received reasonable provision under your Will or on intestacy, there are four classes of immediate family members who have standing to apply to court for reasonable provision:[4]

1. your spouse;
2. a son below the age of 21;
3. a daughter who has never been married; and
4. a son or daughter who cannot maintain himself because of mental or physical disability.

Note that the above references to children apply only to legitimate children who are born within the marriage, legally adopted or legitimised as a result of the marriage of the child's parents.

16. I have a bank account in Hongkong and an apartment in Thailand. Can my Singapore Will cover those assets?

It is possible to write one Singapore Will to cover your worldwide assets, and this is quite commonly done.

However, whether the Will is considered valid is subject to the foreign court's discretion in the future. In general, it is best to write a separate Hongkong Will and a Thai Will to deal with those overseas assets. This question will be considered in Part 4 of this book.

---

4   Based on the Inheritance (Family Provision) Act.

17. What else should I do about my estate planning?

Wills are not almighty. It takes effect only upon the demise of the person making it. You may face other uncertainties such as becoming mentally unsound or critically ill, events which are not covered by the Will. Making an LPA and AMD are some of the other arrangements you should consider to make your estate planning more complete.

Chapter acknowledgements:

With great thanks to Allen Lim of Manulife Financial Advisers for providing me with insurance quotations. He is one of the most competent financial advisers I know.

Chapter 2

Will Trust

by **Keon Chee** with **Samuel Tan**

Our children will inherit more wealth now than in all of history. They could become instant millionaires after we are gone, possibly even without having to work a single day in a full-time job.

Would you find that acceptable? Most likely not.

And yet, as parents we are often so busy accumulating wealth that we don't pay enough attention to how we should pass our wealth to our children.

A huge inheritance can be a lifelong trap for anyone, especially children. Easy money can lead to unmotivated lives. We don't want our children to look in the mirror and ask themselves, "Who am I?"

In this chapter, we look at how a Will Trust (also called a Testamentary Trust) can help you to leave a legacy to your family in a thoughtful way. We answer these three questions:

1. Do I need a Trust?
2. How do I plan a Will Trust?
3. How do I set up a Will Trust?

DO I NEED A TRUST?

Whether a person needs a Trust can be determined by asking this question: do I have vulnerable beneficiaries who cannot handle a sudden, lump sum inheritance?

Case study

Mary has a son, Tommy, aged 10. Like many Singaporeans, she is likely to have a million dollars or more when she passes away – adding up the money from her bank accounts, insurance policies and homes. And like many Singaporeans, she believes that writing a Will that makes only immediate gifts should be good enough. She expects to live till age 85, and by that time, Tommy would have grown up and be able to manage a lump sum gift.

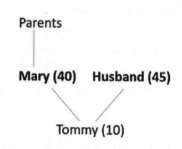

Parents

Mary (40)   Husband (45)

Tommy (10)

Figure 2.1 – Mary's Family

But what if she passes away tomorrow? As morbid as the question may be, it must be asked. The answer is that Tommy would become an instant millionaire as young as at 21. What a Trust can do for Mary is that it can hold on to her money to be released to Tommy over a period of time. Her Trust could have instructions to give a $3,000 allowance every month until a certain age, such as 35. When Tommy turns 35, any remaining funds could be given to him and only if he has achieved a certain goal, such as graduation from university. There are countless variations that Mary could consider because Trusts can be so flexible.

Ask yourself:

• Do you have young children?

• Do you have adult children who love to spend and do not save?

- Do you have elderly parents who need a regular allowance?
- Do you wish to pay for the university education of your nieces and nephews?

If you answered yes to any of the above questions, you would need to consider a Trust for yourself.

HOW DO I PLAN FOR A WILL TRUST?

There is a fact-finding exercise I use for all my clients who come to see me about estate planning for their families.

There are four questions which apply to everyone, whether rich or poor, young or old, employee or business owner. We ask about your family, what assets and liabilities you have, and on your passing, what immediate and delayed gifts you wish to make.

A. FAMILY	B. ASSETS & LIABILITIES	
Parents	Assets	Liabilities
	Bank accounts	Mortgage
	Insurance	Car loan
Mary (40) Husband (45)	Investments	Other loans
	Net Estate = $2.5M	
Tommy (10)		
C. IMMEDIATE Gifts	D. DELAYED Gifts	
$100,000 to Parents	Ongoing: $3,000 per month for Tommy's maintenance until he is 35.	
$100,000 to Husband		
Remainder to Trust	One-off: Up to $200,000 for first college degree, either local or foreign.	
	When Tommy reaches 35: 80% to Tommy and 20% to Singapore Children's Society.	

Figure 2.2 – Results of Mary's Fact Finding

A. Family

Who are your family members?

Family members are usually our main beneficiaries. Mary's main beneficiaries are her parents, her husband and Tommy.

B. Assets & liabilities

What assets do you own? What liabilities do you have?

What Mary owns and owes are all situated in Singapore. She estimates her net worth at death (NWAD) to be $2.5 million.

C. Immediate gifts

What immediate lump-sum gifts would you make on your death and to whom?

Mary plans to give $100,000 in total to her parents and to her husband, and the remainder of her money would be given to Tommy through a Trust.

D. Delayed gifts

What delayed gifts would you make?

On her death, Mary wishes to transfer the remainder of her estate (about $2.3 million) to a Trust, which is like a protected piggy bank. A person called a trustee will be appointed to hold and safeguard the money for Tommy over a period of time.

Brief definition of a Trust

A Trust is a legal arrangement where a Settlor transfers his assets to a trustee to hold and administer for the benefit of his beneficiaries such as his family. Legal ownership of the assets is given to the trustee, while beneficial ownership is given to the beneficiaries.

Mary instructs the trustee to:

- Give $3,000 a month to Tommy for his ongoing expenses. When he comes of working age, the $3,000 can supplement his income. The amount is enough for basic living expenses, but not enough for Tommy to quit his job to live a lavish life.
- Pay for Tommy's first university degree up to $200,000.

- Terminate the Trust when Tommy reaches the age of 35. Any remaining funds should be divided between Tommy (80%) and the Singapore Children's Society (20%), which is Mary's favourite charity.

We have kept the example very simple in order to focus on what a Trust can do for families. As you can see, there is nothing too complicated about the discussion because it is all about what Mary wants for her family, and she knows more about that than anyone else.

Of course, there are many more questions that can be asked, such as:

- Does she have siblings, grandparents or close friends she wishes to benefit?
- How are the assets owned? Solely or jointly with other persons?
- Does she own foreign assets?
- What is the nationality of her family members?
- What is their religion?
- Does she own any privately held businesses?
- What if Tommy passes away before he turns 35?
- What if the Trust runs out of money?

These and many other questions do pop up during our fact-finding sessions. Thankfully, the Trust is flexible enough an instrument that it can handle these and other sorts of family situations.

HOW DO I SET UP A WILL TRUST?

Let's look at how we can legally set up Mary's trust as seen in Figure 2.3.

The delayed gifts that Mary wishes to make can be specified in a special Will called a Will Trust. A Will Trust is a Will that makes both immediate and delayed gifts.

Here's how a Will Trust can be set up:

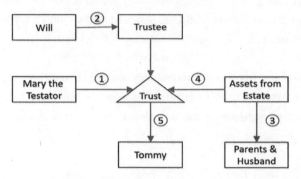

Figure 2.3 – Setting Up Mary's Will Trust

① Mary writes a Will that specifies that a Trust be created upon her passing.

② She appoints a trustee in her Will to hold the money in the future. The trustee is the person who is given control over her money with the legal obligation to administer it for the benefit of Tommy.

③ When Mary passes away, $100,000 is given to each of her parents and husband as immediate gifts.

④ Her remaining estate (currently $2.3 million) is transferred to a Trust account.

⑤ The trustee manages the trust account and follows the instructions found in the Will to distribute various monies to Tommy until he is age 35.

Mary is happy with her estate plan. It allows her to make immediate gifts to her parents and husband. She is able to maintain Tommy until he is 35, an age at which she feels he should be able to manage his life and finances. She is able to realise her values within the plan – she wants Tommy to have a college education and there is a gift to satisfy her charitable intentions.

CONCLUSION

We learned what a Trust is and how it works. A Will Trust is the most basic and affordable type of Trust we can consider. Most of us need a Trust because we may have vulnerable beneficiaries in our families – a young child, a spouse who cannot manage money or a parent who could be taken advantage of.

The Trust is set up only on the testator's death since the Trust instructions are found in a Will. This means that you can rewrite your Will Trust whenever your family circumstances change.

We continue our discussion on Will Trusts in chapter 7 on Planning and Funding a Will Trust.

FREQUENTLY ASKED QUESTIONS
1. Who can we appoint as trustee to hold the money?
The trustee is someone who takes over the legal ownership of the Trust assets, and is responsible for handling the assets held in Trust and distributing the assets to beneficiaries according to your wishes.

A trustee can be a trusted person such as your sister, a person who should have the welfare of your beneficiaries at heart and who understands your wishes for them. Some families prefer to appoint a neutral party to be trustee, such as a Trust company. In Singapore, such companies are licensed and supervised by MAS, thereby providing an important level of scrutiny by the authorities.

2. How much does it cost to have a Will Trust?
Be prepared to pay around $1,000.

If you think that is affordable, then you are absolutely right. The Will Trust is a basic trust that many families can consider for a start.

If you think that is expensive, please consider this – think of a Will Trust as a Will with additional and special instructions that requires a Will writer to plan and draft for you. The time taken to discuss your situation, draft your Will Trust and have it attested easily takes three or more hours. Your family deserves an experienced and concerned Will writer to ask you questions and to listen carefully to your wishes and family situation, and to come up with a plan that takes care of your family for 10, 20 or more years.

You may have heard that Trusts can cost $10,000 to set up; these are likely to be Living Trusts rather than Will Trusts. Living Trusts are Trusts that are set up during your lifetime rather than after your lifetime as in the case of a Will Trust. You may be surprised to learn that Living Trusts are more commonly used than Will Trusts. We will discuss Living Trusts in chapters 8 and 9.

3. If my Trust beneficiary passes away before the termination date, where do the remaining funds go?

You can specify that the remaining funds go to another surviving beneficiary or if there are no human beneficiaries remaining, the funds remaining can benefit an entity such as a charity. It's up to you.

4. When should I review my Will Trust?

Your Will Trust never expires, but major life events or a change in estate planning goals can necessitate changes. For example, if you have a new baby or if you are divorcing your spouse, then it's definitely time to update your Will Trust.

5. What assets can be put into a Trust?

Almost any asset of material value can be put into a Trust, including:
- shares
- property
- cash
- insurance policies
- fine art and jewellery

Even yachts and aeroplanes can be placed in Trust. It depends on the trustee's expertise and willingness to manage the asset.

6. How will the funds in the Trust be invested?

You can leave instructions with the trustee to invest the trust funds in a certain way. For example, you may specify that the trust company place the funds only in safe instruments such as fixed deposits and bond funds. Or you can specify that at least 80% be placed in safe instruments and up to 20% in riskier stocks and equity funds.

If you do not leave instructions on how to invest your trust funds, the trustee is generally obliged to protect the capital while ensuring that the returns on the trust fund keep up with inflation and pays for trust administration expenses at the least. The trustee would also consult your family and beneficiaries on whether they have certain preferences on asset allocation, type of investments and which asset manager to bring in to help with managing the investments.

There are indeed a multitude of options that can be considered and where the trust fund amount is large and requires regular monitoring, a document called the Investment Policy Statement is drawn up. This document is a formal agreement between the trustee and asset manager to manage an amount of trust monies. We learn more about this in chapter 13.

7. What if the Trust runs out of money?

Before we discuss how to distribute to our beneficiaries, we should see if there will be enough funds for them. Financial planning is essential when we plan our Will and Trust.

The amounts that our beneficiaries need to have a basic life are not difficult to calculate. And where there are not enough funds for the family, life insurance can be purchased to pump up the estate or a savings plan can be put in place. For example, if Mary wants to ensure there is $1 million for Tommy until he is 35 years old, she could purchase a 25-year term policy for a female non-smoker for about $90 per month.

Chapter 7 explains how we can calculate how much our family needs and how to fund the requirement.

8. How long can my trust last?

In Singapore, Trusts can last for up to 100 years. However, the terms of the trust will usually allow the trust to end earlier. For example, if and when a beneficiary reaches a certain age or when the funds dip below a certain amount.

9. Can the trustee refuse to act?

If you name an individual as trustee in the Will, that person has no legal obligation to accept the appointment in the future. However, if you appoint a professional trustee such as a licensed trust company, it will almost always act in the future. The reason is that the professional trustee charges a nominal fee for being appointed in the Will. The fee professionally obligates the trustee to keep its word. Secondly, the trustee is happy to act because it earns fees when it does.

10. What if the Trust company goes bankrupt?

Client Trust funds are segregated from the Trust company's accounts. If the Trust company gets in trouble, segregated client Trust funds are not affected. If the Trust company loses its license, client funds are transferred to another licensed Trust company. While there would be some administrative inconvenience when a Trust company gets in trouble, client Trust funds should not be affected.

Chapter acknowledgements:
With great thanks to Allen Lim of Manulife Financial Advisers for providing me with insurance quotations. He is one of the most competent financial advisers I know.

Chapter 3

Lasting Power of Attorney

by **Keon Chee**

Through a Lasting Power of Attorney (LPA), you can appoint a person or persons to step in to manage your personal welfare and financial affairs if and when you ever become mentally incapacitated.

The LPA is considered to be as essential an estate planning instrument as the Will. That is because if you do not have an LPA and you lose mental capacity, your family will have difficulty paying your bills, accessing your bank accounts and dealing with your business interests.

Without this relatively simple document, your family would have to go to court to appoint a deputy to manage your affairs. That court process takes time, costs money, and the judge might not choose the person you would have preferred to act on your behalf.

Case study

Roger had just retired from his engineering job when he became mentally incapacitated at age 70. He was in the midst of selling his home and buying a smaller one. He was unable to perform the transaction because of his dementia. His daughter, Sandra needed to complete the sale of the condo on his behalf and to access his bank account for subsequent transactions.

As Roger did not have an LPA, Sandra had to apply to be his deputy with a lawyer assisting with the application. The cost was $6,000 and it took six months for the deputyship to be approved.

Note: A deputy is an individual who is appointed by the court to make decisions for a person who has lost mental capacity and who did not have an LPA.

There are many excellent resources available online about the LPA. The source of the most reliable information is the Office of the Public Guardian (OPG) itself, which is the division of the Ministry of Social and Family Development (MSF) that oversees the administration and the integrity of the LPA. They have over the years greatly simplified the application process and other procedures. To best benefit from this chapter, you need to plan on getting your LPA done as soon as possible. Go to the OPG's website at www.msf.gov.sg/opg/ to print a copy of the latest LPA Form 1[1] for reference as you read through this chapter.

GETTING YOUR LPA DONE

The process of setting up your LPA is summarised in Figure 3.1:

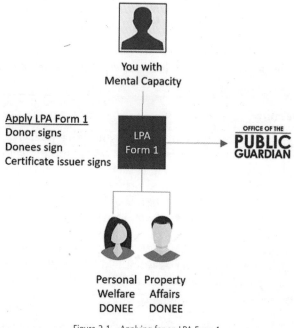

Figure 3.1 – Applying for an LPA Form 1

You the donor who is at least of age 21 and mentally capable:
- Complete the LPA Form 1 application. It takes about 30 minutes to complete.
- Choose a Certificate Issuer to certify your mental capacity and intention to make an LPA.
- Have the LPA registered with the OPG.

As the person making the LPA, you are the "donor" with powers to donate if you lose mental capacity. The persons you appoint to make decisions on your behalf should you lose mental capacity are the "donees".

Comparing the donee roles
There are two types of donees: Personal Welfare Donees (PWD) and Property Affairs Donees (PAD).

Powers of the donees[2]
In the event you are certified mentally incapable, your donees have powers to decide on and act in your best interest.

Your PWD can, among other powers, decide on:
- where you should live
- your day to day care decisions (what to wear and eat)
- handling your letters/mail
- who you may have contact with
- healthcare and medical treatment decisions

Some matters your PWD cannot decide on for you include marriage, renouncing a religion and gifting of any body part.

Your PAD can, among other powers, decide on:
- buying, selling, renting and mortgaging your property
- operating your bank accounts
- managing your CPF monies

---

2 The powers of and restrictions on donees are extracted from the OPG website.

- paying household expenses
- purchasing any equipment you may need

Some matters your PAD cannot decide on for you include executing a Will, and making a nomination on your insurance and CPF savings.

Choose your donees carefully

Given the wide-ranging powers that a donee has, you should be very careful who you choose as donee.

***

Case study

Former China tour guide Yang Yin was jailed for nine years in March 2017 for cheating wealthy widow Madam Chung Khin Chun. After first meeting in 2006, the pair became close. Yang Yin moved into her bungalow with his family in 2008.

Madam Chung appointed Yang Yin to be her sole PWD and PAD in 2012. Madam Chung, who has no children, was diagnosed with dementia in 2014. In four years, Yang Yin drained her cash savings from $2.7 million to $10,000. In a 2010 Will, he stood to inherit all of the widow's assets worth $40 million.

***

These are some of the most common choices that families make when choosing donees:
- Husband and wife appointing one another.
- A parent appointing a child.
- Siblings and relatives appointing one another.

Certain people such as singles and childless couples, who may not have family members or close friends to rely on, can consider appointing professional donees to act for remuneration. A list of professional donees can be found on the OPG website.

Sometimes, the choice of donee seemed right at the time of appointment but not so after a period time. For instance, these may not be desirable situations:

- Frank appointed his wife, Becky, as his donee. Frank loses mental capacity while they are in the middle of divorce proceedings. His LPA is invoked with Becky acting as his donee.
- Betsy and Lindy are single and best friends. They appointed one another as donees. Lindy loses mental capacity a few years later. Betsy learns what a tough job it is to care for Lindy and she isn't getting paid for the time she spends away from work to care for Lindy.
- Jackie appointed Michael, her son, as her donee. When Jackie lost her mental capacity, Michael had just started a new job and a new family. He found himself unable to cope.

Making your LPA should therefore not be a one-off exercise. Over the years, you may get married, have children, get divorced, remarry, start a business, suffer a death in family and go through many other life events. When you experience major life events, you should review your LPA and other documents.

THE COST OF MAKING AN LPA

There are two costs to making an LPA – the cost of certificate issuing and the cost of application.

THE COST OF CERTIFICATE ISSUING

Once you have filled in the LPA Form 1, you need an LPA Certificate Issuer to certify that you are mentally capable and that you understand the purpose of making an LPA, including your intention to appoint the persons named as donees, the powers given to the donees, and that you are not being forced or deceived into making an LPA.

The certificate issuer charges a fee for this service, which typically ranges from $50 to a few hundred dollars. The certificate issuer may be:

- a medical practitioner accredited to issue LPA certificates;
- a medical practitioner who is registered as a specialist in psychiatry; or
- a practising lawyer.

You may be tempted to go for a certificate issuer that charges the lowest fee based on your DIY filled-in LPA Form 1. Be careful that while the LPA is very simple to make, the decisions you make on who your donees are and the powers given to them have far-reaching consequences for you and your family. You are encouraged to speak to a certificate issuer who would take the time to explain the following to you:

- How the powers of the donees work.
- How donees can act solely or jointly, and which may be better for you.
- Whether your choice of donee could pose some future risk.
- How to revoke your LPA if you change your mind.
- How to reduce potential abuse by your donees.
- How to customise the LPA if you wish to have special instructions to deal with your assets, investments, where you live and who should run your private business.

Unless you have a strong understanding of the LPA, you would want these explanations made and they take time. Therefore, be willing to pay a reasonable fee for the issuer's professional time.

The cost of application

This is the OPG's fee to accept and register your LPA. The cost of applying for LPA Form 1 is $75 for Singapore citizens. To encourage more Singaporeans to apply for the LPA, the cost of applying for LPA Form 1 has been waived till 31 March 2021 as seen in Table 3.1.

Table 3.1 – Cost of LPA Form 1 Application

	LPA Form 1 Fee (incl. GST)	LPA Form 2 Fee (incl. GST)
Singapore Citizens	$0 *(fee of $75 waived for another 2 years until 31 March 2021)*	$200
Singapore Permanent Residents	$100	$250
Foreigners	$250	$300

Source: www.msf..gov.sg/opg/AnalyticsReports/LPA_Fees_Table_Jun2020.pdf

WHY YOU NEED AN LPA – THE SOONER, THE BETTER

Singaporeans have the highest life expectancy in the world.[3] That means more years with our loved ones, but it also means that we would experience a higher chance of dementia.

This is because age is the strongest known risk factor for dementia according to the UK Alzheimer's Society. Above the age of 65, a person's risk of developing Alzheimer's disease doubles roughly every five years.[4] In Singapore, according to the Institute of Mental Health, one in ten people aged 60 and above has dementia.[5]

You might expect that dementia only happens to elderly people, but this is not true. Of those reported to have mental incapacity by the OPG,[6] the majority are not elderly at all:

- 65% are below 70 years old, and
- 35% are above 70 years old.

---

3 "Singaporeans have world's longest life expectancy at 84.8 years", *The Straits Times*, 20 June 2019.
4 "Risk Factor for Dementia", Alzheimer's Society, Factsheet April 2016, www.alzheimers.org.uk.
5 "Faster and easier application process for Lasting Power of Attorney from August", ChannelNews Asia, 20 July 2019.
6 "Office of the Public Guardian – Indicators of Activities for Calendar Year 2017", www.msf.gov.sg/opg/Pages//Indicators-of-Activities.aspx.

Given the known risks of dementia and our longevity, you might expect that a good number of Singaporeans have signed up for the LPA. Unfortunately, that is not true. As of June 2019, just 67,000 Singaporeans have made an LPA. If you compare that number to 582,000, the number of Singapore residents who are aged 65 and above,[7] you might agree that Singaporeans have not done enough for themselves and their families.

CONCLUSION

When you lose mental capacity and you did not make an LPA, you cause great inconvenience and stress to your family. Get your LPA done, the sooner, the better. The time and cost to do so are modest.

There is a higher likelihood of dementia as we age, so let's be prepared. Our families will be relieved that we did.

FREQUENTLY ASKED QUESTIONS
1. Can we do something to reduce the risk of dementia?
We can lower the risk of dementia through our everyday lifestyle choices like being physically active, eating healthily, not smoking, drinking less alcohol and exercising your mind (taking a course, playing crosswords).[8]

2. Are Alzheimer's disease and dementia the same thing?
Dementia is an umbrella term to describe a set of symptoms that occur when brain cells stop working properly. Dementia is caused by a number of diseases that damage the nerve cells in the brain, the most common of which is Alzheimer's disease.

3. I'm starting to have memory loss. Is that a sign of dementia?
We sometimes experience memory problems when we are depressed, have insufficient sleep or are suffering the side effects of medication.

---

7 "Population and Population Structure", Department of Statistics Singapore, www.singstat.gov.sg.
8 "How to reduce your risk of dementia," Alzheimer's Society, www.alzheimers.org.uk.

In order to be deemed mentally incapable, a person, such as John, would not be able to:

Ability	For example, after receiving information relevant to making a decision:
Understand information	John cannot paraphrase what he just learned
Remember information	John cannot recall what he just learned long enough to weigh it up and communicate it
Weigh up information	John cannot explain the pros and cons, or why
Communicate a decision	John cannot communicate what he learned whether through speaking, writing or sign language

4. What is the difference between an LPA and a Will?

A Will takes effect only after the Will maker passes away. The LPA takes effect when the donor loses his mental capacity while he is still alive.

The Will deals with the distribution of a person's assets to his loved ones on his death. The LPA deals with the donor's assets largely for the donor's own benefit. The ownership of assets remains with the donor whereas with a Will, the assets are distributed.

5. Are the PWD and PAD roles similar to those of guardian and trustee?

A person who has lost mental capacity cannot make decisions for himself. The PWD provides the appropriate support for the donor in terms of care and concern. This is analogous to what a guardian provides for a child under the age of 21 or what a deputy provides for an adult above age 21 who lacks mental capacity.

As for the PAD, his role is analogous to that of a trustee. The PAD acts as an extension of the donor to provide care and concern over the donor's property. Unlike the trustee, the PAD does not have legal ownership of the donor's property whereas the trustee does. The PAD and the trustee are similar in that neither has beneficial rights over the donor's property.

Donee	Main Role:	Analogous to:
PWD	Care and Concern of Donor's Welfare	Guardian
PAD	Care and Concern of Donor's Property & Assets	Trustee

6. Do I need LPA Form 2?

LPA Form 2 is for donors who wish to have more flexibility in appointing donees (such as appointing more than two donees or more than one replacement done) or who wish to grant specific and customised powers to donees which cannot be given in LPA Form 1. Form 2 must be drafted by a lawyer.

Some situations for which you might consider LPA Form 2 include:

- You want your Singtel and Berkshire Hathaway stocks kept and not sold.
- You want to be put into a specific nursing home.
- You own a private business and you want two trusted directors to run the operations.
- You want to appoint a licensed trust company to be your PAD to provide funds to your family during your mental incapacity.

In each of these situations, customising your LPA is necessary and LPA Form 2 allows such customisation. This would not be possible using LPA Form 1, which contains standardised terms.

7. Can I revoke my LPA after I have made it?

Yes, you can. You may have a change of heart about who your donee is or the powers you wish to give. You can revoke your LPA as long as you are mentally capable to do so.

Your LPA may be revoked automatically in certain conditions such as:

- you the donor or your donees pass away;
- you the donor or your PAD becomes bankrupt;
- you the donor and your donee who is your spouse get divorced (unless the LPA states that the LPA should not be revoked in the event of divorce); and
- your donee loses mental capacity.

8. How do we use or invoke an LPA?

Suppose John is suspected to have lost his mental capacity and you are his PAD. His LPA may need to be invoked in order to, for example, close his bank account. This is the procedure to take:

- Bring John to a doctor to certify his mental health condition. If John is deemed to have lost mental capacity, the doctor will make the appropriate declaration on the Medical Report for Activation/Deactivation of Lasting Power of Attorney (LPA) form.
- Approach the bank with John's LPA, the Medical Report and NRIC documents of John and yourself (the donee).
- When the bank has verified the documents, you can then close the bank account on John's behalf.

9. How can I prevent abuse by my donees?

Your donee must act in your best interest. The OPG is empowered to investigate cases where the donee may be abusing his position and taking advantage of the donor.

The LPA can also include restrictions that limit the powers of the donee.

In spite of this, abuse can still take place as in the case of Madam Chung. These are some additional safeguards that can be considered:

- Tell your family and close friends that you have made an LPA and who the donees are. If you do so, they are more likely to check on you if your LPA is ever invoked.
- Appoint professional donees to act on your behalf.

- Appoint donees to act jointly where both donees have to agree before an action is taken. Of course, if the donees are at loggerheads with one another, a joint appointment can cause delays.

10. Is my LPA recognised overseas?

Your made-in-Singapore LPA is recognised only in Singapore. If you lose mental capacity while overseas, your Singapore LPA would not be recognised in that foreign country.

This also means that your LPA will work only on assets that are in Singapore. Your LPA cannot deal with your bank account in Australia or your condo in Malaysia. For those overseas assets, you will have to consult a legal practitioner in that foreign country about their mental capacity laws there.

Chapter acknowledgement:
With great thanks to Tan Shen Kiat of Kith & Kin Law Corporation for reviewing this chapter. He is one of the very best lawyers I know on mental capacity issues and the most passionate.

Chapter 4

Advanced Medical Directive

by **Keon Chee**

The Advanced Medical Directive (AMD) or Living Will as it is called in the US and the UK, lets others know what medical treatment you would want, in the event you cannot express your wishes yourself and death is imminent. If you do not have an AMD, medical care providers may prolong your life using artificial means, if necessary. With today's technology, physicians can sustain you for weeks or even months.

Medicine can do extraordinary things, but it has its limits. There will come a time when you have to be helped through the dying process and receive palliative care (which consists of medical procedures to relieve pain, suffering or discomfort). Planning the details of your death may sound gloomy, but we do need to respond to the need to be clear about our end-of-life-care. It is an effective way to take the decision-making burden off our family members.

Even younger people should set up an AMD. Severe trauma or a fatal illness can occur at any age. Preparing an AMD will eliminate any disagreements about end-of-life care.

The Terri Schiavo case

On 25 February 1990, at age 26, Terri Schiavo sustained a cardiac arrest at her home in Florida.[1] She had massive brain damage and she was diagnosed to have gone into a persistent vegetative state. For several years, doctors attempted various therapies to return her to a state of awareness, without success.

In 1998, her husband petitioned the court to remove her feeding tube. Her parents opposed. The court determined that she would not have wished to continue life-prolonging

---

1   "Terri Schiavo case", Wikipedia, 1 April 2020.

measures, but it was only seven years later that the feeding tube was disconnected from her. Terri died on 31 March 2005, 15 years after suffering cardiac arrest.

The Schiavo case caused a spike in America for Living Wills. It is estimated that one in three American adults have Living Wills[2].

WHAT IS AN AMD?[3]

The AMD is a legal document that you sign in advance to inform the doctor treating you that in the event you become terminally ill and unconscious, you do not want any extraordinary life-sustaining treatment to be used to prolong your life, where:

- "terminal illness" means an incurable condition from which there is no reasonable prospect of recovery where death is imminent;
- "extraordinary life-sustaining treatment" means any medical procedure or measure which will only prolong the process of dying when death is imminent, but excludes palliative care.

Making an AMD

Download the "Making of Advance Medical Directive" form from the Ministry of Health website at www.moh.gov.sg and fill it in.[4] We encourage you to register the AMD.

To make an AMD:

- You have to be 21 years old and above and not mentally disordered.
- You need to have two witnesses, one of whom must be a doctor. The doctor has to certify that you are not being forced into making the AMD, are not mentally disordered and understand the nature and implications of making an AMD.
- Your AMD is valid only when it is registered with the Registrar of Advance Medical Directives. The Registrar will send you an acknowledgement when the directive has been registered.

2   "Two out of three U.S. adults have not completed an advance directive", www.sciencedaily.com, 5 July 2017.
3   The contents in this section are largely summarised and excerpted from the websites of the Ministry of Health (www.moh.gov.sg) and the Agency for Integrated Care (www.aic.sg).
4   "Form 1 – Making of Advance Medical Directive" is available at https://www.moh.gov.sg/docs/librariesprovider5/forms/form1amd(270905).pdf.

Very few people in Singapore have made an AMD from the time it was first available in 1997. As at end-2015, there were about 25,000 persons who made an AMD.[5] If the take-up rate is similar to that of America's (one in three adults), then there should be over 1 million AMDs registered, based on an adult population of 3.2 million residents aged 20 and above.[6]

CONCLUSION

There is no way today that you can plan out every possible scenario of how you wish to be cared for when you are on your deathbed. Decisions such as how long to stay on the ventilator, whether or not to use a feeding tube, whether or not to use dialysis if multi-system organ failure occurs, may be best left to the attending doctors.

With the AMD, you are leaving instructions that "if I should suffer from a terminal illness and if I should become unconscious or incapable of exercising rational judgment so that I am unable to communicate my wishes to my doctor, no extraordinary life-sustaining treatment should be applied or given to me." It may not be wise to burden your family to second-guess what you would have wanted.

FREQUENTLY ASKED QUESTIONS

1. How much does it cost to make an AMD?

While the AMD form is free, you have to pay a fee to the doctor who will advise you on the AMD and acts as a witness.

2. How does the hospital know I have made an AMD?

The hospital does not know who has made an AMD as it is confidential. However, if your attending doctor has reasons to believe that you are terminally ill and unable to make your wishes known to him, he can check with the Registrar of Advance Medical Directives on whether you have made an AMD.

5   "Let's talk about Advance Care Planning to die with dignity", *The Straits Times*, 16 December 2017.
6   "Population and Population Structure", www.singstat.gov.sg.

3. Can an AMD be used as euthanasia or mercy killing?

Euthanasia/mercy killing is the deliberate ending of the life of a person suffering from an incurable and painful disease by unnatural means, such as the administration of lethal chemicals. The person who receives euthanasia may not be in a situation where death is imminent. The AMD Act is explicitly against euthanasia.

4. When will an AMD be enforced?

The AMD will only come into force once you have been determined to have a terminal illness and a Certificate of Terminal Illness has been issued.

Three doctors, including the patient's hospital doctor, must unanimously certify a patient's terminal illness. Two of the doctors must be specialists.

Chapter acknowledgement:

With great thanks to Tan Shen Kiat of Kith & Kin Law Corporation for reviewing this chapter. He is one of the very best lawyers I know on mental capacity issues and the most passionate.

Chapter 5

Advance Care Planning

by **Keon Chee**

Zuri is 50. She has a fully paid up home, $5 million in the bank, sufficient life and health insurance, and plans to retire when she's 60. She plans to spend $60,000 per year in her retirement. Expecting to live until 90, she expects to spend a total of $2 million, including expenses for any emergencies that may arise. Her Will leaves the home to her husband, a small gift to charity and the remaining $3 million will be transferred to a Trust to benefit her children. Her husband is her Lasting Power of Attorney (LPA) donee and her Advanced Medical Directive (AMD) instructs her doctors not to keep her alive when death is imminent.

She's set for a peaceful retirement, having her estate planning documents done – her Will, Trust, LPA and AMD. However, she remarks, "My documents are all kind of dry and skeletal. Is there some place where I could explain the choices I have made, the values I uphold and how I should be cared for in case I get seriously ill but not quite dead yet? Because one day when I'm unable to communicate, I want my family to know these things about me." This is where the Advance Care Plan (ACP) comes in.

WHAT IS AN ADVANCE CARE PLAN?

The ACP is a non-legally binding document that describes your personal values and beliefs, what you want and not want in certain medical situations and who you wish to be your spokesperson to speak on your behalf when you are no longer able to do so for yourself.

How is an ACP different from an LPA and AMD?

The LPA is a legally binding document. It appoints donees to act on your behalf should you lose mental capacity to make your own decisions regarding your personal welfare and property affairs.

The AMD is also a legally binding document. It informs the doctor treating you that you do not wish to have any life-sustaining treatment to artificially prolong your life, should death be imminent.

The LPA and AMD could technically contain the same planning strategies for everyone. That's because they are based on standard forms to meet the needs of most people.[1] The LPA and AMD are the hardware in your later life plan. They bind the persons involved (the donees and the doctor) to act accordingly. The ACP, on the other hand, complements the LPA and AMD by connecting the dots to the choices you have made in your legal documents. The ACP can help to explain your values and choices, whereas the LPA and AMD do not.

The ACP is part of Later Life Planning

The ACP is one of the documents of "Later Life Planning". The term "Later Life Planning" is commonly used in the UK to describe the planning that one does in retirement. The planning may include writing a Will, making an LPA and AMD, and arranging for a nursing home and funeral services. It is a term that is not quite used in Singapore[2] and I am proposing to use it, albeit loosely, to describe the sort of planning that you should consider doing as you near retirement age.

I illustrate Later Life Planning for my clients as depicted in Figure 5.1.

Figure 5.1 – Typical Components of Later Life Planning

---

1 We are referring to LPA Form 1 which is the LPA form option that 98% of Singaporeans choose.
2 As of August 2020, I Googled "later life planning Singapore" and nothing showed up.

It consists of:

- The LPA which deals with mind matters.
- The AMD which deals with body matters.
- The ACP which is the software that explains the choices made.
- The Grant of Probate (discussed in the next chapter) which deals with our afterlife matters such as ensuring we have enough funds to clear our estate.

The diagram is a huge simplification, of course, but it gets the point across to the people I speak to and it enlightens them enough to prompt them to plan. The technical and legal details can be discussed when each document is being explored and set up.

TYPES OF ACP

There are three types of ACP, depending generally on your health condition.

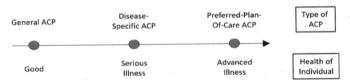

Figure 5.2 – Types of ACP

- General ACP – suitable for relatively healthy individuals, or individuals with early chronic disease.
- Disease-Specific ACP – for individuals with progressive, life-limiting illnesses possibly with limited lifespan, the need for nursing home care and high chance of mental incapacity.
- Preferred-Plan-of-Care ACP for individuals with more advanced illnesses who may pass away within a year.

GETTING YOUR ACP DONE

If you do not have a serious illness and you are not pressed for time, download the ACP Workbook to help you:[3]

---

3   You can download the ACP workbook here: www.livingmatters.sg/start-the-conversation/overview/.

- document your personal values and beliefs;
- explore what you want and not want in certain medical situations;
- choose a spokesperson to speak on your behalf when you are no longer able to do so; and
- write down your wishes and share your plan.

After completing the ACP Workbook, share it with your loved ones and family doctor.

You can make a formal completion of your ACP by engaging an ACP facilitator who is a trained healthcare professional. This can be done at various ACP Centres.[4]

If you have a serious medical condition or you require more guidance in completing your ACP, you can engage an ACP facilitator at the outset. ACP Centres include most public hospitals like Tan Tock Seng Hospital and Singapore General Hospital.

Case study – Pansy Leong

Pansy Leong is my mother. She was born on 30 July 1927 in a provision shop in Serangoon Road. A midwife assisted in her birth. "My mother already had 11 children. Giving birth to me was like laying an egg."

Her Chinese name is Leong Moon Oi. Her mahjong *kakis*[5] gave her the name Pansy because they found her Chinese name too difficult to pronounce. No one else ever calls her Pansy but I've always liked the name Pansy for her. It's the name of a young, feisty girl. It's also the name of an elderly woman with a young spirit.

At 93, she is mentally alert. When I leave home for work, I would ask her if I look good, and she'll tell me whether my clothes look smart or mismatched, and whether my hair is messy. If my tummy is getting too round, she'll say, "Stomach in, chest out."

The loves of her life, besides being around family and playing mahjong, is cooking. In her early 40s, she took

---

4   A list of ACP Centres can be found here: http://singaporehospice.org.sg/acp-directory.
5   Friends and buddies (in Singlish).

cooking classes with a restaurant chef called Tham Yew Kai, which inauspiciously translates to Bland Oily Chicken in Cantonese.

When she was 88, she had four operations on her spine and hip, each taking four to six hours. After a serious fall three years ago which damaged the nerves around her arms and shoulder, she stopped playing mahjong. She gets around today with a Zimmer frame, the same frame that my father used until he passed away in 2014 at the age of 96.

I have helped her with her Will and LPA, and I should be helping her with her AMD soon. I've been going through the ACP workbook with her for nearly a year now. Not that it takes that long, but she'll have stories about her younger life that I couldn't stop listening to. The ACP workbook opened my eyes and heart to my mother's life, her dreams, her hopes, her pains, her joys. I wish I had taken my father through the ACP workbook because there is a deep sense that I could have come to know him better.

When we got to the end-of-life questions, her answers came out fast and clear:

- I'm not afraid of pain or death. It's my time and I can be with your father soon.
- I want you to be my spokesperson when I cannot speak for myself anymore.
- When I am terminally ill, don't keep me alive. Let me go.
- Let my family and the doctors decide what's best for me.
- As long as I can, I want to be independent. To bathe myself. To change my clothes.
- Give me a lawn burial because I am afraid of being burned. No wait, put me in a niche next to your father.

CONCLUSION

Whether young and healthy or elderly and ill, you should consider doing the ACP. Start with the ACP workbook to answer questions about your relationships, your lifestyle preferences, your beliefs and the care preferences you wish for when you are too ill to speak for yourself. You will find yourself walking through your life as you may never have done before and you may even end up writing a mini autobiography.

For me, helping my mother with her ACP was a decluttering exercise that allowed her to focus on what is most important in her life and to tell me that she has had a good life and she is ready to go. You, too, can have such a conversation with yourself and your loved ones.

Chapter 6

Grant of Probate

by **Keon Chee** with **Patrick Tan**

"... leaving your family to decide what happens to your body and organize your funeral/memorial is like asking someone to plan your wedding and reception but giving them no details, no budget, a very tight timeline, and then never really knowing if you would have liked it or not."
Sharon Hartung, *Your Digital Undertaker*

Daniel just died. This is the mess his family has to settle – He wrote a Will last year but no one can find it. He didn't keep a record of his assets. He has a bank account and an apartment in London. He owns 50% of a corporate gifts business and there's no plan in place for who should take over his shares and role. Daniel leaves behind Jenny, his wife, and two daughters. Daniel and Jenny are both Singapore citizens.

Having a Will isn't the end of it. Your family could still run into difficulties if no one can find your Will or knows where your assets are, or the executor cannot act for whatever reason, or your estate has insufficient liquidity to pay for your final expenses.

In this chapter, we look at what it takes to have a hassle-free Probate, where there are enough funds to pay for expenses and your assets are transferred to your family seamlessly.

ASSETS DO NOT AUTOMATICALLY TRANSFER ON DEATH

When you pass away with a valid Will, your assets do not automatically transfer to your family. If you are giving the cash in your DBS account to your husband, he cannot just show up at the bank with your Will and death certificate to ask for the cash to be transferred to him. There is a sequence of steps to take before the transfer can take place:

1. The executor named in your Will takes your Will to court to have it validated.
2. The executor is conferred the position of personal representative (PR). The PR has the authority to take legal ownership of your assets.
3. A court document called the Grant of Probate (the Grant) is extracted with the name of the PR stated. It is the Grant that DBS and other institutions will ask to see and it is the PR that DBS will release the cash to.
4. The PR (who is the executor) follows the instruction in the Will to give the cash to your husband.

PLAN TODAY FOR A SMOOTH & TIMELY TRANSITION

Plan for a smooth send-off to your afterlife. None of the steps are complicated. Put a plan in place that you can update over time. Work with your estate and financial planners to:

1. write a Will;
2. consider a third-party executor in your Will;
3. keep records of your assets and documents;
4. safekeep your Will;
5. appoint a probate lawyer; and
6. plan for sufficient liquidity to pay for estate expenses.

1. Write a Will

This is absolutely a must for the majority of us. We won't even discuss what happens if you don't write a Will because steps 2 to 6 below would not be useful to you.

2. Consider a third-party executor in your Will

An executor's job is not easy as any person who has performed the role will tell you. This is especially true when you are the executor of a person who was close to you, like your spouse or family members. The executor of Daniel's estate has to:

1. locate Daniel's Will;
2. make funeral arrangements;
3. call in his assets;
4. obtain Probate;
5. pay his debts;
6. distribute assets according to his Will; and
7. render final accounts

This can take several months to over a year to complete.

Individuals commonly appoint their spouse or relatives to be their executor. What if at the time of your death, your appointed executor cannot act because he died before you, is mentally unsound or is unable to take on the role because of grief?

Always have a substitute executor named in your Will who can act in place of the first appointed executor. For example, your Will might say – "I appoint A to be my executor. If A cannot act for whatever reason, then I appoint B." You could still run into the nice problem that you survive everyone and none of the appointed executors are available to act.

A good option is to appoint a third-party professional executor who is not related to the family and is someone who is "longer lasting":

- You can appoint a lawyer as executor. He could be the lawyer who is drafting your Will. If the appointed lawyer cannot act in the future for whatever reason, another lawyer in the same firm of a certain seniority can act in his place.
- You can appoint a corporate executor rather than an individual executor. In Singapore, licensed trust companies can act as a corporate executor in your will.[1]

---

1   Not many trust companies are willing to act as executor in Wills on a regular basis. Those that are willing would normally do so only if there is a defined trust role for them in the future.

Never fail to ask what if your appointed executors cannot act. You should be satisfied that at any time, the risk of not having an executor to act for you is low.

3. Keep records of your assets

Don't be like Daniel, who left Jenny to deal with his disorganised estate. Keep your documents in one place, preferably in a single file and box containing these documents:

- Your Will.
- An informal schedule of assets.
- A list of bank accounts and passwords.
- Usernames and passwords to email and social media websites.
- Names and contact details of people to notify in the event of your death, such as the names of your executor, financial planner and lawyer.
- Personal documents such as your birth certificate, passport and marriage certificate.
- Financial and asset documents such as title deeds, mortgage agreements and car registrations.

Table 6.1 is a sample record of Daniel's assets and liabilities (let's assume he did have a Schedule). We'll call it the Schedule of Assets, which is the official name of the court document but we need to identify Daniel's version as an informal version whose format is different from the official Schedule. The point is that Daniel should maintain such an informal Schedule for himself during his lifetime to list what he owns, how he owns the asset and whether there is any liability attached to the asset. This is very useful because it shows what Daniel's net estate is and what liabilities may be due after his death.

Table 6.1 – Schedule of Assets (Informal)

Movable Assets

	Asset	Country	Ownership	Amount
1	Cash in Bank	Singapore	Sole	1,000,000
4	Listed shares	Singapore	Sole	2,000,000
5	Private company shares	Singapore	50% of company	4,000,000

				Sum Assured
8	Whole life insurance	Singapore	Sole	1,000,000
9	Term insurance	Singapore	Sole	2,000,000

Immovable Assets

	Asset	Country	Ownership	Market Value	Loan	Net
10	HDB	Singapore	Joint Tenancy	500,000		500,000
11	Semi-D	Singapore	Joint Tenancy	4,000,000	1,000,000	3,000,000
12	Apartment	London	Sole	2,000,000		2,000,000

Work with your estate or financial planner to compile a Schedule. Once you do this the first time, updating your Schedule is easy whenever there are material changes in your assets and liabilities.

4. Safekeep your Will

You do not want your Will to be missing when it's needed most. There are many ways to safekeep your Will. Please refer to the Frequently Asked Question #13 in chapter 1.

5. Appoint a probate lawyer

It is possible for someone in the family to obtain the Grant. If you do not want the stress and complications of the job for a family member, get the assistance of a probate lawyer to do so instead.

If you had appointed a lawyer as executor in your Will, the same lawyer could be the probate lawyer to help obtain the Grant. This is certainly more convenient for your family.

How lawyers charge for Probate

Lawyers generally charge a fixed fee plus hourly charges for any additional work. Lawyers who have fixed rate packages would stipulate conditions that might include:

- An estate of up to a certain value such as $1 million.

- No more than a certain number of assets such as 10 assets.
- The deceased passed away with a valid Will.
- The deceased was Singaporean.
- All assets are in Singapore.
- The estate is solvent (there are enough assets to settle liabilities).
- A non-contentious probate (a contentious probate could arise, for example, when more than one person wishes to administer the estate and they cannot agree among themselves).

A reasonable fee range for a fixed rate package such as the above might be $2,500 onwards.

In the case of Daniel, his estate is more complicated because he owns assets outside Singapore.[2]

Families usually get quotes from two to three lawyers and are likely to choose the lawyer with the *lowest starting fee*. But do dig further to ask what the total fee may add up to because you do not want too many surprises. Our suggestion is be diligent about understanding what the lawyer will be doing, what constitutes legal work and what doesn't. For example, transferring your home to your family is legal work that the lawyer performs, whereas standing in line to close your DBS bank account is not legal work. There are tasks that you can take on to reduce the cost of Probate.

6. Planning for sufficient estate liquidity

Sometimes the deceased's estate does not have sufficient liquidity to pay for testamentary expenses like for the funeral, taxes and Probate fees. In that situation, someone in the family can pay first and when Probate is settled, the person can get reimbursed.

We have, however, experienced situations where the deceased passed away with a lot of assets but hardly any cash for expenses. We have also experienced situations where family members did not want to help pay for the expenses ahead of time.

2　In Part 4 of this book, we discuss how Singaporeans who own foreign assets can do their estate planning.

As if Daniel's death is not stressful enough for his family, Jenny has to figure out the most affordable way to settle Daniel's estate. But what if Daniel had done some pre-planning to ensure there would be liquidity to take care of expenses on his death? That would surely lift Jenny's spirits.

How much estate liquidity is needed?

Here is a suggested formula to use:

Estate liquidity needed = testamentary expenses + 12 months of family expenses + mortgages + other expenses

Testamentary expenses include payment for the Grant of Probate, funeral expenses and income tax to IRAS on your estate income. We expect that $30,000 should be enough for most estates. For Daniel, the amount may be closer to $50,000 because he owns foreign assets.

We suggest you prepare for 12 months of family expenses in case it takes 12 months to obtain the Grant of Probate. While the Grant can usually be extracted in three to six months, we have dealt with estates where the Grant took 18 months or more to extract. Sometimes, there are complications like beneficiaries fighting, missing persons and assets discovered only months after the person's death.

Family expenses include payments that you were making at the time of your death and these may include:

- Maintenance for the family.
- Car payments.
- House instalment payments.
- Credit card debt and other loan payments.

For Daniel's estate, let's assume his monthly expenses were $10,000 a month or $120,000 for 12 months.

If there are any mortgages remaining, you may want to give the properties to your family fully paid up and unencumbered. He had a $1 million loan remaining on his semi-detached home.

Daniel owns a fully paid-up London property that he is giving to his daughter, Vickie, who is studying in London. It is a UK-sited asset and subject to inheritance tax of 40%. It is charged on the part of his UK estate that is above the tax-free threshold of £325,000.[3] Suppose the apartment is assessed at £1.325 million at the time of his death, his estate is hence liable for:

$$\text{UK inheritance tax} = (\pounds1.325 \text{ million} - \pounds325{,}000) \times 40\%$$
$$= \pounds400{,}000 \text{ or SGD710,000}$$

This tax has to be paid to the UK tax office before the apartment can be transferred to Jenny.

Altogether, Daniel's estate liquidity needs come up to $1.88 million ($50,000 + $120,000 + $1 million + $710,000). As you can see, the total amount needed for liquidity far exceeds the cost of Probate, which is small in comparison.

How to plan for liquidity

Not planning for sufficient liquidity could result in the executor being forced to sell estate assets, sometimes at a time when asset values are low, to generate cash for estate expenses. Daniel's estate liquidity needs are of course higher than for many other people. Whatever your situation, you can quite easily calculate how much your family would need to settle your estate.

Liquidity comes from two main sources:

- Insurance – this is always the most affordable means to provide liquidity. If purchased early enough during Daniel's lifetime, a term policy can be very affordable.
- Non-insurance – this includes cash in Daniel's CPF account, the cash in his bank accounts, his listed share investments and other assets that can be sold. You would agree that non-insurance is a less preferred source.

3   "Inheritance tax", www.gov.uk.

EXTRACTING THE GRANT OF PROBATE

To extract the Grant of Probate, one of the key documents that must be submitted to the court is the Schedule of Assets in a format required by the court. The Schedule is a list of the deceased's properties in Singapore as at the date of death, as well as outstanding debts (which are secured by mortgage), and property outside Singapore. If you have been doing your record keeping of your assets, then this Schedule can be easily put together by your probate lawyer for presentation to the court.

Once the court confirms that there are no other documents required, your lawyer will be able to request for the extraction of the Grant.

A final search is made to ensure that there are no caveats lodged against any assets of the estate. A caveat is a legal document lodged by a person with an interest in an asset. For example, if a person has made a deposit to purchase a home, he may lodge a caveat to protect his interest in the property.

If the documents are in order and all fees have been paid, the court will prepare and issue the Grant of Probate.

CONCLUSION

The Grant of Probate is the document that your executor needs in order to distribute your assets to your family according to your Will. Obtaining the Grant is a procedural matter that is full of details that are best left to a professional like the probate lawyer.

Families who are concerned about the cost of paying for Probate should cast away those concerns. With some pre-planning, it is easy to calculate an estimated amount needed for liquidity and if you do it early enough, you would be able to purchase insurance at affordable rates. Buy more insurance if you can because when your expenses and the value of your assets increase, the amount of liquidity your estate needs would increase too.

Some of the other things we can plan for is to appoint a third-party executor, keep records of your assets and documents, and safekeep your will. We want a hassle-free time for our families when we pass away, and with some planning, your family will be able to give you a smooth send-off to the next world.

Part 2

Special Situations: Family

In Part 1, we looked at the six essential estate planning documents that everyone would require to ensure that their affairs are handled smoothly in the event of their incapacity or death.

The following 14 chapters focus on special situations that you may need to consider due to your family circumstances or goals.

We expand on Trust planning in chapter 6 where, using a Will Trust, we show how financial planning is key to ensuring there is enough of an estate to meet one's planning objectives. Chapters 7 and 8 discuss Living Trusts which, although costlier and requiring administration during one's lifetime, are more able to meet the needs of the families today.

Chapter 10 on retirement planning suggests that you should take care of your own retirement before you think about your gifting goals for your loved ones.

Chapters 11 and 12 are on life insurance, which are essential instruments that provide innumerable benefits – liquidity, estate expansion, estate equalisation, tax mitigation, confidentiality and others.

Chapter 13 looks at how trust funds are invested and managed. With a prudent investment policy, the trust fund can generate sufficient returns to pay for trust expenses, earn a return and extend the number of years that beneficiaries can receive benefits.

What makes a happy and successful family is the topic of chapter 14. It's more than just about money.

In chapter 15, a veteran divorce lawyer is interviewed on what makes a happy marriage and how a couple who are intent on divorce can have an amicable settlement.

Chapter 16 explains the rules of guardianship and adoption along with some case studies.

Chapters 17 and 18 look at how Christians and Muslims have apparently different rules and principles on estate planning but in the end, it's about caring for the family and adhering to God's ways.

Persons with special needs are vulnerable members of the community. Chapter 19 highlights how their caregivers can put in place a care plan and financial plan that are activated when the caregiver is unable to continue providing caregiving.

Finally, in chapter 20, we learn that giving is the foundation of a happy life. We examine various ways in which we can give during and after our lifetime.

Chapter 7

Planning and Funding a Will Trust

by **Keon Chee** with **Samuel Tan**

We took our first steps in chapter 2 to understand what a Trust is and what it can do for families.

Bear in mind that the Trust is merely an instrument. It is the planning not the instrument that makes an estate plan. At this stage of our estate planning journey, it is not wise to dive too deeply into the technical details. We should focus on planning; otherwise, we will miss the forest for the trees.

The purpose of this chapter is to lay out a typical plan for a typical family. We will see that estate planning has to include financial planning at the start, in the middle and at the end. Imagine the perfect estate plan with a sophisticated Will and Trust setup, but it does not have the funds to carry the plan through.

We will continue to use the Will Trust in this chapter for our planning. In the next two chapters, we will learn about Living Trusts, after which we can better answer the question – "Based on the plan we have devised, what trust structure is better suited for me?"

PLANNING FOR DAVID'S FAMILY

David is a 40-year-old company executive whose fact finding is shown in Figure 7.1. He is married to Sally and they have a 5-year old son called Sonny. He earns $15,000 per month, while Sally stays home to care for Sonny. They live in a 3-bedroom condo that is owned solely by David. Sally owns a HDB flat solely that she inherited from her father who has passed away. It is estimated that David's net worth at death is $1.5 million, excluding the condo.

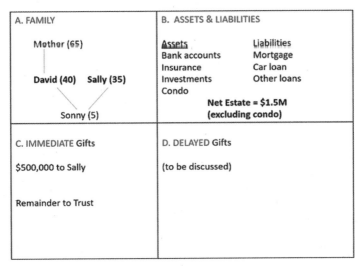

A. FAMILY	B. ASSETS & LIABILITIES	
Mother (65) David (40) Sally (35) Sonny (5)	**Assets** Bank accounts Insurance Investments Condo	Liabilities Mortgage Car loan Other loans **Net Estate = $1.5M** **(excluding condo)**
C. IMMEDIATE Gifts $500,000 to Sally Remainder to Trust	D. DELAYED Gifts (to be discussed)	

Figure 7.1 – Results of David's Fact Finding

On his death, David wishes to make an immediate gift of $500,000 to Sally and create a Trust for his mother. Let's assume Sally has already done planning for Sonny separately.

David's net estate of $1.5 million excluding the condo seems attractive, but we do not yet know if this amount is enough for his family if he passes away. Our planning needs to begin with determining whether there are enough funds for his estate plan and, if not, how to plan for more funds.

Planning a Trust for his mother

David wants to look after his mother's financial needs for the rest of her life by:

1. giving her a regular allowance for ongoing expenses;
2. paying for her health insurance premiums; and
3. paying for any medical or other emergency.

David worked with his financial planner and estate planner to come out with the following plan:

---

1. For ongoing expenses till end of life:

Suppose she lives another 25 years and is to receive $2,500 per month as allowance. The amount to set aside is:

$30,000 per year x 25 years = $750,000

2. For health insurance cover till end of life:

Health insurance premiums go up as we age. We estimate the annual premiums to average $4,000 per year over her lifetime. The amount to set aside is:

$4,000 per year x 25 years = $100,000

3. For emergencies and contingencies:

David wants to limit the amount to $150,000 so that his siblings would also chip in. The amount to set aside is:

$150,000

Total amount to set aside for his mother:

$1,000,000

The ongoing allowance maintains her for the rest of her life. The ongoing payment for health insurance premiums takes care of her medical needs. The emergency amount takes care of unforeseen situations.

We cannot be sure that $1 million is enough or too much. What is important is that a good sum of money has been set aside based on a fairly sound plan and he can adjust his plan at any time after that.

Dealing with inflation

Do we have to keep adjusting the $2,500 per month allowance to David's mother for inflation? There can be a standard clause in the Will Trust to adjust the stated amounts for inflation starting from the day it was drafted. The trustee can refer to an inflation indicator such as the Consumer Price Index to adjust the amounts year after year. There is no need to adjust the stated amounts in the Will Trust unless there are major changes in the needs of the beneficiaries.

Safeguarding the condo

The condo is their much-loved home. It's where the family (including his mother) has lived since Sally and David got married. David would like Sally to have the home eventually and, in the meanwhile, he wants the condo to be safeguarded until his mother passes away.

David's estate planner suggested that he places the home in a Trust upon his passing. The trustee can be a licensed Trust company. Instructions can be left in his Will for the trustee to allow his family to live in the home rent-free and to maintain the home, including paying for insurance and property tax. Then when his mother passes away, the home can be transferred to Sally, or sold and the proceeds given to Sally.[1]

The condo's market value is $4 million and has a mortgage of $3 million. The condo has to be fully paid up for it to be held in Trust. Without it being fully paid up, the trustee would not be able to fully own the condo to do its job.

Financial planning for David

David does not have enough funds to fund his estate plan:

- Trust fund for his mother = $1 million
- Funds to fully pay for condo = $3 million

---

1 Transferring a property to a trustee has a number of technical requirements to be considered, including who might be a suitable trustee (whether an individual such as Sally or an independent trustee such as a licensed trust company), what stamp duties are payable when transferring to a trustee on David's death and what stamp duties are payable when transferring to Sally when Sonny turns 25. These technical matters are beyond the scope of this book.

- Total needed = $4 million
- Total available = $1.5 million
- Shortfall = $2.5 million

David can begin saving for this shortfall. He can also speak to his financial planner about purchasing life insurance of $2.5 million to meet the expected shortfall in funds.[2]

CONCLUSION

People often think that their deaths could be decades away in the future, when in fact, we should be planning for "what if something happens to me tomorrow?"

If you have elderly parents, you really do need to make a plan today that includes delayed gifts. For your children, tell them you have a plan that will not be used until you are elderly and they have grown up, but the plan is there just in case there is an emergency.

A Trust is often thought of as being a complicated and expensive tool that only the wealthy can afford. That is not true at all. With a Will Trust, just about anyone can have a Trust and it can be customised to meet many situations.

Financial planning is essential to estate planning. In conversations with clients, I always emphasise that planning for sufficient trust funds comes before the estate plan itself.

Will Trusts, however, do not satisfy every planning need as they do have some drawbacks. To name a few:

- Will Trusts do not offer confidentiality on death;
- they can be inflexible when it comes to making amendments; and
- they do not offer your assets enough protection from creditors.

The next two chapters look at Living Trusts, which are Trusts that are set up during your lifetime (rather than after). We will see that living trusts shine where Will Trusts do not. In chapter 9, the

---

2   Annual premiums for David's $2.5 million whole life policy is about $45,000 per year.

planning for David will be revisited using a Living Trust instead of a Will Trust. You will then be able to consider which instrument may be better suited for your family.

Chapter acknowledgement:
With great thanks to Allen Lim of Manulife Financial Advisers for providing me with insurance quotations. He is one of the most competent financial advisers I know.

Chapter 8

Aspects of Living Trusts

by **Keon Chee**

We learned in chapters 2 and 7 that Will Trusts are a simple and effective solution for an individual to care for his family. Through staggered payments for ongoing expenses, emergencies and lump sum payments for values-based gifts, Will Trusts should be considered by any family with young children, elderly parents and other vulnerable beneficiaries.

Most of the trusts that I deal with are Living Trusts rather than Will Trusts. A Living Trust is set up during an individual's lifetime (rather than after). While they are more costly to set up, they can accommodate a far wider range of planning situations.

In this chapter, we look at what a Living Trust is, its most important features and how they can be used in certain situations.

WHAT IS A LIVING TRUST?

In a Will Trust, the testator appoints the trustee to set up a Trust after his lifetime. As the Trust arises from a Will, the Trust is not set up until the testator passes away. The trustee has no role until the testator passes away and that could be in 5, 15 or more years in the future.

In a Living Trust as set out in Figure 8.1:

1. The settlor sets up the Trust during his lifetime.
2. An agreement is signed between the settlor who wishes to set up the Trust and the trustee who agrees to look after the Trust. This legally binding agreement is called the Trust deed.
3. The trustee begins the administration of the Trust during the settlor's lifetime.
4. Assets are provided to the beneficiaries based on the settlor's wishes.

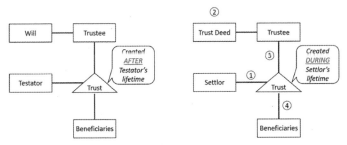

Figure 8.1 – A Will Trust compared with a Living Trust

There are four aspects of Living Trusts that, in combination, are fundamental to understanding why families prefer them over.

1. Living Trusts are confidential

A Will Trust becomes public to the testator's family upon his passing. If Gladys wants to make gifts to her secret friend and does not want her family to find out, she can write a Will and keep it confidential during her lifetime. However, when she passes away, her husband and children can find out what she tried to keep confidential when she was alive.

The trustee of a Living Trust, on the other hand, is required to keep Trust information and documents confidential as a matter of law. When Gladys sets up a Living Trust for her secret friend during her lifetime and places assets into the Trust, she receives two benefits of confidentiality. First, the Trust arrangement is kept confidential from those who are not a party to the Trust. This means that if her immediate family members are not part of the Trust arrangement, the details of the Trust are kept confidential from them.

Second, the assets transferred into the Trust during her lifetime do not need to be probated in a court of law. So if Gladys transfers $1 million into the Trust to benefit her friend, the money would not show up during the probate process.

> **Examples of confidentiality**
>
> Michael Jackson left behind three minor children when he
> died unexpectedly on 25 June 2009. His Will became public
> right after his death and one can easily Google to view it. His
> Will has a clause to put his estate into the Michael Jackson
> Family Trust. We would not know who the beneficiaries
> are in the Trust or how his estate is divided up. That is the
> confidentiality benefit of a Living Trust.

Anita Mui aged 40 died of cervical cancer on 30 December
2003. She set up a Living Trust a few days before she passed away.
Details of her Trust would have been kept confidential, except that
her mother went to court to fight the validity of the Will and Trust.
As a result, details of her Trust are now known to the public.

2. Living Trusts can be revocable or irrevocable

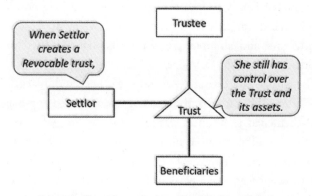

Figure 8.2 – The settlor remains in control with a Revocable Trust

A Revocable Trust can be changed any time before your death.
You can modify it if you have second thoughts about who is a
beneficiary or how the funds should be invested. You can even
terminate the Trust if you decide that it doesn't serve your objectives
any longer.

The assets transferred to a Revocable Trust are still considered your personal property and you can retrieve them when you wish to. However, if you want your assets protected from creditors, a Revocable Trust will fail you: as you continue to have control over your assets, your creditors can still reach them before and after your lifetime.

Irrevocable Trusts in contrast are considered rigid for good reason. An Irrevocable Trust cannot be changed by the settlor after the agreement has been signed. Assets transferred in cannot be taken back by the settlor, almost as if he is putting money into a safe and throwing the key away. For the most part, when you choose an Irrevocable Trust, you form the Trust, place assets in the Trust and step aside for all time.[1]

Example of Revocable Trust

Andy and Teresa are in their early 50s with children in their late teens. They are financially secure with no loans remaining on their homes. They are retiring from their jobs in two years. They want to create a Trust to care for their two children. Their son joined a religious group whose beliefs are, according to Andy and Teresa, "detrimental to society." Their daughter has been filial and will be studying music at NAFA in a year.

Andy and Teresa want a Trust that allows them to have complete control of their assets during their lifetimes. They want to be able to amend their Trust should their children fall in or out of line. They also want to leave something to their future grandchildren for their university education.

3. Living Trusts can be discretionary or fixed

Trusts can be either discretionary or fixed (non-discretionary).

In a Fixed Trust, the settlor specifies the amounts that the beneficiaries are entitled to receive at specified times in the future

---

1   There are situations in which an Irrevocable Trust can be amended or terminated by the settlor and the assets taken back. For example, where the purpose for which the Trust was set up is not relevant anymore, such as where the beneficiary is a person with special needs and he has passed away. Another situation is when the Trust has been depleted of funds.

such as, "Give $5,000 per month for a period of 10 years starting when my daughter Tammy is 25 years old." Such an instruction, along with the Trust being set up as a fixed Trust, provides the trustee with no discretion or power to vary or withhold the amounts to be given because distributions have been pre-arranged by the settlor. If Tammy passes away before she reaches 25, the undistributed funds belong to her estate.

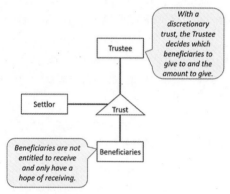

Figure 8.3 – Discretionary Trusts can protect beneficiaries

In a Discretionary trust, as presented in Figure 8.3, the trustee is given discretion as to when and what funds are given to which beneficiaries. The beneficiaries of the trust are not entitled to the funds; they only have a hope of receiving benefits. The funds are also not regarded as part of the beneficiary's estate.

The trustee would use your wishes (discussed in next section) to guide them in distributing funds to beneficiaries. For example, the trustee may be given a guideline to distribute a lump sum of $1 million to a beneficiary when he reaches 25 and is not in an adverse situation such as he is going through bankruptcy or divorce.

This discretion that is exercisable by the trustee has the effect of protecting Trust funds. If the beneficiary is going through an adverse situation, the trustee can withhold the distribution for the time being until the adverse situation has passed.

Example of Discretionary Trust

Daniel and Lency have a young family. Daniel is wealthy but in ill health. He is afraid that if he contracts the Covid-19 virus and passes away suddenly, his young children won't have the maturity to use the money wisely. He sets up a Discretionary Trust, using a licensed Trust company as the trustee. By doing this, he is confident that his trustee will ensure that his children's needs are met, and help to ensure they receive funds only for specified purposes such as maintenance and education.

4. The Letter of Wishes (LOW) offers flexibility

The Trust deed is usually 25 pages or more and filled with legal language. It sets out the terms of the Trust and acts as guidance on how the Trust should be managed. It grants powers and discretions to the trustees. In many instances, the Trust deed is a standard document that is used with minimal modification for numerous families who may have widely different circumstances.

How does the trustee, who is supposed to step into your shoes, know what your true intentions and priorities are? This is the purpose of the LOW as illustrated in Figure 8.4. It is a non-binding letter to provide guidance to the trustee. It is written in an informal way to tell the trustee to use its discretion to administer and distribute trust assets to the beneficiaries.

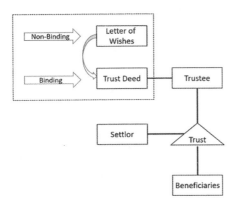

Figure 8.4 – How the LOW complements the Trust Deed

Because the LOW is non-binding, it allows the trustee to adapt to changing circumstances in the future. For example, a statement such as "Pay the tuition fees for the first university degree of my descendants up to 6 years" provides ample guidance to the trustee to give a reasonable amount based on the cost of tuition fees in the future, which could be 50 years or more from today.

The LOW can be amended by the settlor anytime as the need arises. The settlor, usually in consultation with the trustee, can amend and sign a new LOW at usually minimal cost.

An LOW can provide peace of mind to both the settlor and the trustee. The settlor has shared his heartfelt wishes to the trustee, and the trustee has received guidance in exercising its discretionary powers.

EXAMPLE USES OF LIVING TRUSTS

Consider setting up a Living Trust for your family if any of the examples of concerns in Table 8.1 describe your situation. What is described is based on just a snippet of what is possible:

Table 8.1 – Examples of Concerns and How a Trust Can Help

Your concern	Consider this type of Trust	What you can do with the Trust
Spendthrift children	A Discretionary Trust	Provide reasonable funds for your children on a regular basis for maintenance until a certain age such as 35. Avoid lump sum gifts unless children have achieved certain milestones, such as completing university or having stayed employed for a number of years.
You run a business and are worried about creditors reaching into your personal assets	An Irrevocable Trust	When you, the settlor, transfer assets into an Irrevocable Trust during your lifetime, you are giving up control and the benefits of the assets. Those assets therefore cannot be reached by your creditors because you no longer own them. The transfer should not have been done with an intent to defraud creditors; otherwise, those assets could be subject to a clawback.

You are concerned about your own divorce	An Irrevocable Trust	You can transfer assets into an Irrevocable Trust for the benefit of your children so that those assets cannot be clawed back by your divorcing spouse. Of course, you should not be creating the Trust with the intention of unfairly depriving your spouse, especially if those assets are matrimonial assets that are subject to division in the event of a divorce. Any sort of unfair transfer could bring about a clawback.
You are concerned about your children divorcing	A Discretionary Trust	If you are planning to give your children certain lump sum payments in the future, you may specify that the trustee should withhold such payments if your child is having difficulties in his marriage or in the middle of divorce proceedings.
You have persons with special needs in your family	A special-purpose Trust set up and administered by the Singapore Special Needs Trust Company	We have devoted a chapter to this topic. See chapter 19 on persons with special needs.
You are Muslim and you want to set aside more funds for your disabled daughter	An Irrevocable Trust into which assets are transferred during your lifetime	We have devoted a chapter to this topic. See chapter 18 on planning for Muslims.

CONCLUSION

This chapter explained the most fundamental aspects of Living Trusts. We gave a few examples of concerns that families may have and showed how certain Trust features can enhance their planning.

In the next and final chapter on trusts, we will look at three case studies of Living Trusts with structures that are quite commonly used in Singapore.

Chapter acknowledgement:

With great thanks to Linda Wong and James Bates of Kensington Trust Singapore Limited for their review of the chapter and providing their valuable input. They are extremely knowledgeable about Trusts.

Chapter 9

Uses of Living Trusts

by **Keon Chee**

Estate planning is about having management control over your assets while you are alive and after your death. One of the most basic ways to achieve this is through a Living Trust. A Living Trust can be used in countless ways and, with imagination, it can provide wealth and instil values in your future generations.

In this final chapter on Trusts, we look at three types of Living Trusts which Singaporeans and foreigners commonly use:
1. Standby Trust
2. Insurance Trust
3. Investment Trust

Case studies of typical situations will be considered. As always, you should focus on the planning aspect and leave the technical details to your estate planner and Trust advisor.

STANDBY LIVING TRUST FOR A YOUNG FAMILY

Case study
We planned for David's family in chapter 7, where he wrote a Will Trust to set up Trusts to care for his mother and son, and to hold the family home. Today, unfortunately, he has revealed that he has been separated from Sally for the past five years and they plan to divorce soon. He met Ivy three years ago and they plan to get married. On the work front, he plans to quit his full-time job to start a business in the next five years with his best friend, Alan.

He wants to go over his estate plan and is anxious about how to deal with the new elements in his life. David realised that the Will Trust was suitable for his earlier family situation but it is not flexible enough to accommodate his future plans – unless he is willing to continually rewrite what would be an increasingly complex Will Trust each time.

Additionally, he wants his planning to be known to only certain individuals during *and* after his lifetime. With the Will Trust, the Will would have to be probated on his passing and that is when the contents of his planning could be revealed to people he may not wish to share those details with, such as Sally, his soon-to-be ex-wife, and even his mother and siblings. He wants a level of confidentiality that is protected by law. This confidentiality is best achieved with a Living Trust.

Role of protector

Whether the Trust is large or small, how can David be sure that the trustee understands the spirit of his intentions and would perform the trustee's role capably? Is there someone who can oversee the trustee when he is no longer around?

The settlor of a discretionary Trust can appoint a person called a protector to direct or restrain the trustee, someone who may be able to remove the trustee for any misconduct or poor performance.

The powers of a protector are specified in the Trust deed and may include the power to:

1. remove and appoint trustees;
2. approve addition or removal of beneficiaries;
3. approve a change of proper law;
4. approve proposed trust distributions;
5. approve appointment of an agent or adviser;
6. approve investment decisions;
7. appoint replacement protectors; and
8. terminate Trust or approve termination of Trust.

The protector is not mandatory in a Discretionary Trust; it is the settlor's choice. David is keen to have such a role installed. He discusses the matter with the Trust company to select the powers most relevant to his family situation. These powers are drafted into the Trust deed, which makes them binding and enforceable.

The settlor is usually the first protector. David wishes to appoint his sister, Esther, to be the substitute protector after his lifetime. Esther loves his children and understands how a Trust works.

David decides to set up an SLT as presented in Figure 9.1. This is how it works:

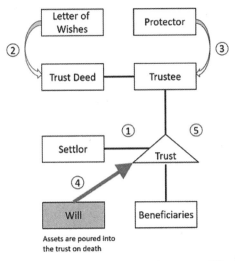

Figure 9.1 – A Standby Living Trust with a Pour-over Will

① David sets up a Trust during his lifetime. He leaves it in standby mode and puts in minimal assets during his lifetime.

② With guidance from the trustee, he writes his Letter of Wishes (LOW) to specify his wishes on how the Trust funds should be managed and distributed.

③ He accepts his position as first protector during his lifetime. His sister, Esther, is the substitute protector after his lifetime.

④ When David passes away, his Will pours his assets into the Trust.

⑤ The trustee begins the job of managing and distributing the Trust funds.

During his lifetime, the trustee meets with David regularly, such as once a year or as needed to review his wishes to see if his documents need to be amended. Usually, it would be mainly the letter of wishes that is amended.

After his passing, the trustee steps into David's shoes to manage and distribute the Trust funds over time.

The instructions that David meticulously set out in his Will Trust can now be transferred into his LOW.[1] When his circumstances or priorities change over the years, David can amend the LOW, usually at a minimal cost. There is no need to rewrite the Will.

Confidentiality of the Trust is ensured because it is a Living Trust; the Trust arrangement is confidential and revealed only to his beneficiaries and to those persons David chooses; if he transfers any assets to the Trust during his lifetime, those transfers are confidential.

INSURANCE TRUST FOR BUSINESS OWNER

Case study

Diane, aged 50, runs her own property development company. She has $80 million in properties, all paid up, and $20 million in cash and financial investments. She is planning to start a substantial residential property project in Thailand as one of the main investors.

Her husband passed away a few years ago and she has two children, aged 15 and 20. She is excited about the project and wants to set aside funds for her children, just in case her project fails and creditors try to reach into her personal assets.

---

1   There is a difference in the language used in the Will and LOW. The language in the Will is formal and binding, whereas the language in the LOW is informal and non-binding.

She purchases a US$10 million universal life policy paying a single premium of US$2.75 million. She's thinking about nominating the policy proceeds directly to her two children. In order to protect the policy from her creditors, Diane can make an irrevocable nomination. While this protects the policy cash value and proceeds from her creditors, she has concerns that her children could each receive US$5 million at a very young age.

Through her estate planner, she sets up an irrevocable insurance trust to hold one or more insurance policies as seen in Figure 9.2:

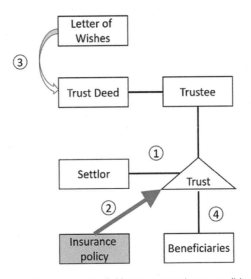

Figure 9.2 – Insurance Trust holding one or more insurance policies

① Diane sets up an irrevocable insurance Trust.
② She assigns the insurance policy to the Trust.[2]
③ She writes an LOW to specify how the proceeds should be managed and distributed on her passing.
④ When Diane passes away, the trustee collects the proceeds and transfers them to the trust, and begins the job of managing and distributing the trust funds.

---

2 Some explaining is needed here. She needs to "give away" the policy in order to protect the policy against future creditors. She does this through an assignment which absolutely gives away the rights of the policy. An irrevocable nomination is not possible because they can only be made to spouse and/or children. Second, the assignment is actually to the trustee which then places the policy into the Trust.

Big multimillion-dollar insurance policies are common these days, thanks to our wealth and the greater availability of competitively priced insurance. A standalone insurance Trust is a popular structure to hold such large policies. With such a structure, wealthy individuals, foreigners and business owners can channel the proceeds of large policies through a Trust, while not disturbing the planning they have already done.

INVESTMENT TRUST FOR A FOREIGNER

The settlor who creates a Living Trust can transfer assets into the Trust during his lifetime to benefit himself and his beneficiaries. A Trust that is activated this way during the settlor's lifetime is an Active Living Trust (as compared with a Standby Living Trust which is activated after the settlor's passing).

Active Living Trusts are commonly used by foreigners who have a tradition of setting up such trusts for confidentiality, asset protection, tax mitigation and succession planning. In the next case study, we discuss a foreigner who sets up an Active Living Trust in Singapore to manage his family's portfolio of financial assets.

Case study

Rudolf, age 60, is German and married to a fellow German. They have three children and they all live in Germany. Rudolf is a keen investor in global securities and has a US$50 million investment portfolio held in his sole name. The assets came from an inheritance from his parents.

He has heard about the foreign Trust regime in Singapore and wants to shift his investment portfolio to Singapore. He has also heard of the excellent asset managers located in Singapore who invest around the region and globally.

He has no plans to be physically located in Singapore and plans to remain in Germany.

Stage 1

He decides to set up an Active Living Trust and transfers his investment portfolio to a Singapore trustee. He wishes to continue managing the portfolio. See Figure 9.3A.

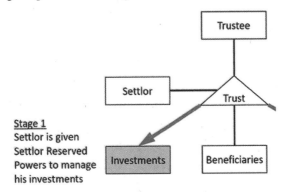

Figure 9.3A – Rudolf manages Trust investments with Settlor Reserved Powers

Since his investment portfolio is now owned by the trustee, he is given settlor reserved powers (as specified in the Trust deed) to allow him to continue to direct the trustee in buying and selling securities for the portfolio.[3] Second, for convenience, Rudolf is given a limited power of attorney by the trustee so that he can deal directly with the broker to buy and sell securities, without having to go through the trustee.

Stage 2

A few years later, Rudolf wants his 30-year-old daughter, Sophie, to help manage the family's investments. The trustee suggests he sets up a foreign company (a company incorporated in the British Virgin Islands (BVI)), for example, whose shares are transferred to the trustee. The portfolio held by the trustee is transferred to the company.[4] See Figure 9.3B.

---

3   Section 90(5) of the Trustees Act allows the settlor to reserve to himself the powers of investment management of the Trust assets.

4   Settlor Reserved Powers can only be reserved to the settlor. Rudolf cannot grant his reserved powers to another person or to an investment committee. See "Reserved Powers Trusts Examined", 16 December 2015, www.collascrill.com.

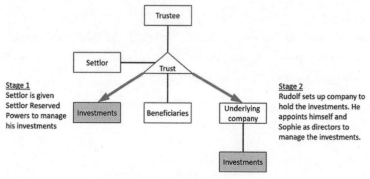

Figure 9.3B – Rudolf and Sophie manage their family investments through the company

Rudolf and Sophie, as the directors of the BVI company, can together direct and manage the investments of the family. There are a few points to note:

- Combining stages 1 and 2 – Rudolf could have combined both stages at the start. In fact, most foreigners already have an underlying company at the time they set up an active Living Trust. We went through two stages in order to explain the thinking behind the eventual structure.

- Qualifying Foreign Trusts (QFTs) – The Trust is likely to be considered a QFT where

  (a) every settlor and beneficiary is neither a citizen nor a resident of Singapore,

  (b) if there is any underlying company, it is incorporated outside Singapore, and

  (c) the trust must be administered by a Singapore licensed trustee company.

  A Singapore Foreign Trust enjoys tax exemption from "specified income" derived from "designated investments".[5]

- Succession planning – When Rudolf passes away, Sophie can continue managing the family investments with minimal disruption to the operations. She can continue as sole director until (if and when) she decides to have another director appointed to join her to continue her good work.

5   You can read more about foreign Trusts here: "Singapore Foreign Trusts", www.kensington-trust.com/resource-center/resources/singapore-foreign-trusts/.

Rudolf has succeeded in meeting his objectives of moving his portfolio to a tax efficient, business-friendly Trust jurisdiction. He is confident that should he pass away, Sophie, his daughter, would have already learned the ropes to continue without him.

CONCLUSION

We have come to the last of the Trust chapters. You should have received a few good ideas about how to plan for your family.

Use the fact find in chapter 2 to see if you need a Trust by first listing out your beneficiaries and assets. Then ask what immediate and delayed gifts you would make if you pass away suddenly. If you have vulnerable beneficiaries like children and elderly parents, chances are that you need a Trust. We introduced the Will Trust as a basic and most affordable Trust to consider.

In chapter 7, we combined financial and estate planning to set up a series of Trusts for a family. We used a Will Trust where the Trust instructions have to be carefully drafted into the Will.

The Living Trust was introduced in chapter 8, where the Trust is set up during one's lifetime rather than after. We got a glimpse of what sort of Trust you may need given a certain situation.

Finally, in this chapter, three case studies were used to introduce three commonly used structures in Singapore. There are, of course, other structures that may better meet your planning needs. Speak with an estate planner or Trust adviser about your family situation.

Chapter acknowledgement:
With great thanks to Linda Wong and James Bates of Kensington Trust Singapore Limited for their review of the chapter and providing their valuable input. They are extremely knowledgeable about Trusts.

With great thanks to Allen Lim of Manulife Financial Advisers for providing me with insurance quotations. He is one of the most competent financial advisers I know.

Chapter 10

Retirement Planning in Turbulent Times

by **Ronald Wong**

"The Young think they are Too young for it
The Old think they Cannot make it
The Rich think they Don't need it
The Poor think they Cannot afford it
Our Government is worried about it
Financial planners have difficulty communicating it
Retirees now Regret not having done enough about it
Yet, we will all eventually face it."

– Ronald Wong

This is an awkward chapter. We have discussed Wills and understand the importance of a Trust – documents to take care of people, things and what is on our minds that matter deeply to us after our departure.

While these documents and tools take care of what happens to us when we die, the event of death might take a very long time to come to pass, especially in Singapore, where we can expect to live beyond the age of 90!

Other questions beckon – what if we live too long? What if we fall sick, and can no longer continue going about our daily routine of work or business, and accumulate and set aside assets for the legacy we wish to leave behind? Are we able to do something that is suddenly of the most critical concern: are we able to take care of ourselves, or will we become a burden to the loved ones we initially thought about? We have yet to die, even though by then some may find that death could be a better and more merciful option.

In today's environment plagued by the COVID-19 virus, retirement is as much a nightmare as dying! Markets are volatile, many established businesses have closed for good, succumbing to the macroeconomic forces that took them by surprise.

The financial crisis brought on by COVID-19 is actually one crisis out of many that we have experienced in the past (such as the The Asian Crisis of 1997 and The Financial Crisis of 2007–2008) and one of many that we will experience in the future. And each time a crisis happens, we and especially retirees suddenly find that our retirement nest eggs have shrunk significantly, battered by the storms thrown up by the crisis. Why? How could this happen? In my humble opinion, it all boils down to a lack of holistic planning.

PLAN FOR YOUR RETIREMENT – A CLICHÉ WORTH REVISITING

Retirement planning is nothing new. We are living longer and the chance of outliving our retirement savings is real. The CPF Life payout provides a basic standard of living, insufficient to support our expectations of a "comfortable retirement".

We have far fewer babies now, and so we are not able to depend on our children as retirees did in the 1970s and 1980s. In those days, an average family nucleus of three to five children could take care of their elderly parents financially. Filial piety was stronger then, residing in the centre of core family values.

The population today is ageing rapidly and in a country like Singapore, this puts a huge burden on the State to provide basic healthcare and elderly support. Tax revenue cannot be effectively utilised to build the nation, burdened by expensive caregiving for the elderly. So we need to raise GST and bring in more foreigners to support growth, and this sometimes drives citizens crazy largely due to the fear of job losses. We know we cannot expect the government to take care of us in the future as we age – we should never expect that as it is our own responsibility, and retirement planning is all about providing for our golden years in dignity, with financial and emotional independence.

The cost of living is rising faster than we can ever imagine. A cup of kopi now costs more than $1.50 in some places, as compared to just $0.60 slightly over a decade ago! Medical inflation is hovering around 8 to 10% annually over the past decade.

If these facts are not grim enough for you to stop and think, something is amiss!

New Age Thinking and Retirement

I have been teaching Retirement Planning for the Certified Financial Planner (CFP®) program for over 15 years. I have found that the acronyms I create to help my students learn technical materials to pass their exams have also helped to inspire and remind them to do their own retirement planning. What I am sharing in this box has evolved over time.

"You may believe in 'FIRE'
You may believe in 'DIRE'
But believe me, you may not be able to RETIRE

You might wanna be called 'HENRY'
You may also like be known as 'DESIREE'
But someday you'll just be a RETIREE

Start planning for your retirement adequacy properly ..."
– **Ronald Wong**

These days, we have to grapple with New Age doctrines about retirement: the "FIRE Movement", the "DIRE Movement", the HENRYs and the DESIREEs. Different people that I have met have come up with their own ideas of how retirement should be planned.

Even these New Age retirement doctrines are being challenged these days, no thanks to COVID-19 and other crises. The FIRE ("Financially Independent, Retire Early") movement seems to have lost steam, with significant capital market drawdowns impairing the desired 5 per cent drawdown rate to an already simple retirement lifestyle – some who FIRE-ed are expected to return to work. The HENRYs ("High Earnings Not Rich Yet"), characterised by high income earners and small business owners, suddenly got hit and either got retrenched, or lost their entire businesses and income generation capability.

The DIRE ("Don't Intend to Retire, EVER") found themselves in a predicament as they have not saved enough passive income and have also lost their jobs. What about the DESIREEs ("Determined Entrepreneurs Seeking Innovative and Rewarding Experiences Everyday")? These millennial entrepreneurs dabbling in artisan craft, tech and niche marketing experiences, such as drop shipping, have not been spared either.

A BALANCED APPROACH TO RETIREMENT PLANNING

So how do we navigate the environment today or on any day? My advice is to take a balanced approach to RETIRE – **"Retirees Expecting Tangible Income Receipts Everyday".**

I would like to suggest the following six simple steps:

Step 1: Keep working, even in retirement!

Our economic life value is the most critical wealth creation resource we have, and we should always guard it closely, and enhance it exponentially. As we age, we may be less energetic than those who are younger, but our experience makes up for the loss of vigour. We must keep learning and developing our craft in whatever field we are in, and learn new tools and gain new experiences to maintain our relevance in the world. Personally, I have found coding a very valuable skill to learn, as it reinforces my ability to think analytically, and to combine algorithmic frameworks and creativity to new world problems. Due to COVID-19, we also need to develop a new type of soft skill – connecting with people virtually.

Even in retirement, we should not stop working. Retirement is never about not working in the first place, but about having the *choice* to pursue our passion, purpose and aspirations, while not having to worry about whether we are able to feed ourselves every day.

Step 2: Save a third in CPF and manage it prudently

If you are an employee below the age of 55, you do not have a choice in any event. Under the Central Provident Fund Act, an employee contributes 20% of his gross salary into his CPF account (CPF-OA/SA/MA) and his employer co-contributes another 17%.

Manage this "enforced savings" well for future retirement. There are many things one can do with one's CPF savings – provide for upward mobility, provide for retirement, provide basic healthcare and leave behind a legacy. Do not use 100% of your CPF-OA on a property. That would be putting all your eggs in one basket. Leave aside one-third to save and invest for retirement.

By the way, do not forget to set up a proper CPF nomination of beneficiary to ensure you utilise your right of choice to decide how you want to give away your CPF savings upon your demise. Otherwise, you will allow the Singapore Government to do it for you under the intestacy laws.

Step 3: Save regularly

Clichés are often good not to be ignored – "pay yourself first" is one. We would never save optimally if we only think of saving after paying off our expenses. Always set aside a portion of your income first before spending and you will always have an overflow of wealth in the future.

Here is my suggestion to help you get GRIPS on savings. I would suggest a start of 10% for each of the following elements, but these are just ballpark figures. One should manage the ratios in their own personal way that is manageable for them, and it should never be a burden to do so.

- *Generosity* – give to charity cheerfully. An ancient book says "Give, and you will receive. Your gift will return to you in full – pressed down, shaken together to make room for more, running over, and poured into your lap. The amount you give will determine the amount you get back." – I believe in this, absolutely.
- *Retirement* – set aside a portion for your future retirement. If you need $3,000 a month, saving $300 a month for a year will sustain you for one month of expenses in your future retirement, and if you utilise the law of compounding and invest in a wise and prudent manner, the amount you save will multiply your retirement income manifold.
- *Invest* – set aside a portion for general wealth accumulation. In an environment of low interest rates (such as today when AAA-rated bonds and Singapore Savings Bonds are low), investing is a better way to grow your money, potentially allowing you to "catch the wave on recovery". Of course, you should only do so with the guidance of a competent and qualified professional such as a CFP* Professional.
- *Personal development* – this was discussed this earlier. Commit to lifelong learning and increasing your economic life value. You can also use your SkillsFuture Credit given by the government to do so.

- *Save for the future* – a portion of your income should be committed to your general savings account to build up liquidity to buffer against any emergency. The old adage of having savings to cover three to six months of expenses may not hold true for everyone, as depending on circumstances, some might need less (for example, in the case of single individuals with no dependants) while some much more (such as sole proprietors, who are also breadwinners and have to care for many young and elderly dependants).

Step 4: Have a Portfolio of Insurance

An insurance policy is often perceived as the next best gift God provides to His stewards. Insurance policies provide certainty, preserves our financial wellbeing and retirement savings from destruction, and creates wealth. One should have a portfolio of insurance policies to protect against life's critical events:

- *Daily uncertainties such as accident and hospitalisation* – statistically, a person has a high chance of meeting with an accident or hospitalisation. Unforeseen events such as falls, dengue, etc, can creep up at the most unexpected time and deal a heavy financially blow in terms of lost income and medical bills, and having an adequate mix of hospitalisation (for example, Integrated Shield Policy, Hospital Cash, Early Critical Illness policies) and personal accident plans (such as Accidental Death and Disability, TCM and bone-setting coverage, etc) is critical.

- *Catastrophic events that impair our ability to work* – in such a situation, the person may be struck with a severe or total disability or a critical illness such as cancer or stroke which impairs the ability to continue working. Here's where term insurance and critical illnesses coverage will be an absolute lifesaver in terms of income replacement and wealth protection. In the event any of these happen to you, the policy should ideally help you kickstart a secure retirement, if proper planning has been done.

- *Risk of living too long* – a person should have insurance policies in the form of endowment and retirement income policies. Such policies provide a contractually guaranteed stream of cashflow and liquidity, irrespective of market conditions. One will find such contractually guaranteed payouts valuable in ensuring a minimal standard of living, complementing CPF Life.

At the end of the day, do not forget that when you set up a Trust, the most efficient way to fund it is through an insurance policy. As an insurance industry veteran, Ben Feldman, once said: "Insurance is like buying discounted money."

Step 5: Have a basket of investments

Investing is the only way we can beat inflation these days, and investing should not be something to be afraid of. Whether you are one who is absolutely risk averse or a speculative punter, there is a suitable investment strategy you can adopt to help you invest safely and profitably over the long-term horizon. Seek the advice of a qualified financial planner who will be able to help you understand your investment attitude and tolerance to risk and aversion to losses, and develop an asset allocation strategy to own a diversified portfolio to achieve a secure retirement.

Step 6: Give it a handful of time in the hands of a competent professional

Building retirement wealth is not magic. It takes time, and it takes expertise. To do so safely, you need to be patient. Markets fluctuate and you might go through turbulent times, but stick to the plan. The first five steps will help you to create a resilient retirement planning strategy. Now you need to take action and, if you have not already done so, I would suggest that you speak to a professional, such as a CFP* professional who is trained and qualified in various aspects of retirement, investment and financial planning to help you.

TAKE ACTION

> "The journey of a thousand miles begins
> with one step."
> **– Lao Tzu**

And if I may add, "in the *right direction*".

Retirement planning is not rocket science. However, it requires personal ownership and commitment, and the earlier you begin, the easier it will be. Often, many of us have already started at least thinking about it, but for some reason we may not have revisited it for a while. I would like, through this short chapter, to encourage you to start taking action for your retirement security, even as you think about what happens after your departure from this world, in considering Wills, Trusts and Special Situations that may happen.

This book is about taking action to get your personal and financial matters in place. Retirement is a critical part of it. Let your retirement plan protect what you are trying to leave behind, so that your Will and Trust instructions can fulfil their intended purposes without someone like your executor or trustee having to deviate from your intentions because your assets are insufficient to make your desired gifts to your family and loved ones.

If you plan well, you can "Rest in Peace" and need not "Rise if Possible"!

Chapter 11

Traditional Life Insurance

by **Eric Seah**

I have been in financial planning for 26 years. I joined the insurance industry right after I finished my National Service. Financial planning was my first job and it will be my last.

One of the disadvantages of being in the industry this long is that some of my clients have already passed away. Other than helping the family with collecting insurance payouts for the family, I found myself unable to help further when they asked me about how the deceased's estate would be distributed and when.

In 2007, I started taking classes in estate planning, Wills, Trusts, LPAs and others. As I took more classes, I became better at helping my clients and their families. I have since worked with hundreds of families and businesses, and I want to share my personal experience on why insurance is so important in estate planning. This chapter discusses life insurance only.

KEY BENEFITS OF LIFE INSURANCE

Life insurance is an amazing estate planning tool. Two key benefits are:

1. Immediate access to funds

When you pass away, your estate will be subject to probate, which can take many months to complete. While that is going on, your assets in the estate are tied up and cannot be accessed by your family. This could leave them without enough funds for household expenses and to pay bills. In comparison, the funds from a life insurance policy can be made available very quickly.

If you had made a nomination, the insurance payout can be as soon as one to two weeks. If you did not make a nomination, your family can still claim up to $150,000 per insurance company before probate is completed.

2. Leveraging your assets

One of the reasons insurance payouts are generous is because our life expectancy in Singapore is high. You should use this fact to your advantage. If you are a 50-year-old female non-smoker in good health, you can purchase a $1 million term life policy with an option to increase the death benefit to $1.5 million after ten years for $22,104 a year. Then if you pass away at 85, the payout on the policy is $1.5 million. In that case, you will have made 15 years of payments or $331,568 to create a $1.5 million estate for your family. That represents a net gain for your estate of $1,168,432.

Furthermore, there is no tax to pay on the insurance payout. That makes life insurance a very effective way to maximise the amount of money your family can receive.

ESTATE PLANNING IS PART OF FINANCIAL PLANNING

Figure 11.1 shows the financial planning triangle that I use to plan for my clients.

Starting from the bottom, I show my clients how to:

1. Protect their families in the event they pass away suddenly. They may get an amount of life insurance that is equal to a certain number of years of their income.
2. Accumulate funds for retirement by investing in units trusts, investment linked policies and other investments.
3. Preserve their estate such that their families can give the maximum amount possible for their families. This can be done through purchasing insurance to pay for mortgage debt, bank loans and company personal guarantees. Sometimes, clients want to create a nice legacy for their families to give them a

comfortable living, even though the family may have enough funds already for basic living.

4. Distribute the funds in their estate after they have passed away. This is where I work with service providers like lawyers, accountants, Will writers and Trust companies to provide the legal documents to help my clients to properly distribute their estates to their families.

Figure 11.1 – Financial planning triangle

MAIN GOAL OF FINANCIAL PLANNING IN ESTATE PLANNING

One of the main goals of financial planning in estate planning is to maximise the amount of assets for the family. We see in Figure 11.2 that on a person's death, his assets can be seen to be poured into a funnel. After his debts and obligations are paid, the net estate is available for distribution to the family.

I will now explain four main uses of life insurance that I have helped my clients with in order to maximise their net assets.

FOUR MAIN USES OF LIFE INSURANCE

I have helped my clients with the use of life insurance in four main areas of use. I will explain each use with a case study.

1. To enhance legacy

Henry bought a $2 million life insurance policy for his son and to leave some money for his church. As his son is young, he has used a Trust to hold the policy. When he passes away, the payout will be managed by the Trustee to give regular sums of money to his son for his upkeep, medical expenses and education. He also sets aside $50,000 for his church to be given $10,000 per year for five years.

2. To pay debts

Doris owns a $3 million condo as joint tenants with her husband. The condo has a mortgage remaining of $1.5 million. Doris bought a life insurance policy and mentioned in her Will that the remaining mortgage should be fully paid for by the insurance payout. Doris wants her husband to own the condo after her death without any debt remaining.

3. To equalise the estate

Paul's wife passed away a few years ago. He has a son and daughter. He has $5 million he wants to give his son. He has a condo worth $2 million that he wants his daughter to receive. In order to equalise the gifts for his children, Paul bought a $3 million insurance policy and nominated his daughter to receive the proceeds.

4. To protect the business

Judy owns a successful car parts trading company that she wants to pass to her 25-year-old son. She is concerned that if she passes away suddenly,

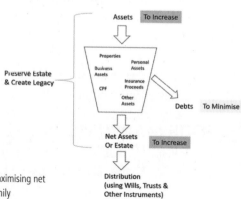

Figure 11.2 – Maximising net assets for the family

her son may not be ready to take over yet. The company has $1 million in liabilities and she has signed some personal guarantees. She buys a $2 million policy that on her death would pay up the $1 million of liabilities and provide a financial buffer of $1 million for her son to stabilise the company.

CONCLUSION

Life insurance is not only very flexible, it has helped hundreds of my clients meet their financial needs when a loved one suddenly passes away.

Life insurance is cheaper the younger you are when you purchase a policy. Plan ahead to get the best deal.

Work with an estate planner who can help you legalise the distribution of your estate with instruments like Wills and Trusts.

Chapter 12

Variable Universal Life Insurance

by **Louise Gan** and **Thomas Lim**

As a businessman in the last two decades in a neighbouring country, you have grown your business by leaps and bounds. You own majority shares of your business and continue to expand your business since it gives your family a comfortable living and high level of wealth. You acquired local and overseas properties and bought a varied portfolio of listed shares and bonds with the recommendation of your Singapore private banker, just to diversify. You have two grown-up sons, to whom you are contemplating passing the business eventually.

Your business is the largest part of your wealth portfolio and you hope to maintain absolute confidentiality when you transfer the shares to your beneficiaries, away from the scrutiny of your business competitors. Markets are volatile, which means the value of your assets fluctuates with it.

Regulations across countries have become increasingly demanding during the last few years. Taxation of wealth has become a priority for many governments, along with increased transparency and cross-border reporting. It is getting very cumbersome to consolidate your investments in different currencies and financial institutions annually for your tax reporting with the recent implementation of common reporting standards.[1] You are not particularly comfortable updating the authorities on the type and amount of assets you possess because of possible data breaches to unwelcome parties.

---

1   See chapter 35 for an explanation of common reporting standards (CSR).

You are looking for a plan for your family that gives you:

- confidentiality;
- asset protection;
- tax efficiency;
- control; and
- succession planning.

WHAT IS VARIABLE UNIVERSAL LIFE INSURANCE (VUL)?

VUL (or commonly called Private Placement Life Insurance (PPLI)) is a permanent life insurance policy that allows you to put your assets into a "variable account" comprised of financial assets. VULs are flexible in what insurers can accept as an asset. For simplicity, we will restrict our discussion to the most common type of asset accepted and that would be financial assets, which includes cash, stocks, bonds and unit trusts.

The dual nature of VUL provides you with valuable life insurance coverage, along with a cash-value component that permits you control over where you want to allocate the cash-value portion of your policy for greater earning potential.

The premiums that you transfer into a VUL need not be cash. It can be your financial assets that you have actively managed through the years. When the assets are transferred to the insurer, the insurer becomes the owner of the assets while the client becomes the policyholder of the VUL plan and the beneficiaries can be your loved ones and family members.

In comparison with traditional life insurance, the premiums paid are managed by insurance companies and any bonuses declared are subject to the insurer's performance and discretion. The policy owner does not participate in the decision making of how the premiums are invested or how much bonus is declared. For VUL plans, the policyholder can retain full control of investment assets and continue to invest them himself. He also has the flexibility to withdraw the profits of his investments.

Table 12.1 presents some of the main features of different types of insurance plans to help you compare the VUL with other types of plans that you may be familiar with.

Table 12.1 – A Comparison of a Few Types of Insurance in Singapore

	Variable Universal Life	Universal Life	Whole Life	Term
Coverage Duration	Life, flexible	Life, flexible	Life	Fixed, 1 year to age 99
Premium	Assets or cash	Cash only	Cash only	Cash only
Control over Investment Strategy	Policyholder	Insurer	Insurer	NA
Currency	Available in different currencies	USD only	SGD/USD	Available in different currencies
Investment management	Client/Client's Asset manager	Insurer	Insurer	NA
Accumulate Cash Values	Yes	Yes	Yes	No
Top Up/ Withdrawal Flexibility	Yes, subject to limits	Yes, subject to limits	No Top up. Withdrawal features in some plans	NA
Appeal to Customers	Flexible, transparent charges, potential investment upside, simplified CRS reporting, tax efficiency	Flexible, transparent charges, policy values grow with crediting rate. Usually invested in fixed income with guaranteed minimum returns	Guaranteed lifetime cover with bonuses subject to insurer discretion, cash values have guaranteed and variable portions	Low premium outlay, guaranteed cover for the specified period

Case study

Mr Hartono owns US$10 million of financial assets consisting of listed shares and bonds in a Singapore private bank. He is satisfied with his asset manager's performance of 6% to 8% returns annually. He withdraws dividends for his annual holidays and reinvests any profits from his portfolio with the bank.

With the recent implementation of common reporting standards, he needs to report annually to his country on the values of the assets. Any profits and dividends received by him will be consolidated in his annual tax reporting and would be subject to income tax.

He is used to having a diversified portfolio in various countries and currencies. This has helped him to make his money work harder for him. To consolidate these financial data annually for his local regulator is a cumbersome process and he is always concerned about managing the regulatory and fiscal complexity in different countries.

He is also concerned about how to pass the assets to his two children and whether his investments will be sold in a distressed market price if cash is required to fund his $5 million liabilities and last expenses.

SETTING UP A VUL PLAN

Hartono contacted a specialist insurer to set up a VUL as illustrated in Figure 12.1. Hartono has the flexibility to add on some insurance to provide liquidity to his estate when he passes away. He decided to also set up a trust to hold the VUL; then on his death, the proceeds of the VUL distributed to his family can be staggered over time.

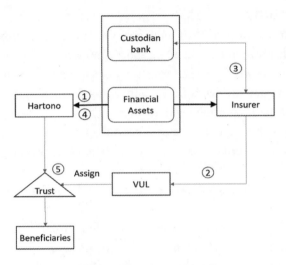

Figure 12.1 – Hartono sets up a VUL and Trust

1. Hartono transfers US$10 million of financial assets as premium. He applies for US$5 million of insurance cover in the VUL.
2. The insurer sets up a VUL with Hartono as the policy owner. The VUL periodically deducts from the investment account for insurance charge for the US$5 million cover.
3. The investments remain with Hartono's custodian bank. The insurer becomes the new owner of the investments.
4. Hartono is given a Limited Power of Attorney (LPOA) by the insurer to manage the investments.
5. He sets up an Irrevocable Trust and assigns the VUL to the Trust.

The VUL is unlike other insurance products. It is a wealth management tool where the client can place his investments into the VUL and continue to manage the investments under the VUL.

The Irrevocable Trust gives Hartono creditor protection, which is especially important for businessmen who are usually personally liable for the loans and debts of their companies.

DURING HARTONO'S LIFETIME

The VUL policy is a "holding vehicle" or "wrapper" for Hartono's investment assets. During his lifetime, he is able to:

- Manage the investments held within the VUL policy with an LPOA provided by the VUL insurer.
- Withdraw profits anytime he wishes (although there may be tax consequences for doing so).
- Achieve increased confidentiality and ease of reporting as his investments are held within an insurance policy, and annual reporting will be based on the value of the policy only, not on the types and values of underlying assets.
- Benefit from tax deferral. Depending on Hartono's and his beneficiaries' tax residence, the investment gains achieved within the VUL can potentially accrue tax-free within the policy. This tax deferral provides a very favourable tax-free compounding effect.

After Hartono's lifetime

Suppose the financial assets in his investment account grow to US$20 million during his lifetime. Along with US$5 million of proceeds from the insurance add-on, his trust receives US$25 million, that is, US$20 million of investments and US$5 million of cash. The funds can subsequently be managed by a suitable investment manager, while the trustee oversees the distribution of funds to his beneficiaries after paying for any liabilities, taxes and duties.

IS VARIABLE UNIVERSAL LIFE SUITED FOR YOU?

In our view, VUL is geared towards someone who already owns multiple life insurance policies and has investment portfolios whether self-managed or under management with private banks and asset managers. A person with such a profile is most suitable for VUL, because he can obtain multiple times of additional coverage through their existing investment portfolio, enjoy tax deferral benefits and maintain confidentiality of the policy's underlying assets.

People who purchase VULs need to have higher risk tolerance. VUL policies may offer flexibility and higher potential growth compared to traditional life policies, but they do not provide the guarantees that traditional policies do.

VULs are suitable for business owners and investors who are comfortable managing their assets directly. This flexibility to self-manage the underlying assets might do more harm than good for those who are less investment savvy. They may be better off getting traditional plans and have the insurers invest the premiums for them.

VULs can meet many business applications, including business continuity planning, keyman insurance and retirement planning. In many instances, VUL's ability to wrap a client's assets makes it both flexible and more complex. As a result, VULs require experienced financial professionals for structuring and setting up.

As you already can see, VULs are suitable for more affluent clients who typically have US$1 million or more in financial assets to set up the VUL.

CONCLUSION

Like any product, VUL plans have costs involved in the setting up and for the annual maintenance of the plan. You should weigh the costs against the investment potential, confidentiality and tax deferral benefits. Investment returns and tax savings would generally more than justify the costs.

Getting a VUL requires planning. It nudges the client to organise his assets, consider his exposures and start thinking of his plans for succession for his beneficiaries. Such a topic is not a priority when clients are busy in their quest for more wealth. However, if he had used a lifetime to build his empire, he owes it to himself and his loved ones to organise the fruits of his labour. No other person is more familiar than he would be to decide on the optimal way to manage and transfer these assets. He can speak to an experienced adviser who can advise on what solutions are available as well as gathering suitable legal and tax resources to put the right structure in place.

Chapter 13

Trust Investments

by **Keon Chee** with **Adam Wang**

You have set up a Trust. One day when you are no longer around, a portion of your liquid funds (such as cash in bank, proceeds of insurance policies and property sales) will be transferred to the trustee who will take legal ownership of the funds. The trustee will, over a period of 10, 20 or more years, manage those funds for the benefit of your family and other beneficiaries.

You would understandably be concerned about how the trustee manages those Trust funds. Questions such as these are typical:

1. Will the trustee charge an arm and a leg?
2. What if the trustee invests and loses money?
3. How can I check on the trustee?
4. Could the trustee be investing in very risky investments?

The trustee has to abide by the Trustees Act (which regulates the operation of Trusts and trustees in Singapore), the terms of the Trust deed and the wishes of the settlor in the Letter of Wishes. The Trustees Act provides guidelines that are sufficient for any trustee to manage Trust funds in general. The Trust deed and Letter of Wishes provide more specific guidelines that are relevant to the settlor's unique family circumstances, such as keeping the funds in fixed deposits only or investing mainly in low risk investments or avoiding structured products.

To appreciate what the trustee does with Trust funds, we present a case study of Tom who has just passed away and has funds transferred to the trustee for investing. Trust companies have the power to invest Trust funds but they normally do not have an investment license to do so. As a result, the power to invest is commonly delegated to an external investment manager. You would want to know how the trustee engages the investment manager and what safeguards are in place to ensure your investment objectives will be met.

We invited an investment manager to give us their views on how they might invest for Tom's family.

CASE STUDY – INVESTING TOM'S FAMILY TRUST FUNDS

Tom set up a Standby Living Trust five years ago. He passed away three months ago at age 50. Probate has been cleared, debts have been paid and immediate gifts have been made. Now his net estate of $10 million is being passed to the trustee (a licensed Trust company).

The sole beneficiary of the Trust is his daughter, Michelle, who will be turning 15 soon. The distribution plan is illustrated in Figure 13.1. The Trust is for Michelle's education, medical expenses and maintenance of $5,000 per month until age 45. At age 25 and every 5 years thereafter until age 40, she is to receive a lump sum of $500,000 to do whatever she pleases. When she turns 45, the Trust is to be terminated and the remaining funds distributed to her. If she does not survive until age 45, the remaining funds are to be given to the Singapore Buddhist Welfare Services.

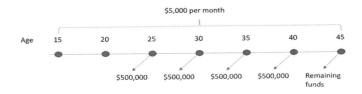

Figure 13.1 – Distribution Plan for Michelle

Tom wrote in his Letter of Wishes (LOW) that the Trust funds should be managed by an investment manager without naming anyone specific. Tom indicated that the rate of return should be 5 to 8% per year. The portfolio should consist of at least 60% lower risk bond investments and no more than 40% in riskier investments like equities. Since Michelle is 15 and the Trust is to be terminated when she reaches 45, the investment horizon at the start is 30 years.

THE TRUSTEE'S POWER TO INVEST

Trust companies in Singapore are guided by the Trustees Act, which lays down the overall rules on how the trustee is to deal with Trust funds. The trustee is given general powers to invest in any kind of investment (including land, commodities, stocks and bonds).[1] This wide investment power is treated as a default provision – it is overridden if the Trust deed restricts the ways Trust funds can be invested. Further wishes come from the LOW.

The trustee has to observe standard investment criteria, which means that in making investment decisions, the trustee should consider what is suitable for Michelle's benefit and whether there is a need for diversification.[2] What is meant by suitable is not defined, although it is generally accepted that the trustee should invest solely for the financial interest of the beneficiaries.

Diversification should be considered but it is not a requirement as it may be overridden by the Trust deed and LOW, which may specify that the Trust should have very focused assets, such as, for example, insurance policies only or the shares of private companies only.

The trustee's investment powers may be delegated to an investment manager[3] based on the trustee's arms-length selection from a panel of investment managers. However, it is often the case that the beneficiaries' family has their own investment managers in mind. For example, Tom's wife may have a preferred investment manager that she would like to engage.

Regardless of the investment manager selected, the trustee remains liable for the acts or defaults of the investment manager

---

1   Trustees Act, section 4.
2   Trustees Act, section 5.
3   Trustees Act, section 6.

in the same manner as if they were the acts of the trustee.[4] In other words, even though the trustee can get an investment manager to invest the funds, the trustee is ultimately responsible for what happens to the Trust funds.

For this reason, it is vital that you are satisfied that the investment manager candidates are asked certain questions about their background, such as:

1. What is your track record? Compared with your competitors?
2. What is the size of your assets under management?
3. How long has your core team been investing?
4. Do the investment managers invest themselves?
5. How do you charge?
6. How do you conduct your research?
7. What references can I contact?
8. How timely is your reporting?

When the investment manager has been selected, the trustee needs to formalise a written agreement to engage the investment manager. This agreement is called the Investment Policy Statement (IPS). While it is the trustee who has to present this agreement, it is usually in consultation with the investment manager that the details are hammered out. The IPS is an important document for the trustee and the beneficiaries to help ensure that the investment goals established for the particular Trust fund will be met.

WHAT AN IPS LOOKS LIKE

There is no prescribed format for an IPS in Singapore legislation.

I have used an IPS format that contains common priorities that families seek to satisfy. With this IPS format, we provided the scenario of Michelle to our guest investment manager, Kredens Capital Management[5] and together we devised a sample IPS. The sample IPS has been placed at www.legasyplanners.com/epbook so that this book is not overloaded with technical content

---

4 Trustees Act, section 27(6).
5 Kredens Capital Management (KCM) is a Registered Fund Management Company (RFMC) regulated under the Monetary Authority of Singapore (MAS). KCM trades in global financial markets. Their investment expertise ranges across equities, fixed income and forex markets.

The sample IPS is in no way ready for your use and you would have to tailor it to your particular situation.

Comments from the Investment Manager about the IPS

Tom's family would normally have a few meetings with KCM. The points below are an example of the dialogues that take place, with each dialogue helping to refine the IPS.

KCM's comments about the 30-year investment horizon:

- The key investment objective is capital preservation and stable cashflow, in order to provide monthly distributions and an annual drawdown of principal every five years between ages 25 and 40. Given the investment objective is 5 to 8% p.a., which can be well covered with our investment strategies, we should be able to meet Michelle's financial needs. We would specifically require at least an inflation-adjusted annual return of around 2.6% p.a. based on: (a) monthly dividends of $5,000, which is quite readily generated from an investment portfolio of $10 million (0.6% p.a.), (b) a drawdown amount of $500,000 every five years between ages 25 and 40 (1% on annual basis) and an annual inflation of 1% (MAS core inflation was 1% in 2019).

- The investment horizon is very long. The portfolio will have a strong holding power to invest in long-term investment grade fixed income securities and less liquid and higher return instruments (growth stocks, real estate and even private equity).

- As the investment approaches the termination date, the investment portfolio will gradually exit illiquid positions and move into more liquid instruments (short-term fixed income and blue-chip stocks).

Any bespoke strategy given the profile of the beneficiary and family?

- Given the client is based in Singapore, geographical diversification would be important to manage country and sovereign risk.
- As a bespoke investment manager, we are able to accommodate any unique preferences of the family. Some families may be inclined towards socially responsible green funds that can deliver both returns and environmentally positive outcomes like clean air and solar energy. Or they may tell us to avoid "sin stocks" that are involved in gambling and manufacturing weapons.

REVIEW PERFORMANCE AND THE IPS

Once an IPS is in place, the trustee has the duty to continually review the arrangement and exercise any power of intervention if they consider there is a need to do so.[6] Before the meeting with the investment manager, it is prudent for the trustee to:

- gather performance figures;
- have a sense of the investment climate during the investment period and the next; and
- go through each statement of the IPS.

Then during the periodic meeting with the investment manager, you may want to ask:

- How has the market been? Where do you think it's headed?
- Can you go through the performance figures and compare them to the benchmarks?
- Does the IPS require amending?

The trustee is, in the end, liable for the acts or defaults of the investment manager. Hence, not only do these and other questions have to be asked, the meetings and discussions should be recorded and noted down in formal minutes.

6   Trustees Act, section 41M.

CONCLUSION

Your Trust fund will be managed for many years after you are gone. During your lifetime, actively understand how your funds would be managed. Even better would be to transfer a sum of money into your Trust during your lifetime and let an investment manager manage those funds with your oversight. The annual trustee fees can typically be expected to be offset by investment returns. The better your Trust funds are managed, the more there would be for your loved ones.

We suggest that you work with professional investment managers, especially when your Trust fund could be many million dollars in size. Professional investment managers are guided by legislation and are regulated by MAS. Of course, not every professional manager can give the returns, attention and care that your family deserves, but with reasonable due diligence and the use of an Investment Policy Statement, the chances of managing your family's Trust funds successfully would be boosted.

Chapter 14

Pillars of Wealth

by **Victor Tang**

My wife and I have seven children. They range from ages 8 to 21. When people learn that I have seven children, they ask – why so many? Why seven or why not eight or even more?

We knew from the start that we wanted at least two. When our second child Pollyanna arrived, we trained her to sleep through the night from 7pm to 7am within one and a half months from birth. In fact, we were successful in training all seven of our kids this way. When our eldest turned two, we were enjoying the success of managing our two children so much and we still had time for ourselves. So it just seemed natural to have more.

We named our first born Makarios. We wanted a powerful name to mark the occasion, a name to tell the world that we would have a wonderful and successful family. The name should also be Biblical because as Christians, we wanted a name that honoured God and to be always reminded of our faith and duty. Makarios means supremely blessed – the perfect name for him and for us!

We went for parenting classes three years before our children were born. We were such active contributors in the parenting classes that we were considered model parents even before we had any children. We prepare for many things in life and spend years in training for our professions, and hence we didn't want to take parenting for granted.

What I would like to share in this chapter is how we created a model of wealth for our family over the past 25 years. My wife and I realised that we needed a model that went beyond dollars and cents, a model that each member of our family could refer to and follow, one that would lead to a happy and successful life.

PILLARS OF WEALTH

There are many definitions of family wealth, but ultimately it is up to each family to decide what it values most and to work towards that. We call ours the Pillars of Wealth as shown in Figure 14.1.

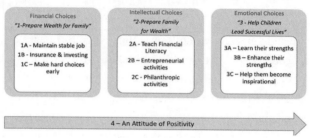

Figure 14.1 – Pillars of Wealth

It is a model that has worked for us and is still evolving, just as the family is evolving around the model. While I am not advocating the model for everyone, I must say that whenever I share it with the families I work with, they readily identify with it.

THE FIRST PILLAR: CAPITAL

Building up a strong pillar of capital includes:
- maintaining a stable income;
- insurance and investing for the family; and
- making the hard choices early.

Being financially stable means that our income and capital are sufficient to cover our essential expenses and allow us to live comfortably. Of course, financial stability will look different to each person and your definition will be personal to you.

Financial stability has an impact on most areas of life. A lack of it can harm your mental wellbeing through stress and may even lead to ill health if you cannot afford basic goods like food and healthcare. Financial stability also gives you the ability to deal with unexpected costs and emergencies.

As I am writing this chapter, I am recovering from a serious ankle injury that will put me out of work for a while. On the day before the circuit breaker began, I was playing basketball with my eldest son. I stepped on Makarios' foot and landed awkwardly on my ankle. I heard a snap, much like a twig breaking, coming from my ankle as it inverted. The pain was excruciating and I had to be carried off and sent to hospital. There was no fracture and the MRI revealed that my ligament was ripped apart and torn off at the point of attachment to my ankle bone. The doctor's orders were to stay home and minimise movement for the next four months, which meant I could not meet clients and my income could be severely affected.

This incident certainly served to emphasise to me the importance of building capital. Maintaining a stable job, ensuring that the family is provided for through insurance in the event of the breadwinner becoming unable to work, and investing for the family – these are the key tenets of a strong pillar. I am blessed to have been able to build up sufficient savings to tide my family through this economic slowdown.

I must declare that I am not wealthy in the sense that many of us may be familiar with, and if the pandemic lasts 12 months or more, we will begin to struggle. Instead, we are stable because as a family:

- my job as a wealth manager gives me a stable income;
- each of us is adequately insured in case we fall ill or have an accident; and
- we have invested our family wealth into various funds that have given us good income and returns.

The third element in building a strong capital pillar is to make hard decisions early.

In my late 20s, I was serving full-time in a Christian Media Centre set up by the Southern Baptist Convention in the United States. It was a very fulfilling job. I was also regularly speaking on radio and TV in Singapore on parenting and estate planning.

When our subsequent children arrived, I realised I wanted to have more time and flexibility for my family. I joined a financial institution as a wealth manager and scaled down on my radio and TV work. This was a difficult decision because I was thriving in my work and my bosses loved my work.

The second big decision we made was not such a hard decision but perhaps it was a drastic one. We decided to homeschool our children, all seven of them. When Makarios was four years old, we attended a talk about building life's principles and were surprised to learn about homeschooling as part of the session. We were curious at first when we were presented with this idea. After more learning and research into this education model, we were impressed and we took off from there.

Our eldest son had not started formal schooling yet. We created a school environment at home to bring the children through primary school, secondary school and junior college. If you can imagine a public school such as St Andrews or ACS with over 100 students in each grade from primary 1 to junior college, well, that's exactly the environment that we created at home for them.

If you are curious how homeschooling works, our children are assessed by MOE at certain times to ensure that they are meeting the compulsory education requirements. They have to take MOE examinations at primary 4 and PSLE, and in between we gave them the freedom to pursue any interest they wanted – to learn to cook, play musical instruments, read widely, pick up multiple hobbies while keeping up with the mainstream curriculum.

The third decision we made early was to have only one shared mobile phone for all our children until they entered national service for the boys or university for the girls. The one mobile phone was used by everyone to receive messages from school, and to take along when one of the children was out doing an errand.

This gave us time and mental space to gel more as a family. Our meal times, for example, are full of talking, laughing, singing and learning about one another. Having one mobile phone was just one of the family habits we developed where we would always ask ourselves, "Is this good for everyone in the family?" Whether it is planning for a vacation, planning a meal or changing the colour of a room, we wanted everyone to be decision makers and stakeholders, and having just one mobile was one of the family decisions we made and kept.

THE SECOND PILLAR: EDUCATION

With the first pillar erected to "prepare wealth for the family," and expecting that wealth would flow to our family to create financial stability, the next pillar is to "prepare the family for wealth." This would consist of lessons and activities to teach:

- financial literacy;
- entrepreneurial activities; and
- philanthropic activities.

Being a father of seven, I have acquired a niche in teaching financial literacy to children and advising on wealth transfer from one generation to the next. For some families, it is the transferring of values that is the most challenging. Thus, I have been dedicating my time to help families achieve breakthroughs in this area.

Here are some lessons that have worked for my family. In the early years of our children's growth, we felt it was necessary to inculcate the value of a dollar in their young minds. This is a topic not to be avoided because it appears to be difficult or should it be emphasised too much in case children become too calculative. We shared with our children that money does not just magically transfer from our phone to the cashier and that we cannot just walk away with anything we like without paying a price for it. The introduction of how money performs in the real world to a toddler could be demonstrated with a few rounds of walking them through the withdrawal of money from a physical bank and using it to buy what we need from the supermarket. We would also wait in line together at the bank to deposit money. We let our children hand the notes to the teller, and that helped them understand that money has value and is also saved up.

When our children were of primary school age, we introduced the concept of budgeting to them. One of our favourite activities was to get the children involved in cooking a meal. We would discuss the recipe and the ingredients needed, and gave them a budget of $10 or $20 to buy the needed ingredients for the meal, leaving the spending up to the children assigned for the task. This fun activity of going to the supermarket to pick up things and paying for them emphasised the value of the dollar, as they are forced to realise how much $10 or $20 is worth.

When they got older and were able to manage their allowance, we introduced this budgeting formula:

Allowance + Earnings = Savings + Sharing + Spending

When they received their allowance, they had to first take out a portion for savings. We would ask each of them what they would save for that may take about three to six months. Sometimes it may be a toy or a good pair of jeans. This showed them that they should pay themselves first.

Entrepreneurial activities taught them to earn so that they could appreciate how one could become financially stable. We brought our children to flea markets to have them sell items. They planned what they would sell and how they would sell the items. Makarios sold *nasi goreng* that he fried. He received a taste of how hawkers made a hard-earned living. My daughters Pollyanna and Roshoshanna sold homemade muffins, while my sons Ebenezer and Imagodei sold wooden guns they crafted out of recycled wood. For any flea market event, my youngest daughter Nesherina will be selling her homemade slime. Eshonmelo, our seventh child, will be using his self-taught Street Panna skill (playing a soccer ball through your opponent's legs) to earn some tokens.

They went through the process of buying raw materials, making and selling the items. Cost and price were concepts they came to understand, and they realised that whatever they made could have value. Similarly, they started to see that some things cost very little to make but are sold very expensively, such as branded goods, which they decided they should avoid when trying to spend money prudently.

On philanthropy and sharing, we are planning to do more of such activities on a regular basis. We have started by asking our children to keep their money in percentages allocated according to the budgeting formula for saving, sharing and spending. Every now and then, they would pool their sharing percentages together, to bake cakes and cookies, buy snacks, some basic toiletries and cooking needs. We would then deliver these goods personally to individual households, senior citizens' homes and foreign worker dormitories. These were simple exercises, but the lessons that they took away were priceless. They learnt to appreciate the joy of giving and gained an understanding that the gift of money is not merely for the sole purpose of bringing happiness to themselves, but that being in a more fortunate position meant they could share what they have with those who are less fortunate.

THE THIRD PILLAR: MINDSET

For the children, building up a strong mindset pillar includes:
- learning about their strengths;
- enhancing their strengths; and
- becoming inspirational to others.

We know the strengths of each of our children, and we feel that is our duty as parents to enhance their strengths by giving them adequate resources and encouragement to help them develop their strengths even more.

Makarios dreams of becoming an entrepreneur and successful businessman. At age 20, while in the army, he started a video production and website business. He has completed over ten projects, each earning him an average of $5,000. His aim is to be able to support himself for tertiary education. He has secured an offer from NUS to do a double degree in Economics and Psychology.

He reads very widely and is self-motivated, highly skilled and never lacks ambition. This is probably attributed to the early years of homeschooling when he was free to learn anything that was of interest to him. We devoted much time on him, being our first child, just as we have done so for our other children, but as he is the eldest, we had hoped he would be a role model and inspirational to his younger siblings. Fortunately, he has turned out to be a fine young man, adored by his siblings.

Our second child, Pollyanna, is 19 this year and has a keen interest and talent in ballet. In 2020, she hired a dance studio to teach ballet to twelve students. After paying for the studio rental, she gave all her earnings to us and is happy that we can use it in areas to further develop her. She has completed the International Baccalaureate programme and is using her International Certificate of Christian Education to apply to NTU for a place in their Biological Sciences (Hons) course.

THE FOURTH PILLAR: POSITIVITY

Positivity means to be able to:
- reframe the situation;
- focus on the positive side; and
- build emotional resilience.

Just before the circuit breaker was implemented, my family had planned on going for a holiday together to Angkor Wat. Due to COVID-19, our plans were cancelled. After much discussion, we decided to go to Cameron Highlands which is closer to home.

However, as the virus situation escalated, we decided to play it safe and spend our holiday in Johor Bahru.

We managed to find a nice place to stay for a few days. However, the Malaysian government made the decision to close the border between Malaysia and Singapore at the end of the next day. After a night of family discussions, we decided to leave the next day. After lunch, we set out on the road home. With everyone rushing back to Singapore, the traffic seemed bearable at first, with the car edging forward only every few seconds, and soon after every ten minutes.

Squeezed in our 8-seater car, we started feeling the effects of claustrophobia. Before everyone could start getting annoyed and impatient, we took turns to belt out our favourite karaoke songs, played bonding games and had picnics where we sat. My eldest son took over the steering wheel when I had to tend to the younger children. We were at the Causeway for 11 hours before we got back to Singapore. The slight change in perception of the situation gave us an enjoyable trip despite the setbacks thrown at us.

However, things are not rosy and positive all the time. As a family, we have our moments of stress and strife. Maintaining positivity requires focus and attention, and one has to be conscious about staying positive. Positivity makes us physically and psychologically healthier and more productive and successful.

CONCLUSION

In the end, we want happy and successful children. I am always keen to learn from other parents and families. As I connect with my clients, relatives and friends, I find boundless wisdom in them and I profoundly appreciate the priceless lessons learned.

The Pillars of Wealth model is the result of our lifelong commitment to our children and to God, and we know that it will be continually adjusted and we hope our children will one day adopt it for their own children.

Chapter 15

Marriage & Divorce

by **Keon Chee** with **Angelina Hing**

If you want to know why marriages break apart, and what it looks like when they do, talk to a divorce lawyer. In fact, talk to a divorce lawyer who was a judge overseeing divorce cases. Better yet, talk to a divorce lawyer who is happily married and knows a lot about how to stay together. Readers of this chapter are in luck, as I know just the right person.

Angelina Hing has spent more than 18 years handling divorce, custody disputes, child care payments, nuptial agreements and essentially every conceivable divorce scenario. She has seen couples, transformed from loving one another "till death do us part" to sworn enemies ready to destroy one another.

In spite of the often grim circumstances she faces in her daily work, Angelina is a true marriage warrior.

ON HAVING A HAPPY MARRIAGE
Keon
I read that a quarter of married people are thinking of divorce.[1] Is marriage doomed?

Angelina
I believe that most of us, if not all, need companionship. Intimate life-long companionship nourishes the soul. Marriage, being a committed life-long commitment, teaches a lot of life lessons if parties are prepared to learn. It teaches forgiveness, forbearance and it forces one out of the default self-centred mode especially when kids turn up. Learning such lessons brings about multiple fruits of joy.

---

1   "1 in 4 married couples in Singapore are thinking of divorce", *The New Paper*, 16 October 2016.

Our founding father Mr Lee Kuan Yew and his wife, Mdm Kwa Geok Choo, are such role models. Reading their love story never fails to touch my heart. If you read their story, you would find unwavering commitment to each other, through health and illness; understanding each other's roles and work commitments and support for each other. They clearly communicated a lot with each other. What struck me is that they were both highly intelligent, and they both knew what they wanted to see in their life partners. They knew what they needed in a soulmate. They clearly knew themselves well.

Keon

Do you believe that there is such a thing as a soulmate?

Angelina

Yes, I do. That would have to be my life partner. He has to be my best friend, someone I can communicate deeply with, and with whom I can be myself. So, my husband and I were in fact very good friends for a few years, before we realised that we had feelings for each other which were beyond platonic.

Keon

What advice do you have for people thinking about getting married?

Angelina

For couples who are thinking of getting married, if it is for any reason other than the fact that you are so in love, for example, to please your grandma or because you like his Porsche or her good looks, DON'T.

For those who are madly in love, my advice will be to do the following:

(a) A "360-degree assessment" or survey of what people who care for you think about your spouse-to-be. I would do this early on in the relationship, and not wait until the wedding has been booked and deposits paid. Do it naturally, slowly, over a period of time. Get a sense of what your parents and your entire clan think of him, what your close friends think and what his friends think (it would actually be good to get to know his friends, especially childhood ones). Do not be afraid of getting feedback. You may not agree with all of them, but it would give you a fair sense of a third party's perspective of your significant other, and their thoughts on your relationship. That is often helpful. If you find yourself afraid of finding out, that should sound alarm bells.

(b) Attend a pre-marital counselling course. There are many available, religious and non-religious ones. I would recommend doing one which is comprehensive and over a period of a few months rather than a 1-day workshop. This one of the most important decisions of your life and a life-changing one. You want to be as prepared as you can be for it.

I attended one with the church many years ago before my husband and I got married. It was very useful and alerted me to various issues which I would otherwise not be aware of.

(c) No matter how you may feel, always seriously weigh any concerns people who know and love you have. Where there are frequent areas of conflict as a result of a personality trait of your partner or a conviction or belief which he is adamant about, ask yourself whether you are able to live with it, every day of your life. Be realistic and brutally honest with yourself. This is one decision you do not want to regret making, ever.

(d) Know yourself. You need to know yourself and your needs. This seems basic, but I have come to realise that not many people actually know themselves for who they are. Many live trying to meet the expectation of others (or what they perceive are expectations of society) and deny who they really are. In fact, by going through (a),(b) and (c) above, it would help with getting to know yourself.

Keon

If your partner is unwilling to go through a 360-degree assessment or a pre-marital counselling course, could that be a bad sign?

Angelina

Yes, I feel that it would be a litmus test of sorts, and if the partner is unwilling to meet any of your friends/relatives, and unwilling to attend a pre-marital counselling course, this should raise alarm bells. It is important to understand what the underlying reason is. Whatever the issue is, it should be dealt with before walking down the aisle. This is something I do not think anyone can afford to sweep under the carpet. The consequences are too dire.

Keon

How do couples stay happily married?

Angelina

The ABCs of marriage success:

(a) Always keep communication lines open, no matter how difficult. Communicate honestly and respectfully as much as you can. Work at giving each other a *safe space* (where there are no accusations and judgement, only a desire to understand) to do so. Never give up trying. If necessary, enlist professional help to facilitate that.

(b) Be aware of the stressors in life, the different seasons such as illness, birth of a child, death of a loved one and try to find ways to cope with these different seasons. For example, cut back on work if it is financially viable to enable more time and energy to be devoted to the area of need; make deliberate effort to set aside time for each other to rest and reconnect. Awareness is the first step.

(c) Committed to contend with the storms of life, and stick by each other. For a marriage to work, commitment must be mutual.

Keon

How do you make sure you perform the ABCs when sometimes you just want to avoid issues because "he will never change"?

Angelina

I believe that everyone needs to take ownership of his own actions. If you feel there is an issue, you need to take ownership and deal with it and not make assumptions or presumptions. That would not be fair on the other party. For example, if a wife feels neglected because her husband has been very busy at work, the onus is on the wife to communicate how she feels to her husband, not in an accusatory manner, but in a manner that speaks honestly of her feelings. But if she chooses not to have an open, honest and respectful communication with the husband, and instead acts out in a passive-aggressive manner, it would only be a matter of time before the relationship deteriorates. Similarly, if the husband does not respond in a loving and respectful manner when the wife tries to communicate her needs to him and discuss ways to address the issue together, it would also adversely affect the marriage in the long term.

As reflected by John Gottman of The Gottman Institute: "Trust is built in very small moments in which one person turns toward their partner when they are in need. When our partner responds positively, by 'being there' for us, that builds trust."

Keon

Are there any marriage books you might recommend?

Angelina

I have found these books to be useful in my own marriage journey:

The 5 Love Languages by Gary Chapman
I found this book very enlightening as the concept of the love

languages helped me understand myself and my husband better. It also helped me understand why I always felt so let down by my husband's reaction when he opens a gift which I had put so much thought into and spent so much effort in acquiring. After my husband and I read the book, I discovered that "receiving gifts" is not his love language at all! I could have saved myself a lot of pain if I had known this earlier!

Men are Clams, Women are Crowbars: Understand Your Differences and Make Them Work by David Clarke
This is another book which I found very enlightening. It opened my eyes to the fact that a man (my husband at least) processes problems differently from me. What seemed most natural to me, which was to sit down and talk through issues as soon as they arise, was not at all natural for him. He needed time to process. And to process meant that he would withdraw, which drove me absolutely nuts. This book shed a lot of light on our respective psyche and enabled us to come to an understanding and compromise as to how we should deal with issues when confronted with them.

ON DIVORCE
Keon
Let's talk now about divorce. What are the main reasons that cause couples to get divorced?

Angelina
When there is a breakdown in the ABCs of a happy marriage. And, often, it starts with A. When parties stop communicating, the downward spiral begins. For some couples, a third party gets involved. From my experience dealing with hundreds of cases over the years, I must say that I have not seen a case where adultery takes place while the marriage is healthy.

Keon

But what, in your experience, are the main real reasons that couples divorce? Is it money, adultery, incompatibility? I've read that unreasonable behaviour is the main legal reason but not the real reason.

Angelina

Unreasonable behaviour is the broadest "ground". Hence the most common. But from my perspective, the real reasons for the breakdown is as explained above. The legal threshold just does not explain the actual reason for the breakdown.

Keon

Are there situations where a couple should get divorced because it's just not working out?

Angelina

I think that fundamentally, if at least one party is no longer committed to the marriage, the parting of ways would be inevitable. Bear in mind that commitment entails being determined to make changes to make the marriage work.

Marriage is a partnership. The partnership cannot continue if one partner is not committed to it. Commitment entails doing whatever is necessary to keep the partnership going, which often means making changes to habits, work arrangements, communication patterns and mindsets. It involves a lot of hard work. Not many are able or prepared to do so. For example, if a partner decides that his work which involves a lot of travelling and he is not prepared to give it up or explore with his management ways in which the travelling can be reduced, this may reflect a lack of commitment in the partnership.

I see an increasing trend of cases where a partner suffers from some form of personality disorder. This would definitely make it difficult for the partnership to continue as the partner who is ill very often has no capacity to self-reflect, much less make any changes to his habits, communication patterns or mindset.

Keon

Is it possible to have a "happy divorce"?

Angelina

I would hesitate to use the word "happy", but amicable, most definitely.

The most amicable divorce would be one where all the issues are discussed and resolved between the parties *before* filing the Writ for Divorce in the Family Justice Courts. These would be issues relating to the reason relied on for the divorce, the children's living arrangements after the divorce, the maintenance of the children and spouse (if applicable) and the division of matrimonial assets.

Keon

Is this a simplified divorce track?

Angelina

Yes, in the court process, there is a simplified divorce track. Under this track, no one needs to attend any court sessions. A case can only be on this track if all issues are agreed upon between the parties at the time when the divorce papers are filed in court.

So how does one attain this? Communication is key. Understandably, effective communication between the parties at this point in time is often difficult. This is where mediation would come in. Mediation can take place with or without the presence of lawyers. The role of the mediator, in situations where parties wish to divorce, is to facilitate the discussion such that parties would be able to come to an agreement on all issues such that the divorce can be filed on an uncontested basis and be on the simplified divorce track. This would be the objective in a *divorce mediation*.

ON MEDIATION

Keon

Do you feel that divorce mediation should be made mandatory when divorce is already the couple's shared objective?

Angelina

Divorce mediation is currently mandatory in law, once a parent who has a child below 21 years of age, commences divorce proceedings in the Family Justice Courts. This divorce mediation is conducted by a Judge-Mediator. I am, however, advocating that the couple should contemplate going through private divorce mediation *before* commencing divorce proceedings in court. This is because, if all the issues are resolved before the court is involved, costs would be lower (because the process is a lot simpler and the entire court proceeding is uncontested and completed administratively), and the relationship between the couple would tend to be less strained. Without attempting to resolve the issues *before* filing court papers, the act of commencing a court proceeding itself often ignites very negative feelings in the receiving party. This can make it more difficult to resolve matters amicably afterwards, at the mandated court-annexed mediation.

Keon

This sounds costlier?

Angelina

Yes. Most lawyers charge based on time. The longer the matter takes to resolve, the higher the costs. Hence, whether from the perspective of maintaining an amicable relationship with the divorced spouse for the sake of the children, or from the perspective of costs, it would make sense to manage the conflict between the spouses and attempt to resolve the post-divorce issues earlier rather than later, and preferably, without the involvement of the court.

There are occasions when the couple is contemplating divorce, but they are not absolutely sure about it. They can consider *marital mediation*. As marital mediator, I would mediate the marriage issues and facilitate a discussion and crystallise the issues which have been troubling the parties in their marriage. Once the issues are crystallised, the parties would have to decide whether they would like to work on their marriage, now knowing what the specific issues are. Some couples require the assistance of a counsellor to work on these issues. I work with a few counsellors who would be able to help them.

But if the couple decide that the issues are too many and too daunting to work through, and they feel that the parting of ways would be their choice, then the *marital mediation* would evolve into *divorce mediation*.

CONCLUSION

Keon

Thank you, Angelina. Is marriage really as good as it sounds?

Angelina

Marriage is a journey of discovering the depth of intimacy one can have with a soulmate after going through thick and thin; continuous lessons of forgiveness and forbearing of each other's failings and learning to put the other person's interest above your own. The result is the joy and sweetness of being one; that is the hope and motivation of this life-long, life-changing journey.

****

Appendix –

Technical Supplement to Marriage & Divorce

This supplement applies only to non-Muslim civil marriages in Singapore according to the Women's Charter.

ELIGIBILITY TO GET MARRIED

In order to be eligible to marry, you must fulfil these requirements:
- Must be at least 21 years old. Those between 18 and 21 are required to obtain consent from their parents or guardians and attend a Marriage Preparation Program.
- Must be unmarried.
- Cannot be of same gender.
- Must follow marriage rules of solemnisation.
- Cannot be too closely related.
- At least one of the parties is a Singapore citizen or Singapore permanent resident.

TWO STAGES OF DIVORCE

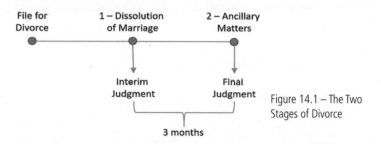

Figure 14.1 – The Two Stages of Divorce

Stage 1 deals with meeting the legal requirements of divorce.
Stage 2 deals with child custody, the division of matrimonial assets and spousal maintenance.

The Certificate of Final Judgment concludes all divorce proceedings. Unless there are special reasons and the court allows, the Certificate of Final Judgement can only be extracted at the expiration of three months from the date of the Interim Judgement.

STAGE 1 – DISSOLUTION OF MARRIAGE

The parties must satisfy the legal grounds for divorce in order to dissolve the marriage.

Who can apply to divorce in Singapore?

Either or both spouses are:

- domiciled in Singapore at the point of divorce commencement;
- habitually resident in Singapore for at least three years, before divorce commencement; or
- married at least three years, unless spouse suffered exceptional hardship or exceptionally unreasonable and cruel behavior.

Facts relied upon for divorce

It has to be shown that the marriage has irretrievably broken down due to one of these facts:

- adultery – defendant has committed adultery and plaintiff finds it intolerable to live with defendant;
- unreasonable behavior – defendant has behaved in a way that plaintiff cannot reasonably be expected to live with defendant;
- desertion – defendant has deserted plaintiff for at least two years; or
- separation – parties have separated for either three or four years, depending on whether defendant consents to divorce.

STAGE 2 – ANCILLARY MATTERS

Ancillary Matters deal with the couple coming to an agreement regarding the children and financial matters.

Custody

- Custody – to determine who has the authority to make major life decisions for the child, in areas such as education, health and religion. Parents are usually given joint custody.
- Care and control – to determine who the child lives with on a day-to-day basis.
- Access – to determine when the parent without care and control is allowed to spend time with the child.

Financial matters

- Division of their matrimonial assets.
- Maintenance payments for spouse.

What assets are considered matrimonial assets?

Assets acquired:
- during marriage;
- before marriage by one or both parties and used by both parties and their children while the parties are living together; and
- before marriage by one or both parties which has been substantially improved during the marriage by either or by both parties.

Maintenance

- The court may order a man to pay maintenance to his wife or former wife, or order a woman to pay maintenance to her incapacitated husband or incapacitated former husband.

MARITAL MEDIATION

When a couple is considering divorce, they may consider marital mediation with the intention of working things out. The mediator assists parties in identifying the main issues in the marriage and facilitates a discussion and agreement between the parties as to how they think the issues may be dealt with.

Marital Mediation may evolve into Divorce Mediation.

Note: Marriage counselling, on the other hand, has a more therapeutic element.

DIVORCE MEDIATION

One of the main goals of divorce mediation is help the couple come to an agreement regarding custody and financial matters, so as to end the marriage in a more amicable way. A desired outcome is an uncontested divorce where no court attendance is required. This minimises stress, time and cost.

There are two paths to divorce mediation:

Private mediation

- These sessions are voluntary.
- The parties may go through mediation before filing any court papers (pre-writ). If they can agree to all the ancillary issues, they can proceed to file on the simplified track (uncontested divorce).
- Mediation can also occur post-writ. If a settlement is reached, the parties can proceed to record the terms of the divorce in a court order made by consent, at the next available date given by the court.

Court-annexed mediation

- These sessions help divorcing couples agree on ancillary issues and focus on cooperation as opposed to being involved in lengthy, costly and acrimonious court proceedings.
- The sessions also seek to help parents understand the impact of divorce on their children and how to minimise this impact.
- Where there are children under the age of 21, parents are mandated to attend such sessions.
- If an agreement is reached, the Judge-Mediator can record the court order by consent, immediately.

Chapter 16

Guardianship

by **Chong Yue-En**

The word "guardian" could conjure up a few possible mental images – perhaps that of an authoritative figure like a soldier who is standing guard to keep the land safe or that of a strict governess figure whom you would have a healthy dose of fear of, or perhaps you might think of a guardian angel, who comes to your aid in your time of need. I would submit that a guardian has characteristics of all three figures as a person who is appointed to protect or defend something or someone.

Indeed, the need of a guardian is critical in the following situations: where the parents of a child have passed away, where the parents of a child are situated in a different country and are physically unavailable or when both parents may be medically unavailable to care for their child, due to a brain injury or quarantined for contracting COVID-19. In these situations, a guardian needs to be present to make decisions for the child pertaining to the child's education, accommodation and daily care, religious instructions, medical needs, etc, in place of the child's parents.

CARE FOR A CHILD THROUGH GUARDIANSHIP

The overriding spirit of guardianship is that the welfare of the child is of paramount consideration, and this guides the court in its discretion when deciding on guardianship matters.[1]

For the purpose of this chapter, we will focus more on the two main methods by which a guardian is appointed when the parents are unable to perform their roles, either by the courts[2] or by way of a Deed or Will.[3]

---

1   Section 3 of the Guardianship of Infants Act.
2   Section 17(1)(d) of the Supreme Court of Judicature Act.
3   Section 7 of the Guardianship of Infants Act.

Appointment by the court

In a recent court case,[4] the Family Division of the High Court in Singapore allowed the grandaunt of three children to be appointed as their guardian, having found "no evidence that the mother of the children was willing to be, or capable of being a responsible parent to these children." It is suggested that in the event where both parents are deceased, a family member could be appointed guardian of the child by the High Court. Again, this would be due to the family member satisfying the court's requirement that the child's welfare is best served by doing so.

Appointment by parents under Will or Deed

The more common method of appointment of a guardian is by way of Will or Deed (called a testamentary guardian). In their respective Wills, the father or mother of the child can appoint a person to be testamentary guardian to care for the child if the said parent passes away while the child is still under the age of 21.

Both the mother and father are able to name the same person to be the guardian under their respective Will. Alternatively, the mother and father are able to name a different person in each of their respective Wills. However, it is recommended that the two people that they are choosing are able to work together to jointly care for the children, assuming that both parents have passed away.

Note that when either the mother or father appoints a person to be guardian under his Will or Deed, this person would automatically step in to act jointly with the surviving mother or father should the parent that appoints him passes away. The surviving parent can object to working together with this person; however, this person has the right to bring the surviving parent to court if the appointed guardian deems the parent to be "unfit" to care for the child.

At this point, you could possibly imagine the tension and conflict that could arise from such a legal challenge and it is important that

---

4   VET v VEU [20202] SGHCF 4 at [42].

when advising clients on choosing the testamentary guardian, the other parent of the child is consulted, in order to prevent such legal conflicts from arising in the future.

Finally, the mother and father have the option to appoint the same set of guardians (for example, a married couple who are related to one parent or are good friends of the couple) who would act jointly only after the death of the surviving parent.

Temporary Guardianship

It is quite common for foreign couples who work in Singapore and who have their minor children with them to make enquiries on the appointment of temporary guardians. While their Wills typically name family members as testamentary guardians, these family members are likely to live in a foreign country. If something untoward happens to the parents, it would take some time before their testamentary guardian can arrive in Singapore to care for the children. A temporary guardian is someone who lives in Singapore and can care for the children while the testamentary guardian is making his way here.

I would recommend that at least a deed of guardianship be executed by the parents and the persons whom they wish to have as temporary guardians, so that this could serve as evidence to the court of the parents' intentions should there be such an unfortunate need.

ADOPTION

Another way that a non-parent can have "guardianship" of a child is through adoption.

Under Singapore law, these following points have to be noted:
1. The potential adoptee parent has to be above 25 years of age.
2. The age difference between the potential adoptee parent and the child should be 21 or more years.
3. A male potential adoptee parent cannot adopt a female child.

However, the court still retains the discretion to allow the non-biological parent to adopt even if these three criteria are not fulfilled.

Unlike guardianship, adoption has more severe consequences for the natural parents of the child. Under guardianship, the natural parents of the child still remain the parents of the child and the child would still be able to inherit from his parents under intestacy. However, with adoption, this legal relationship between the natural parents and the child is severed and a new legal relationship is created between the adoptive parents and the child.

The court would have to consider what is in the "best interest" of the child before deciding if the child can be adopted.

In a recent case, the court found that it would be in the child's best interest that he be adopted by the family who had brought him up since he was born, and declined to returning the child to the care of his natural mother who was coming out of prison.[5]

CARE FOR A MENTALLY INCAPACITATED ADULT

Apart from children, there is another vulnerable group of individuals who require someone similar to a guardian to care for them. This group would be adults without the mental capacity to make decisions for themselves.

Examples of such adults are adults with special needs or intellectual disabilities, those in persistent/permanent vegetative states, those with mental disorders or mental illness, or those who have dementia.

As discussed in chapter 3, for an adult who only lost mental capacity later on in life, by signing an LPA, this adult would have made the necessary preparations for a person to care for him when he loses mental capacity.

However, for adults who were born without mental capacity, a person called a "deputy" has to be appointed to care for the needs of such persons above the age of 21.

---

5   Re B [2020] SGFC 46. As of July 2020, the natural mother has instructed her solicitor to file an appeal; however, the court finding in this case could be interpreted as there being no presumption that a child is best raised by his natural parents, and instead, any decision on the upbringing of a child rests on ensuring the child's best interest.

CASE STUDIES
Let's look at a few case studies to see how the principles described above can be applied. We highlight some of the key actions that could be considered.

Family A
Tom and Sally are a married couple from China and they have one son, John. Tom's and Sally's relatives all reside in China. One day, Tom and Sally are involved in a car accident, with Tom passing away and Sally suffering from irreversible brain damage, which puts her in a vegetative state. John is only four years old and is alone in Singapore together with the domestic helper.

With no planning, Sally becomes the sole guardian of John, but Sally is unable to care for John because she has lost mental capacity. John will likely be made a ward of the court, where the court makes the major decisions for John, until a member from either Tom's or Sally's family applies to be appointed as his guardian.

With some planning, Tom could have appointed a testamentary guardian for John in his Will. Tom and Sally could have executed an LPA in order to appoint someone to care for them in the event that they lose the capacity to care for themselves.

Family B – Blended Family
Sarah is a divorcee and David is a widower. Both of them have one child each from their previous relationships, as they enter into their new marriage. Both the two children get along well with one another and they have often wished that they could consider David and Sarah as their "mom" and "dad" rather than just "step-mom"and "step-dad".

It is suggested that Sarah and David consider adopting their stepchildren. Note that David will have to seek Sarah's ex-husband's consent to adopt Sarah's child.

Family C – Unmarried Family

Lucy and Peter both love each other but did not want to get married to one another. They have three children, who are their biological children. However, they are all considered illegitimate under Singapore law because they were born out of wedlock.

The children can become legitimised if Lucy and Peter get married one day.

If they do not marry, Lucy and Peter should write Wills to appoint each other as testamentary guardians so that if, for example, Lucy passes away, Peter can be appointed the guardian of the children under the Will.

However, they may not be able to adopt their own children in the same way that a married couple can do so.

CONCLUSION

There are vulnerable individuals such as minors and persons without mental capacity who need care and concern. Some individuals like minors require care and concern until they become adults. Some other individuals like persons born without mental capacity require care and concern for all of their lives.

The overriding principle is always that the welfare of the minor or the mentally incapacitated person is paramount.

Whether the person in question is a young child or an elderly individual, there are a variety of benefits that come from planning the future care of such vulnerable persons. As a parent or caregiver for example, you might find peace of mind knowing that you have done what you can to provide for those under your care with the support they need if you pass on before them. Indeed, guardianship can help safeguard a child's rights and protect mentally incapacitated adults from scam artists and from being abused.

Chapter 17

Christians

by **Samuel Tan** with **Benny Ong**

"Abundance isn't God's provision for me
to live in luxury. It's His provision
for me to help others live. God entrusts me
with His money not to build
my kingdom on earth, but to build
His kingdom in heaven."
– Randy Alcorn

As Christians, we come to the realisation that it is all about God.

The purpose of our lives starts when we establish that personal, intimate relationship with God. Prior to knowing Jesus, each of us were on treasure hunts of our own. Some sought riches and power, while some others sought happiness and peace of mind. Jesus once told a story of a man who, on discovering hidden treasure in a field, gave up everything he had to obtain the treasure (Matthew 13:44-46).

Such is the value of discovering that treasure, the kingdom of God.

So if we are Christians, we have already discovered the ultimate treasure that brings about this life-changing joy. But before we pack our bags and move into our heavenly home, there's quite a lot to do especially where it comes to estate planning.[1] We have to put our affairs on earth in order and be wise and good stewards of His resources. Estate planning is essential for Christians so that the wealth we manage may be used towards God's greater good.

---

1   We refer to estate planning as discovering your family's needs after your lifetime and which usually incorporates the Will, Trust and LPA at the minimum.

HOW I CAME INTO ESTATE PLANNING

As a child, I did not think that growing up in a broken home would affect me much as an adult. The negative influences and emotional scars lingered on into my adult life. In my master plan, I was set to accomplish all that my parents had not – to have plenty of money, to achieve my earthly aspirations and to be the loving father and perfect husband.

Quite frankly, after a rollercoaster of a childhood, I was only interested in taking the path of least resistance and one that makes a lot of money. Little did I know that through my painful experiences that God was preparing me for His plans, a miraculous entry into and journey through law school and a career in estate planning!

A Christian approach to estate planning was to me a revolutionary concept and it has changed my life and the lives of my loved ones, and the families I work with. Let me now tell you all about it.

BIBLICAL STEWARDSHIP

In the beginning, all the way back to the Garden of Eden, God created and placed Adam in the Garden to work and tend to it.

It was clear that man was created to work and that is the stewardship of all of God's creations here on earth.

"Every faculty you have, your power of thinking or of moving your limbs from moment to moment, is given you by God. If you devoted every moment of your whole life exclusively to His service, you could not give Him anything that was not in a sense His own already."
– **CS Lewis,** *Mere Christianity*

Everything belongs to God absolutely and we are managers of what God allows us to oversee. This forms the foundation of Christian stewardship.

As Christians, we affirm God's ownership over everything we have. We understand that we are not owners of material assets, we are merely administrators of the assets that the Lord has entrusted and blessed us with. With this in mind, planning an estate to pass those resources on in a way that honours God and furthers His work is clearly a believer's responsibility.

> "The earth and everything in it, the world and its inhabitants, belong to the Lord."
> **– Psalm 24:1**

THE GOOD STEWARD PLANS AHEAD

My first job as an estate planning specialist taught me rather quickly that estate planning can be a used as an opportunity to protect and bless your family or as a weapon to hurt and punish them. Advancing enormous wealth to financially inexperienced young adults and children can have devastating consequences. They are at a stage in their lives where they are trying to forge part of their identities and finding their purpose in life. The mere presence of this inheritance may distract them from working, and may potentially be very overwhelming and isolating for them.

Let me share an incident that would forever change my attitude towards families and estate planning. A junior estate planner's client had just passed away and in his Will, he left $2.5 million to his 23-year-old daughter in a lump sum. Her mother knew that her daughter would not be able to cope with what she was about to receive and she wanted my help to stage an intervention, but there was nothing we could do. A couple of years later, we learnt that mother and daughter had intense fights over the inheritance and that the daughter had left home. Her friends knew of her inheritance and convinced her to fund their business ventures, which eventually failed. She dropped out of university to try to keep the businesses afloat, even taking on loans after fully utilising her inheritance. When all had failed, she fell into deep depression and tried taking her own life.

I remember sitting in the consultation room alone, reflecting on the earlier news from her mother. I realised that things had to be done differently and pleaded with God to help me see my work from His perspective.

Over time, God humbled me and revealed His estate planning "secrets" through His Word. Armed with these "secrets", His hand has been in my estate planning work with clients ever since, believers and pre-believers.

> "In his pride the wicked man does not seek him;
> in all his thoughts there is no room for God"
> **Psalm 10:4**

As Christians, we are called to protect and nurture our family, to lead our family and that glorifies God. A carefully crafted estate plan is an important resource for the faithful Christian steward.

God is not stopping us from storing treasures in our earthly storehouse. God does not forbid us to be wealthy. Some of us, however, may not be using our earthly treasures in God's way such as in the case of David.

David was not intentional in planning his Will

David is married to Ruth and they have two young children aged 10 and 12. He has two elderly parents that are dependent on him. Ruth has never gotten along well with her parents-in-law.

David had been procrastinating on planning his Will despite knowing the consequences of not getting one. Being promised a hassle-free and quick way to get his Will done, David heeded his friend's advice and decided to DIY his own Will using a template he found on the Internet.

Without an experienced estate planner to guide and plan with him, David quickly did up his Will and got it attested with the help of friends as witnesses. In his Will, he indicated that his wife will get a third of his estate, while the other two thirds will be divided between his two minor children in equal shares. There were no provisions in his Will for his dependent parents as he assumed that he would survive his parents.

David passed away shortly after that due to a heart attack.

While his wife inherited a third of his estate, his two young children were set to inherit their substantial shares of his estate at age 21, regardless of their maturity and readiness to manage such wealth. His elderly parents were left with nothing.

With a *properly planned* Will, David could have better blessed the lives of all his loved ones.

Could David have done things differently? Definitely!

A wise old man once told me that "you know what you know, and you don't know what you don't. Don't be afraid to seek proper counsel."

Seek advice from a professional and for Christians, a professional that shares similar beliefs. To me, he need not be a Christian but he should have a belief in and understanding of stewardship principles, which religions in general encourage.

"An inheritance obtained too early in life is not a blessing in the end."
– **Proverbs 20:21 NLT**

No parents would hope to bury their child. They would like to see their children grow up and achieve their dreams. However, it is not for us to "know the times or dates the Father has set by His own authority" (Acts 1:7 NIV). Let us not be like David and let us include the near future in our plans.

Now before we worry about facing the unknown, we should adopt a practical view of the future when it comes to crafting our estate plans.

There is no such thing as the "perfect" Will, where we only plan for the best case scenarios and that we will live to a ripe old age. Let us not speculate on the distant future but draw our minds to plan for the present and the near foreseeable future (three to five years).

Let's learn from Josiah.

Josiah sets up a Trust for his children

Josiah and his wife, Margaret, have three young children.

He understands that should anything happen to both him and Margaret in the near future, their young children are set to receive regular payments for their upkeep.

Keeping Proverbs 20:21 close to his heart, he was not going to allow any lump sum inheritance to potentially ruin their lives.

With the help of an experienced estate planner, Josiah and Margaret set up a Standby Living Trust with a Trust company.

With a conservative approach, they made it clear in their Trust deed and Letter of Wishes that the children will stand to inherit their shares fully only when they attain the age of 35, an age at which many of us would have achieved a certain level of financial maturity, been in full-time employment for a while and experienced the fruits of our own labour.

The parents carefully planted milestones and gifts in their Letter of Wishes, so as to continue to build their children up in life, encouraging and blessing them along the way.

> Once every few years, Josiah and Margaret would meet up with their estate planner to review their situation and plans for their family.

Too much, too soon. Soon ripe, soon rotten.

We do not reap soon after we sow. We have to ensure that sufficient time and space is given for our heirs to mature and grow, and when they are ready to take on the responsibilities of stewardship, the release of their inheritance will bless them greatly and the generations after them.

Let's next look to Noah, who has planned for his giving for beyond his immediate family.

Noah plans for his employees

Noah owns a food production centre, known for its traditional Nonya delicacies, and many of the staff have been working there for more than 20 years. He inherited the business from his father and would like to ensure that the business continues after he is no longer around.

He sought help and guidance from a Christian estate planning specialist to get a business succession plan in place, including a customised Lasting Power of Attorney. He made sure that his trustees and donees would appoint a worthy successor to continue the business, stating leadership qualities he would like to see in the next leader and recommending a few names.

If Noah were to lose his mental capacity due to dementia, his donees would conduct interviews for qualified people to fill leadership roles.

His plan included who his successor would be when he passes away. That would be his son and daughter, who are only starting to help in the business.

The business continued to grow and his loyal elderly employees were greatly blessed, without having the need to seek employment elsewhere!

Business owners often think they would live a very long time and neglect to make retirement plans. While we can, we should be looking to the day when we cannot run our businesses any more.

Due to our self-centered instincts, Paul reminds us that as Christians, we should "in humility count others more significant than ourselves" (Philippians 2:3) and if God has placed it in our hearts to bless others in our estate plans, do it with a grateful heart. That is a test of character!

When Noah inherited the business from his father, he recognised that he had inherited the employees along with the responsibilities of a dutiful Christian business owner. The heartbeat of every Christian business owner is to be like Moses seeking God for a worthy successor to bring the Israealites to the Promised Land, being guided in everything that they do!

THE PLANS AND THE BLESSINGS

"If you read history you will find that the Christians
who did most for the present world
were precisely those who thought most of the next. It
is since Christians have
largely ceased to think of the other world that they
have become so ineffective in this."

– CS Lewis

Now with an eternity perspective and all the estate planning tools at our disposal, would it not be exciting to show the world the wonderful legacy that we Christians will leave behind? When we keep our eyes on God, seek Him in all that we plan, He will establish our steps!

The Christian approach to estate planning ensures that we pass on responsibilities and valuables to our children and, in turn, they will do the same for their children and beyond. When the day arrives for each of us, will we see the faces of our loved ones up in heaven and will we hear the words "Well done my good and faithful servant"?

I can't wait!

While the world encourages "control from beyond the grave", we should adopt something different. Let us keep our eyes on God and focus on "goodness from beyond the grave".

Chapter 18

Muslims

by **Masagoes Abdul Karim**

"Allah SWT will not be merciful to those who are not
merciful to mankind."
– Sahih Al-Bukhari Book 73 Hadith 42.

In Islam, God encourages Muslims to seek wealth and to share it.

God instructs Muslims after completing their prayers to work
hard to achieve wealth. The Holy Qur'an says:

"And when the Prayer is finished, then may ye
disperse through the land, and seek of the Bounty of
Allah: and celebrate the Praises of Allah often (and
without stint): that ye may prosper."
The Holy Qur'an 62:10[1]

Wealth is considered to be a gift from God. God, who provided
it to the person, has already made a portion of it for the poor, so the
poor has a right over one's wealth through zakat. Zakat is an Islamic
obligation that an individual has to donate a certain proportion of
his wealth each year to charitable causes.

A Muslim who accumulates wealth during his lifetime needs to
plan for how his wealth is distributed upon his death. The Qur'an
has established rules on how one's assets should be distributed upon
death. These inheritance rules are called faraid and Muslims are
obliged to follow them.

Faraid is similar in concept to what many European countries
term as "forced heirship". Generally under such a regime, at least
two-thirds of the assets of a deceased Muslim should be distributed

---

1   All Qur'an quotes are taken from Yusuf Ali's translation found at www.quranexplorer.com.

according to faraid rules, while up to one-third may be freely distributed by an Islamic Will (called a Wasiat in Islam).

WRITING A WILL (OR WASIAT)

The Qur'an grants Muslims the right to dispose upon death up to one-third of their property through a Will. The assets referred to are those as at the date of death, not at the date of writing the Will.

The writing of a Will is considered of utmost importance for a Muslim, although it is not a requirement:

> "It is the duty of a Muslim who has anything to bequeath not to let two nights pass without writing a Will."
> – in the Muwatta of Iman Malik[2]

The Will is made by a person during his lifetime. The one-third of his estate that can be given can be to whomever he wishes, as long as the beneficiaries are not amongst those who will benefit from the remaining two-thirds.[3] However, more than one-third can be bequeathed if those entitled under the two-third portion agree to do so.

The formalities of an Islamic Will in Singapore are similar to those for a non-Muslim Will in terms of formalities. However, in terms of substance, there are some important differences, including:

- The Will must be signed before two adult witnesses;[4]
- The Will cannot benefit his faraid beneficiaries. For example, Ahmad cannot write a Will to benefit his wife. He can, however, write a Will to give Benny, who is not a Muslim, or to Amir who as an adopted child is not a faraid beneficiary; and
- Ahmad cannot Will away more than one-third of his estate.

---

2 The Muwatta is the first written collection of hadith comprising the subjects of Muslim law, compiled and edited by the Imam, Malik ibn Anas.
3 This rule applies to followers of the Sunni school. Shiite rules allow bequests in a will to be made to legal heirs whereas Sunni rules do not. To keep things simple, we will assume the Sunni school is being referred to unless otherwise stated.
4 The formalities of a Muslim will can be referred to here: section 111(2)(a) Administration of Muslim Law Act.

How Faraid Rules Disposes of Two-Thirds of a Muslim's Wealth

Faraid rules are used to determine which of the relatives of the deceased are entitled to inherit and the amount each is to receive. Of the deceased person's assets, two-thirds (if one-third has first been distributed according to his Will) or all of his assets (if the deceased did not write a will) may be distributed.

There are just three verses from the Qur'an that give specific rules on inheritance: Chapter 4 verses 11, 12 and 176. From these three verses, together with the traditions of the Prophet Muhammad (pbuh) (hadith), and through juristic reasoning (qiyas), the laws of inheritance have been developed in painstaking detail with large volumes of work written on the subject.

Let us go through an example to see how faraid works.

Ahmad passes away and leaves behind $1,000,000. He is survived by his wife, one son, one daughter, father, mother, one sister and one brother. How would his assets be distributed assuming he had not written a Will?

We can use the trial calculator provided by the Singapore Syariah court[5] to give us an idea of the distribution:

The assets of Ahmad, in the event of his/her death, shall be divided into 72 (seventy two) shares as follows:-

			Shares
1.	Father, Father 1 , will get	1/6	12
2.	Son, Son 1 , will get	asobah	26
3.	Mother, Mother 1 , will get	1/6	12
4.	Wife, Wife 1 , will get	1/8	9
5.	Daughter, Daughter 1 , will get	bilghair	13
		Total	72

Please note this calculation is for user's own information only. The user may print a copy of the calculation. Please note, however, that no individual, authority or court of law is obliged to accept the calculation as binding it in any way.

As you can tell, the inheritance breakdown can get complicated. Our task here is to appreciate the intricacies of faraid rules and that Muslims have the responsibility to plan for their families in the event of death.

---

5 An Islamic inheritance calculator can be found at www.syariahcourt.gov.sg

You may have noticed that:

- His daughter receives 13 shares, while his son receives twice as many (whereas if Ahmad is non-Muslim, his children share equally under non-Muslim intestacy law).
- His siblings get nothing (because there are family members who are more closely related to Ahmad, that is, his son and daughter).
- His parents get a share (whereas if Ahmad is non-Muslim, his parents would not get a share under non-Muslim intestacy law).

Why is Islamic inheritance "unfair" for women?

Males get more than females under inheritance because males have more responsibility for the females and the family in general (The Holy Qur'an 4:11). Also, women are favoured financially over their male counterparts in these situations:

1. Before marriage any gift given to a woman is her own and her husband has no legal right to claim it after marriage.

2. On marriage, she is entitled to receive a marriage gift and this is her own property.

3. Even if the wife is rich, she is not required to spend a single dollar on the household. The full responsibility for her food, lodging and comfort is her husband's.

4. Any income the wife earns through working is entirely her own.

We see that the female's financial position may not be as unfair as it first seems to be.

WHAT IF FARAID RULES DO NOT MEET AHMAD'S NEEDS?

The important question for Ahmad is whether the above distribution is satisfactory to him. What if Ahmad's daughter is physically disabled and unable to find a suitable marriage partner while his son is a very successful businessman? What if Ahmad's spouse now bears the responsibility of looking after his parents and children when her inheritance is just one-eighth of his assets?

Can Ahmad give away some of his assets to his needful daughter and spouse during his lifetime and not run afoul of faraid?

The following is a list of possible situations in which Muslims can consider to ensure that their assets are distributed in a way that is fair to their family situation or does not unfairly deprive a faraid beneficiary, and is beneficial to society and compliant with Shariah. Each is briefly explained:

1. Making a Gift (or Hibah)
2. Charitable giving
3. Making a CPF nomination
4. Making an insurance nomination
5. Purchasing property under joint tenancy
6. Making a Will with non-binding wishes
7. Setting up a Private Trust

1. Making a Gift (or Hibah)

It is lawful for a Muslim to dispose outright during his lifetime part or all of his property.[6] A Muslim should not, of course, bequeath before death all of his assets to his favourite spouse or child, for he should secure the welfare of dependents while not denying the rights of beneficiaries.[7] The Holy Qur'an says:

> "Let those (disposing of an estate) have the same fear
> in their minds as they would have for their own if they
> had left a helpless family behind: let them fear Allah,
> and speak appropriate (comfort)."
> **– The Holy Qur'an 4:9**

---

6   According to former Chief Justice Suffian of Malaysia in the case *Reman bin Mihat* (1965) 2 MLJ 1.
7   Irwan Hadi Mohd Shuhaimy, "Fatwa on Revocable Insurance Nomination", Financial Planning for Muslims Conference in Singapore, 30 August 2012.

When one makes a gift, it is done voluntarily without receiving or expecting any consideration in return. The transfer must be done during the lifetime of the donor in order for the gift to fall outside of faraid rules. In our example of Ahmad above, he could make a gift of $50,000 to his spouse during his lifetime, knowing that it is she who would hold the family together after his death. The gift of $50,000 would then not be "clawed back" into his estate for faraid distribution.

2. Charitable Giving

The alleviation of poverty and suffering lies at the heart of Islam. It is for this reason that charitable giving is strongly encouraged in Islam, both as a means of purifying one's wealth and to alleviate poverty and suffering.[8] The Holy Qur'an says:

> "To spend of your substance out of love for Him, for your kin, for orphans for the needy, for the wayfarer for those who ask and for the ransom of slaves; to be steadfast in prayer and practise regular charity."
> **–The Holy Qur'an 2:177**

There are three main forms of charitable giving in Islam: zakat (already discussed), waqf and sadaqah:

- Waqf (or Trust) – Waqf is like an endowment[9] or trust and is normally set up during a person's lifetime to fulfil charitable purposes. If a person makes an asset waqf, such as a building, the building henceforth ceases to be his property. Once the property is dedicated, the ownership is "transferred to God", and held in Trust. This allows the property to be used perpetually for charity.
- Sadaqah (or Voluntary Charity) – Sadaqah means "voluntary charity" (as opposed to zakat which is "prescribed charity").

---

8   Rianne C. ten Veen, "Charitable Giving in Islam", *Islamic Relief Worldwide,* September 2009.
9   An endowment is typically a financial donation made to a non-profit organisation for a stated purpose at the bequest of the donor. Most endowments are designed to keep the principal amount intact while using the investment income from dividends for charitable efforts.

Examples include monetary donations, feeding the poor, supporting orphans and widows, saying a cheerful word or smiling, advising or counselling others, and volunteering in the community.[10]

3. Making a CPF nomination

A CPF nomination may be considered as hibah as it is made by the contributor during his lifetime, according to a fatwa.[11] Ahmad could use a CPF nomination to provide more to his daughter and wife in order to balance his gifts to his family.

4. Making an insurance nomination

An insurance nomination (whether revocable or irrevocable) may be considered as hibah as it is made by the contributor during his lifetime, according to a fatwa.[12] Ahmad could purchase an insurance policy and nominate his daughter and wife in order to balance his gifts to his family.

5. Purchasing property under joint tenancy

The surviving joint owner of a property would receive the rights to a joint tenancy property on the death of a joint owner.[13] Ahmad could purchase a condo with his daughter under a joint tenancy. On his passing, the rights to the condo would be passed to his surviving daughter.

6. Making a Will with non-binding wishes

A testator may write a Will to distribute his assets in a way that is not compliant with faraid.

---

10 "What is Sadaqah?" www.islamic-relief.org.uk/about-us/what-we-do/sadaqah.
11 The religious council in Singapore, called Majlis Ugama Islam Singapura (MUIS), from time to time makes Islamic legal rulings called fatwas. A fatwa is regarded as an expert opinion on matters of modern life. In recent years, several fatwas have been issued regarding CPF nominations, insurance nominations, joint tenancy of properties and others. The fatwa on CPF nominations can be accessed here: www.muis.gov.sg/officeofthemufti/Fatwa/CPF-Nomination. Note that fatwas are not binding on the courts. Fatwas can be rejected if the court finds that they are not applicable to the issue. However, fatwas tend to be respected and adopted by the Muslims in Singapore in general.
12 The fatwa on insurance nominations can be accessed here: www.muis.gov.sg/officeofthemufti/Fatwa/English-Revocable-Insurance-Nomination.
13 The fatwa on joint tenancy can be accessed here: www.muis.gov.sg/officeofthemufti/Fatwa/English-Joint-Tenancy.

I once had a widow who had a solely-owned HDB flat that she wanted sold on her death, with the proceeds to be given equally to her three sons and three daughters. She had a statement in her Will that read "It is my request and desire that all my surviving children should share equally the proceeds of the sale of my HDB flat, without making any distinction between male and female heirs."

She had her entire family in my office during the Will signing. While she understood that her wish is not legally binding, she was confident that her children would abide with her wishes on her death.

Depending on the situation, the testator may sometimes ask for more assurance that his wishes are followed by his family. If so, I would often draft a Muslim Will along with a deed of renunciation to be signed by his faraid beneficiaries. If a faraid beneficiary signs such a renunciation, it means that he is willing to forgo his legal share to another family member. As you can imagine, some beneficiaries do refuse to disclaim their share. Hence, I have to weigh the situation each time because family situations are never the same.

7. Setting up a Private Trust

A Muslim can transfer some of his assets into a private Trust. Such assets may be considered hibah, where the Trust is an Irrevocable Living Trust and the assets are transferred in during his lifetime. Once transferred into such a Trust during his lifetime, the transferor loses his rights over those assets.

In the case of Ahmad, he could set up an Irrevocable Living Trust into which he could transfer a sum of money to benefit his family.

CONCLUSION

Islamic estate planning is based on the principle that all wealth belongs to God and that anyone who possesses wealth is simply its caretaker:

"Be quite sure that to Allah doth belong whatever is
in the heavens and on earth.
Well doth He know what ye are intent upon: and the
day they will be brought back to
Him and He will tell them the truth of what they did:
for Allah doth know all things."
– The Holy Qur'an 24:64

Social responsibility is deeply rooted in this principle. As wealth is considered to belong to the Creator, it requires forward planning for this life and the hereafter.

Muslims are encouraged to write a Will. Muslims are expected to follow faraid rules regarding the distribution of at least two-thirds of their wealth. Where a Muslim finds that faraid rules may not be suitable for his family situation, there are various tools that a Muslim can use to vary the distribution of his wealth.

As you can see from this short chapter, faraid rules and diverse family situations make Islamic estate planning quite a challenging task. We encourage you to seek proper legal advice in your estate planning.

Chapter 19

Persons with Special Needs

by **Keon Chee**

INTRODUCTION

Persons with special needs (PSNs) are vulnerable people in our society because of their dependence on others for care and support. While anyone can experience neglect, abuse and aggression, PSNs are at greater risk because their ability to respond is limited.

Caregivers are often the voice and hands of PSNs. Behind the scenes, they face day-to-day challenges that many of us don't have to deal with and in many cases, don't understand.

In this chapter, we look at what is meant by special needs. After having worked with families with PSN members, I realise that we have to be careful with the words we use. We then focus on the financial and estate planning that caregivers should consider when they are no longer able to care for the PSNs under their charge.

WHAT IS MEANT BY SPECIAL NEEDS?

If we go by the Merriam-Webster dictionary,[1] special needs means "any of various difficulties (such as a physical, emotional, behavioural, or learning disability or impairment) that causes an individual to require additional or specialized services or accommodations (such as in education or recreation)." This definition is wide.

The definition of special needs gets narrower depending on the context. In the context of children in school, the Ministry of Education (MOE) uses the term Special Educational Needs (SEN) to describe the characteristics of a child who (a) has been diagnosed with a disability, (b) shows greater difficulty in learning as compared to his peers, and (c) requires additional resources beyond what is generally available.[2]

---

1   "Special Educational Needs", Ministry of Education Singapore, www.moe.gov.sg/education/special-education/.

2   "Special Educational Needs", www.moe.gov.sg/education/special-education.

In the context of setting up a trust with the Special Needs Trust Company (SNTC) (to be discussed later), PSNs are defined in SNTC's Constitution as "those persons whose prospects of securing, retaining places and advancing in education and training institutions, employment and recreation as equal members of the community are substantially reduced as a result of physical, sensory, intellectual and/or developmental impairments. This may also include persons with mental disabilities."

The Vernacular – Special Needs or Disability or Disorder?

I used to use the term "special needs person". One day, my lawyer friend told me that that isn't a good term to use and that I should use 'person with special needs'. He gave an illustration that stuck. He said that if a person has a fat tummy while the rest of his body isn't fat, would that person like to be described as "a person with fatness" or "a fat person".

Referring to a person by their impairment is no longer acceptable. Acceptable terminology draws attention to the person first, then mentions their impairment, only if relevant. It is better to say "person with special needs" rather than "special needs person".[3]

Yet the term "special needs" does not sit well with some. A few years ago, during World Down Syndrome Day, a film was shown that highlighted that persons with Down Syndrome do not have needs that are special. Instead, their needs are just like every other human being's: family, education, job, friends, love, etc.[4] In some other instances, the word "disorder" is more appropriate, such as in learning disorder.

Terms evolve. When the words "retarded" and "spastic" were once commonly used, they are today not acceptable and have been replaced by more respectful language.

---

3   "Disability Etiquette", www.cerebralpalsy.org
4   "Changing Perspectives: 'Special Needs' vs 'Disability'", 25 June 2019, https://allin.guide/blog/changing-perspectives-special-needs-vs-disability/.

These days, I use "person with special needs" or PSN for short, although PSN does sound impersonal. Sometimes I use PSN as a noun such as Jenny is a PSN. At other times, I use PSN as an adjective, such as "Jenny is a PSN child". Sometimes when I am not sure, I ask the parent. Or if I am speaking to the PSN, I would look at his face and call his name. And if the PSN has a sibling who is not a PSN, I know never to refer to the non-PSN sibling as "normal" because that would suggest that the PSN is "abnormal." For the rest of this chapter, I will use the acronym PSN and the term "disability" interchangeably.

CONCERNS OF CAREGIVERS – AFTER THEIR LIFETIME

Caregivers have two main after-lifetime concerns: (a) to create a Care Plan for how their child will be cared for, and (b) to create a Financial Plan to ensure there will be enough money for the child. Caregivers commonly ask:

1. Who will care for my child's day-to-day needs when my spouse and I aren't around anymore? Will the caregiver know our child's likes and dislikes, daily routine, medical treatment, hobbies, food preferences, allergies and needs?

2. Between our PSN child and our other children, should we be allocating more to our PSN child? How do we make sure nobody feels resentful?

3. Can our other children look after our PSN child? Is it fair to expect them to care for their sibling, when they have their own families?

4. Will my spouse and I have enough money for our PSN child? How can we make sure that the money to be used for our PSN child's care and lifetime needs won't run out?

5. Do we need to set up a trust? Is it expensive?

A private trust can incorporate a family's Financial and Care Plans for their PSN child. The Trust deed and Letter of Wishes can specify how trust funds are disbursed. The Letter of Wishes can also contain wishes on how the family wants their PSN child to be cared for.

However, not all families wish to have a private trust or can afford one. Furthermore, a commercially run licensed Trust company would not have the expertise or focus on dealing with PSN children and adults. Fortunately, in Singapore, we have the Special Needs Trust Company (SNTC), which checks all the boxes.

THE SPECIAL NEEDS TRUST COMPANY

SNTC is a non-profit organisation that aims to serve lower to middle class families with PSN children and assist members to plan for their future care. It is the only organisation of its kind in Singapore. As depicted in Figure 17.1, SNTC is supported by the Ministry of Social and Family Development (MSF) and the Trust funds of families are invested by the Public Trustee. The principal value of the Trust funds is guaranteed by the government.

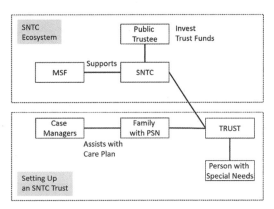

Figure 17.1 – The SNTC Ecosystem & Setting Up an SNTC Trust

Setting Up a Special Needs Trust

Bunny is a mother who has a PSN son with cerebral palsy. She wishes to set an SNTC trust and submits an application. As shown in Figure 17.1, SNTC appoints a case manager who is an employee of SNTC and a trained social worker, to review the application. The PSN child must be resident in Singapore and be either a Singaporean or Singapore permanent resident.

The SNTC case manager works with Bunny to assess her son's needs to develop a detailed Care Plan to estimate the amount of funds her son needs for the rest of his life. The Care Plan also details how her son should be looked after, including his food and future accommodation needs, the therapy and medicines he needs, the people he is fond of meeting and other care and financial matters.

The Care Plan is the result of SNTC's holistic needs assessment to understand Bunny's family and the sources of funds for her son's care. The objective is to be as detailed as possible so that her son can enjoy a similar quality of life when Bunny is no longer around.

The cost to set up an SNTC Trust is $1,500, as seen in Table 17.2.[5] MSF subsidies 90% of this fee and Bunny pays $150. The initial capital required by SNTC is $5,000 in cash. The Trust fund for her son can be topped up any time. Funds can also be transferred in to the Trust after the caregiver passes away through the estate, CPF nominations and the proceeds of insurance policies.

Table 17.2 – SNTC Fees & Subsidies

SNTC Type of Fees	Fee Before Subsidy (S$)	Subsidy by MSF (S$)	Fee After Subsidy (S$)
One-time Set-up	1500	90%	150
Annual Pre-Activation	250	100%	0
One-time Activation	400	90%	40
Annual Post-Activation	400	90%	40

Source: www.sntc.gov.sg

---

5   "A Lifelong Gift for your Loved One with Special Needs", Special Needs Trust Company, www.sntc. org.sg.

The Trust is set up as an Irrevocable Trust, which means that the funds are permanently set aside for her son and cannot be taken back by Bunny as long as her son is alive. A Letter of Intent (LOI), which is effectively a Letter of Wishes, is drawn up by taking planning details from the Care Plan. The LOI contains detailed descriptions, dollar amounts and when those amounts should be disbursed for her son's future care and financial needs.

Before the Trust is activated on Bunny's death, there is no annual pre-activation fee after subsidy. During the pre-activation period, the case manager will conduct reviews with Bunny at least once a year.

When Bunny passes away, there is a one-time activation fee of $40 after subsidy and an annual post-activation fee of $40 after subsidy, regardless of the size of the funds that have been safeguarded for her son. The trust funds are disbursed according to Bunny's wishes as set out in the LOI. If her son continues to live in the community, then the funds will be disbursed to her son's appointed caregiver or to such service providers if the son is institutionalised after Bunny's demise.

Case Study – Planning for their PSN Son

Bunny is a homemaker and is married to Andy, a 50-year-old business owner. Besides their PSN son, they have a daughter who is not a PSN.

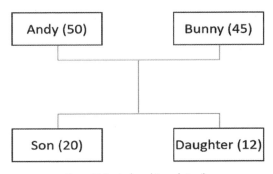

Figure 17.2 – Andy and Bunny's Family

Andy makes a comfortable income. They live in a private condo that is owned by Andy and Bunny as joint tenants. Andy and Bunny wish to set up an SNTC Trust for their son.

A question popped up during the planning with the case manager about how much should be set aside for her son. Bunny estimates that her son would need $2,500 per month or $30,000 per year. They brought in their financial planner to help plan an amount that could take care of her son for the rest of his life.

To get a sense of the total needed, Andy and Bunny learned that a person with cerebral palsy has a life expectancy of between 30 and 70 years, depending on the severity of the condition and quality of treatment received.[6] Since their son is 20 and if he lives to 70, Andy and Bunny should prepare for 50 years of expenses for their son:

Amount needed for son = $30,000 X 50 years = $1.5 million

They decide to top it up to $2 million to leave room for unexpected expenses. SNTC is advised to adjust the monthly amount for inflation over the years.

Setting Up an SNTC Trust for their Son

Figure 17.3 shows how the SNTC trust can be set up for their son.

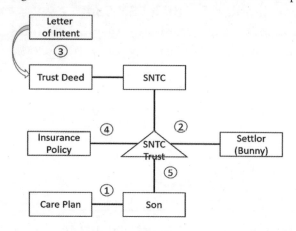

Figure 17.3 – An SNTC Trust for their Son

---

6   "Cerebral Palsy Life Expectancy," www.birthinjuryguide.org.

① Andy and Bunny decided that Bunny, being the main caregiver, should be the person to plan with the case manager. A Care Plan is devised for their son's care.

② It was also decided that Bunny should be the settlor of the Irrevocable SNTC Trust.

③ The LOI stipulates how much funds are to be disbursed for her son and for what purpose.

④ Bunny purchases a $2 million insurance policy on her own life and nominates SNTC to receive the proceeds – to be elaborated below.

⑤ When Bunny passes away, proceeds from the insurance policy are transferred to SNTC, whereupon funds are regularly disbursed for her son's benefit according to the LOI. When her son passes away and there are funds remaining, those funds can be passed to Andy, their daughter, to charity or to whoever she has specified as a contingent beneficiary.

Other Points of Planning

Caregiver parents can also consider:

The Special Needs Savings Scheme (SNSS)

The parent of a PSN can make a CPF nomination to benefit his PSN. However, the CPF savings will be distributed as a lump sum upon the parent's death. This may not be suitable since the PSN is unlikely to be able to handle a potentially large lump sum of money.

A good option is to use the SNSS scheme, which allows parents to nominate their PSN to receive monthly payments from the parent's CPF savings after the parent's demise.

There is no minimum CPF balance required at the time of application. However, at the time of the parent's death, there should be at least a balance of $3,000 so that the minimum monthly CPF payout of $250 can be made. Otherwise, the full amount would be disbursed. Of course, parents can specify that a larger monthly amount be made if desired.

Appointing Guardian / Deputy for the PSN

If either Andy or Bunny passes away, the survivor of them becomes the sole guardian of their children who are both under the age of 21. If Andy and Bunny have both passed away, their Wills should have named someone to be the guardian of their children. When their daughter reaches 21, she would be considered an adult and the guardianship over her ceases.

Their son has intellectual disability and would not be able to make decisions for himself even after age 21. Andy and Bunny can have guardianship extended beyond age 21 by applying to court to become his deputies even before he reaches 21. They may also appoint successor deputies who can act if both Andy and Bunny are unable to in the future.

Setting up a Private Trust for the whole family

Andy and Bunny should consider setting up a Private Trust for themselves and their two young children. The insurance policy can be re-nominated to the Private Trust instead. The Private Trust can then pass monies to the SNTC Trust as needed for their son's care on an ongoing basis rather than as a lump sum.

CARE FOR THE CAREGIVER

Caregiving is a tough, sometimes seemingly thankless job. When a person is caring for someone day in and day out, he will experience many different emotions - happiness, sadness, loneliness and anger at any time. When caregivers do not pay attention to their feelings, they can experience poor sleep, illness and depression.

A study by the National Council of Social Service (NCSS) showed that close to half of caregivers of persons with disabilities experience caregiver strain, with 4 in 10 being psychologically distressed and more than 6 in 10 felt burdened by the weight of their caregiving duties.[7]

---

7   "Understanding the Quality of Life of Adults with Disabilities", 2017, www.ncss.gov.sg.

The needs of caregivers were highlighted in the 3rd Enabling Masterplan in which caregivers were able to express their key concerns as.[8]

- Preparing for the future when they are no longer able to care for the person with a disability
- Being able to perform their caregiving duty well
- A need for self-care and respite

Caregivers need help and they need to express their feelings so that they can find beneficial ways to deal with them. Doing so would improve the quality of life for the caregiver and the one being cared for.

BECOMING AN INCLUSIVE SOCIETY

I know we don't mean it but some of us can feel awkward around PSNs. You must have seen this: when a disabled person enters the MRT, everyone sort of tiptoes around the person, hoping not to make eye contact and afraid to make conversation.

Singaporeans are generally inclusive and sensitive, except that many of us do not know what to do or what to say around PSNs. We can certainly learn. For instance, how do you help a person with visual disability cross the road? Ask the person if you can help. If he says yes, then offer your hand or elbow. Much can be learned by Googling.

Some companies have created an inclusive workplace. Since 2013, UOB has been hiring persons with disabilities at its UOB Scan Hub, its nerve centre for checking, digitisation and archiving of customer documents. About 30% of the Hub's employees are persons with autism or hearing impairment, and it has been reported: "Their attention to detail and high levels of concentration and accuracy have helped improve UOB Scan Hub's productivity and employee retention rates."[9]

---

8   "3rd Enabling Masterplan 2017–2021 – Caring Nation, Inclusive Society", December 2016.
9   "UOB champions inclusive hiring through first such public, private and people sector collaboration in Singapore", 16 July 2019, www.uobgroup.com/web-resources/uobgroup/pdf/newsroom/2019/UOB-inclusive-hiring.pdf.

CONCLUSION

We are a wealthy nation when it comes to dollars and cents. We are, however, in the *process* of becoming a wealthy nation in terms of being inclusive and sensitive towards PSN persons who are vulnerable and need more care and support.

Caregivers are at the frontline of caring for PSN persons. Theirs is a task that lasts the lifetime of the PSN.

For families with PSN members, SNTC provides an invaluable and affordable service. It is only one of a handful of such government-supported, non-profit organisations in the world that provides trust services for PSNs.

Chapter acknowledgements:

Esther Tan, General Manager of SNTC, for reviewing the chapter and giving her valuable inputs.

Yvonne Chiang, a caregiver mother to a child with autism, for her detailed suggestions and excellent insights.

Bernard Chung, my lawyer friend, for his important contributions to this chapter and his kind-hearted care and work for the PSN community.

Chapter 20

Giving

by **Keon Chee**

Giving is the foundation of happiness. Psychologist Martin Seligman maintains that it takes three types of lives integrated together to bring us Authentic Happiness: the Pleasant Life, the Good Life and the Meaningful Life[1] –

- The Pleasant Life is about having as many pleasures as possible in life. Having a delicious banana split or a beach holiday during Christmas brings positive feelings but they are not long lasting. After the third or fourth banana split, you would be feeling quite sick.

- The Good Life is about using your strengths in the core parts of your life, such as in your work, family, friendships and parenting. If you are good at solving math problems, then you might want to explore a career in IT, engineering and accounting.

- The Meaningful Life is about sharing your highest strengths in the service of something that is bigger than you are. If you are good at teaching and communicating, you could teach English at an orphanage or volunteer as a Bible study leader in church.

Surveys on why people donate their time and money to charity show the top reason to be being of service to others. Tax is rarely a top reason even in countries with high income and estate taxes, like in America and the UK.[2]

In this chapter, we look at how giving should begin at home where we can be examples to our children to encourage a lifetime of positive giving. We also consider the two ways that people can

---

1   www.authentichappiness.sas.upenn.edu
2   A sample of articles that referred to such surveys include – "7 Reasons Why Donors Give", 9 March 2020, www.networkforgood.com and "5 reasons why people give their money away – plus 1 why they don't", 27 November 2017, www.theconversation.com.

donate money – either during their lifetime or after their lifetime. Whether the giving is modest or significant, small and large amounts all make a difference to the causes that need our help.

CHARITY BEGINS AT HOME

Children who participate in giving lead happier lives. As our children grow up, they begin to understand that others may have less than they do. They can learn to share with others in many ways. For example:

- They can give a part of their money.
- They can help people by giving their time and energy.
- They can share or give away clothes and toys they no longer need, by passing them on to others who have a use for them.

Parents can donate and volunteer in projects that involve their children.

Case study

Casey taught English every Saturday for four years at a senior citizens home. He taught them to sing English songs like "Twinkle Twinkle Little Star" and "Silent Night", and brought them to perform at other homes. Many of the home residents who Casey taught were in their 70s and 80s. They were eager to learn because they wanted to be able to communicate with their grandchildren. Casey brought his daughter Sarah along once a month. Sarah loved playing the piano and played Chinese songs for the residents whenever she visited.

Giving while you are alive allows you to find and experience for yourself the charitable causes that receive your time, money and effort. We will focus on the giving of money because that is the most common item of value that people donate. We will refer to Samantha, aged 50, who has a son Frankie, aged 18, as an illustration of a giving journey, and we use examples of various charities to demonstrate how diverse, convenient and flexible donating has become.

Here are four ways to consider for the making of gifts or donations:

- giving directly to a charity of your choice;
- giving through an intermediary, such as a portal;
- giving through a donor-assisted fund; and
- starting your own charity.

Giving directly to a charity

This can be as simple as writing a cheque and mailing it to the religious organisation you attend. Samantha donates $1,000 to the Rahmatan Lil Alamin Foundation (RLAF), which is a charity set up by the Islamic Religious Council of Singapore (Muis) in 2009 to help people affected by serious infectious diseases.

Samantha donates US$30 per month to Doctors Without Borders, a foreign charity that responds to medical emergencies around the world.

Giving through an intermediary

When you donate through an intermediary, your donations and those of other donors are accumulated, managed and distributed to selected charities that, on their own, may not be as effective in raising funds for themselves.[3]

Samantha donates $1,000 to the Community Chest (ComChest), which is the fundraising arm of the National Council of Social Service (NCSS). ComChest raises funds from the community for the benefit of adults with disabilities, children with special needs, persons with mental health conditions, vulnerable seniors and other social services.

---

3 According to statistics revealed by the Commissioner of Charities Annual Report 2018, the 2,277 charities in Singapore in 2017 received $20.5 billion in annual receipts, which include government grants and donations. Of those, 193 large charities received almost $100 million each, whereas the other 2,084 received less than $1 million on average.

Frankie is eager to get give, too. Together, they learned about Giving.sg, which, to them, is the perfect place to begin their family's charitable giving adventure together. The smallest amount one can donate to a charity in one transaction is $10, which is an amount almost anyone, including our children, can afford to give.

Frankie lost his grandfather through illness and wants to benefit seniors. He makes a $50 donation to YWCA Meals-on-Wheels for the Elderly & Children and is excited that his photo is shown on the campaign website as a Recent Donor. To donate, your child has to be at least 18 years of age. If he is between 13 and 17, he can still donate but with parental consent.

Some donors who want their giving more customised to their wishes and have more to give can consider The Community Foundation of Singapore (CFS). CFS can help you set up a donor-advised fund where, if the amount donated is $200,000 or more, it can open a fund in your name and work closely with you to match your interests with community needs. CFS has over 400 charity partners and donated funds are managed by an Investment Committee, which is made up of experienced professionals from the finance industry.[4]

Suppose you are not comfortable giving your money to a charity that then decides on your behalf when and how your money is disbursed. What if the money goes towards a purpose that is contrary to your wishes? Is there a way to give cash directly to needy people and let them decide how best to use it? After all, the $10 given to a needy person may be spent on food, while another needy person may use the $10 on seeds for growing crops.

The American charity GiveDirectly collects your donations and gives money directly to the world's poorest. "We believe people living in poverty deserve the dignity to choose for themselves how best to improve their lives — cash enables that choice."[5]

Starting your own charity

If your family has a significant amount to give, you could consider

4   Community Foundation of Singapore, www.cf.org.sg.
5   "About GiveDirectly", www.givedirectly.org.

starting a private foundation, such as the Shaw Foundation (donated $350 million) and the Lee Foundation (donated $1 billion).[6] Such charities are often founded with private money (from family or corporate sources) and do not raise funds from the public.[7] They thus differ from typical charities such as the Singapore Children's Society and the Singapore Red Cross Society, which seek funds from the public.

The Bill and Melinda Gates Foundation which was launched in 2000, is reputedly the largest private foundation in the world, holding US$46.8 billion in assets. In May 2020, the Foundation committed US$125 million towards developing and distributing COVID-19 diagnostics, therapies and vaccines.

TESTAMENTARY GIVING

Testamentary giving means your donation occurs only after your death. Your gift can be an immediate gift on your passing or it can be staggered over a period of time.

Making immediate gifts

This is most commonly done through a Will. Table 19.1 shows some examples that Samantha can consider:

Table 19.1 – Examples of Testamentary Giving Options

Gift	Intention
I give $100,000 to Causes for Animals.	This is a gift to a specific charity.
I give $100,000 to charities that care for animals.	You can specify a charitable cause and let the executor use his discretion to decide which charities to give to that care for animals.
I give 10% of my residuary estate to Causes for Animals.	The residuary is what is left after specific gifts. You can give a percentage of your residuary.
I give my residuary estate to Causes for Animals if my spouse, children and parents have all passed away before me.	The gift comes into effect only when your individual beneficiaries do not survive you.

---

6   "Long-time Givers: Who's Who", *The Straits Times*, 26 June 2016.
7   "Guidance on Regulation of Grantmakers", Commissioner of Charities' Office, February 2018.

Some individuals who have set aside enough funds for their families may consider nominating charities as beneficiaries of their CPF savings and insurance policies. The funds are transferred directly to the charities named and are not dealt with by their Will.

Making staggered gifts

If the size of your gift is large, such as $100,000 or more, you could use a Trust and specify guidelines on how those funds are managed and used for charity. This allows you to make a lasting contribution over a period of time.

Case study

Samantha wants to make a one-off donation of $1 million to the Lions Home for the Elders. Her estate planner suggested that she considers making her gift through a Trust instead.[8] She agreed.

Then on her death, let's assume the $1 million fund can earn a constant 5% per annum. She instructs that 3% of the capital or $30,000 be distributed to the Home. Assuming Trust expenses are 1%, at the end of 20 years, the fund will have grown to more than $1.22 million and will have distributed $600,000. This is depicted in scenario 2 in Table 19.2:

Table 19.2 – Making an Annual Gift and Still Growing the Trust Fund

	Scenario 1	Scenario 2	Scenario 3
Trustee expenses	1%	1%	1%
Distribute	2%	3%	4%
Return	5%	5%	5%
After 20 years	$1,485,947	$1,220,190	$1,000,000

---

8 Samantha can use either a Will Trust or a Living Trust for her giving.

Giving over a period of time can endow a lasting memorial in your name for the charity or charitable cause that you care for. Your family members will be reminded of your giving every year, thereby encouraging a tradition of social responsibility for future generations.

CONCLUSION

More than six million children die each year from preventable diseases, and over one billion people lack access to clean drinking water.[9] Fortunately, there are unlimited ways to make a positive difference by giving. You and your family can embark on a giving adventure. You will make new friends, achieve a sense of pride and live happier lives.

Giving comes from a place deep within us that wants to share what we have with others. Giving is not about sacrifice. It is not a case of "I give up what I have so that you can have." Rather, it is about "I have something that I would like to share with you." It need not just be about money – it can also be about giving your time, effort and companionship.

---

9 "Giving What We Can", www.givingwhatwecan.org.

Part 3

Special Situations: Business

While the largest companies often dominate the headlines, small to medium enterprises (SMEs) remain the lifeblood of our economy, employing 72% of Singaporeans and accounting for 99% of business enterprises.

Number, Employment and Value Added of Enterprises in 2018

Source: Infographics – Singapore Economy, www.singstat.gov.sg.

SME is a term that often conjures up images of elbow grease, crammed work premises and micro business, but SMEs are big businesses, too. In Singapore, an SME is defined as an enterprise with (a) at least 30% local shareholding, and (b) up to SGD100 million in annual sales turnover or with up to 200 employed workers.

With over 260,000 SMEs, Singapore is very much an entrepreneur's haven. The desire to own our own business is a calling that many of us have, and that drives business owners to succeed.

We often hear the saying "shirt sleeves to shirt sleeves in three generations." While this saying usually refers to family businesses, it is true in general of businesses regardless of culture, country or language.

What type of estate planning do businesses and their owners need in order to overcome this cliched misfortune? We provide some answers in the next four chapters.

We begin with Setting up a Business in Singapore and what makes Singapore attractive for business owners. We then discuss over three chapters how to protect the key stakeholders in a business – the business itself, the shareholders and the family (where it is a family business).

	Chapter 21 Starting a Business	Chapter 22 Protecting the Business	Chapter 23 Protecting the Shareholders	Chapter 24 Protecting the Family
Objective	●	●	●	●
How achieved	Setting up a Private Limited Company	Keyman Protection	Buy-Sell Agreement	Family Business Governance

Finally, in chapter 25, we learn about family offices which are large, structured family businesses, many of which have overcome the third-generation curse.

Chapter 21

Starting a Business

by **Yang Hezhou**

INTRODUCTION

You have decided to leave your full-time job to become an entrepreneur.

You are about 42 years of age. That is the average age of entrepreneurs at the time they founded their companies according to a Harvard Business Review (HBR) survey.[1] The age varies across industries, with younger starting ages in the tech industry and older starting ages in other industries like biotech and oil and gas.

Singapore's entrepreneurs these days are starting their businesses at an even younger age. A survey by the world's largest domain registrar GoDaddy found that 74% of Singaporean millennials compared to the global average of 50% are planning to become their own bosses in the next decade and with 32% of millennials starting their businesses while in school.[2]

Note that the HBR survey points out that older entrepreneurs have a substantially higher success rate. The key reason is that they have more work experience.

In this chapter, we answer four questions that are most relevant for those wanting to start a business:
1. What is a suitable type of business entity for an entrepreneur?
2. Why is Singapore a good place to start a business?
3. What requirements are needed to set up a Singapore company?
4. What are some popular uses of Singapore companies?

We will not go into the details of how to set up a company or to compare different business entities. There are more than enough

---

1   "Research: The Average Age of a Successful Startup Founder Is 45", *Harvard Business Review*, 11 July 2018.
2   "The sweet trap of entrepreneurship", *Singapore Business Review*, 18 December 2019.

online resources available. Rather, this chapter is to share my over 12 years' experience with setting up companies, providing corporate and accounting services, and meeting reporting requirements.

WHAT IS A SUITABLE TYPE OF BUSINESS ENTITY FOR AN ENTREPRENEUR?

In Singapore, businesses fall within the regulatory oversight of the Accounting and Corporate Regulatory Authority (ACRA).

There are many types of business structure available. We will go straight to the most commonly used structure by SMEs and foreigners. This is the private limited company. We will briefly compare the private limited to the sole proprietorship and partnership to highlight some meaningful differences.

Private Limited Company

A private limited company, although it has more compliance requirements and costs more to set up and run compared to a sole proprietorship and partnership, has the following important advantages.

Legal entity and liability

A private limited company has its own legal identity, separate from its shareholders and its directors. In comparison, a sole proprietorship is owned by the sole proprietor and does not have separate legal identity of its own. This means that the sole proprietor is personally liable for the debts and losses of the business. Whereas for a private limited, shareholders are not personally liable for company debts.

After a few years, persons who start off as sole proprietors due to cost and convenience, tend to convert to a private limited comany.

Perpetual succession

A private limited company can have up to 50 shareholders. The company's existence does not depend on the continued membership of any one of its shareholders. When one shareholder leaves for whatever reason, the company can continue to exist.

That is not true for sole proprietorships and partnerships.

Ease of change of ownership

Ownership shares can be easily transferred among shareholders. Operations can continue undisrupted and the legal documentation is straightforward.

Tax efficiency

Singapore companies have the ongoing benefits of:

*   17% corporate tax year in and year out;[3]
*   no capital gains tax;
*   single-tier taxation whereby once corporate income has been taxed, dividends can be distributed to shareholders tax free;
*   over 50 avoidance of double tax agreements (DTAs) to tap on.[4]

We do have to observe some requirements to set up a private limited company, which are:

*   up to 50 shareholders;
*   at least one director who resides in Singapore;
*   a resident company secretary; and
*   a Singapore registered address.

WHY IS SINGAPORE A GOOD PLACE TO START A BUSINESS?

Mention the name Singapore, and most businessmen have a sense of trust and peace about the place. Singapore is well-known as an international financial centre with a pro-business environment, excellent infrastructure, cost-competitive and a highly skilled work force.

---

3   If you are setting up a new company, there are attractive tax exemptions where for the first three years of assessment, the effective corporate tax rate is less than 6.5% of taxable income up to $200,000.

4   A DTA between Singapore and another jurisdiction serves to prevent double taxation of income earned in one jurisdiction by a resident of the other jurisdiction. A DTA also makes clear the taxing rights between Singapore and its treaty partner on different types of income arising from cross-border economic activities between the two jurisdictions. Each DTA is unique; please speak with your tax adviser.

Singapore ranks #1 and #2 on many global surveys including:

- #1 Most Competitive Economy – IMD World
  Competitiveness Ranking 2019;
- #2 in the world for Ease of Doing Business – World Bank's
  Doing Business Survey 2019;
- #2 in the world for Talent Competitiveness – INSEAD's
  Global Talent Competitiveness Index 2019; and
- #2 in the world for Digital Competitiveness – IMD World
  Digital Competitiveness Ranking 2019.

Case study

A foreign client from a neighbouring country had to set up a
Singapore company in order to sign a business contract with
a supplier from Europe. The Europe counterpart was more
comfortable supplying to a company in Singapore where
the legal framework is deemed more structured and reliable.
We set up the company in two days and the corporate bank
account took two weeks.

WHAT REQUIREMENTS ARE NEEDED TO SET UP A SINGAPORE COMPANY?

For Singaporeans who want to start a business in Singapore, using
a Singapore company is an obvious choice.

We will in this section look from the perspective of a foreigner
who wants to start a business in Singapore.

Foreigners can own 100% of the company shares with no
ownership restrictions. To start a Singapore company, foreigners
should observe that:

- Their physical presence is not required in Singapore at the time
  of setting up the company. However, their physical presence is
  required when the bank account is being opened.
- The director and shareholder records are publicly accessible.
- Foreigners can run the Singapore company without having to

live in Singapore. However, Singapore companies must have a local resident director living in Singapore.

- On the other hand, if the foreigner wishes to run the business locally in Singapore, the foreigner would need an Employment Pass or Entrepreneur Pass. With this local presence, the foreigner can be the company's local resident director.

WHAT ARE SOME POPULAR USES OF SINGAPORE COMPANIES?

Here are some popular uses whether or not the person is a Singaporean or foreigner:

- Launching a startup business – As mentioned, there are tax incentives and Singapore is one of the world's most business-friendly places. As an example, a 2017 Startup Genome's report places Singapore as the world's number 1 for startup talent. In fact, Singapore has overtaken Silicon Valley as the world's number 1 for startup talent.[5]

- International expansion – Foreign businesses that wish to expand internationally can use Singapore as a launchpad to expand organically or through acquisitions.

- Holding company – To create a holding company to hold the shares of its subsidiaries. The holding company's main purpose is to provide the financial structure for the business and to ringfence the risks of each subsidiary from one another.

- Trading from Singapore – A foreign business that is serving foreign clients can use a Singapore company to distribute products of the foreign company. International customer transactions can be handled by the Singapore company.

---

5   "Singapore Startup Ecosystem: An Entrepreneurs' Paradise?" 7 October 2019, www.hospitalitynet.
   org.

Case study

Foreigners attracted to Singapore's property market commonly buy properties through a Singapore company. Suppose Mr A wants to buy a semi-industrial office in Singapore. He can choose either to own the unit as a foreigner in his own name. Or he can hold the unit through a Singapore company where he would be the 100% shareholder and foreign director of the company.

The route of owning the investment property using a company is usually preferred. It's always good to consult a tax consultant or accountant before deciding to invest in Singapore.

CONCLUSION

Starting a business in one of the world's most business-friendly countries is easy. Within about two days, the business can be up and running. Then after the setting up, you will have to meet the ongoing requirements of keeping the company going: financial and tax reporting, keeping documents with ACRA updated and others. Fortunately, these obligations are not overly burdensome as well.

The Singapore government wants to attract both capital and talent. We can be quite confident that the business-friendly environment in Singapore will continue.

Chapter 22

Protecting the Business (with Keyman Protection)

by **Michael Seow** with **Yang Hezhou**

*"A leader is one who knows the way,
goes the way, and shows the way."*
– John C Maxwell

INTRODUCTION

SME owners build successful businesses, because they "know the way and go the way." Many single-handedly or with a handful of partners start their businesses, toil through years of effort and sacrifice to create successful businesses that bring wealth for their families and provide jobs for the community.

These are the keymen[1] in their businesses, without whom their companies could sink.

Case study

We know of a successful printing company that was started by a husband and wife team. Henry was the creative director who produced award-winning designs. Lisa was the CEO who brought designs to life from sketches to mass production. Lisa knew the process from start to finish, but only she knew it.

When she suddenly passed away at age 55, a large void was created because Lisa had not "shown the way". The company's customers became dissatisfied by the sudden drop in quality service. Creditors and suppliers lost confidence in the company's ability to pay its bills. Employees got unsettled and many left the company.

Henry was unable to run the company and the 30-year-old company was shut down within six months.

---

1   We use the commonly used term keyman to refer to both genders.

WHO IS A KEYMAN?

There may be a large number of employees in a company, but only a handful are truly essential.

Who exactly is a keyman? If a person suddenly leaves the business:

- Would the business be disrupted because the keyman was responsible for the company's operations?
- Would creditors lose faith in the company's ability to pay its debts and call in loans or refuse to issue credit?
- Would customers delay or withhold business, or even worse, leave for competitors?
- Would suppliers reduce credit terms and working capital is reduced?
- Would competitors come in to take market share, causing overall profits to fall?

If the answer is yes to any of the above questions, the person is likely a keyman.

KEYMAN SUCCESSION – PUTTING A PLAN IN PLACE

If you are the keyman in your company, there will come a time to call it quits and retire. As an employee, this can be as simple as a resignation letter. But if you are a business owner, making an exit can be more difficult. You must decide if you are going to sell your shares, hand it over to someone else, or close the company down.

Whatever the desired outcome, you can plan for your business successor ahead of time. Here is a simple plan to get started:

Start early

If you knew you would suddenly leave your business in one month's time due to a serious illness, when would you start preparing for your exit? Probably yesterday.

204 Planning Your **Will, Trust, LPA & More**

Most business owners are so busy running the business and growing profits that an exit plan is far from their minds.

Make yourself redundant

Lisa could have documented her processes to ensure that she was not the only person who could take a design from inception to production. Have someone or a team who can take over your duties should you become unavailable for any length of time.

Case Study – Apple Continuing to run without Steve Jobs

Steve Jobs created Apple University in 2008 to instil into employees Apple's business culture. The goal is to teach the executive team's thought process to future leaders. Apple University has been called the solution to Apple after Steve Jobs.

The courses use case studies to explain the strategic decisions that Apple made, such as the one to make the iPod and its iTunes software compatible with Microsoft's Windows system.

Source: Wikipedia

Determine when to exit

Would this be in five or ten years? Once you decide on a time frame, work backwards to ensure your plan is in place.

Knowing that you wish to exit the business in five years means that you would know when to share certain business details with your successor so that he can run the business completely without you.

Find the right person to succeed you

This can be as easy as appointing a family member or a loyal senior executive to take your place. Or there may be several possible successors from which to choose — each with their own strengths and weaknesses.

Please consider these questions:
- Who would likely succeed you, if you are not around?
- Can he take over your role immediately or would he need time?
- Would shares be offered to your successor?
- Could this person be headhunted?

Begin by documenting what your company needs in terms of competencies. For example, in Lisa's case, the company needed someone with specialist skills who could perform the value chain of activities from design to production. Audit the competencies that the company's senior employees have in order to find out what might be missing. Then look at the gaps that need to be filled.

Case study – Li Ka Shing Had a Plan[2]

Li was a high school dropout who became known as 'Superman' for his deal-making abilities. By the time he stepped down as chairman of his US$100 billion business empire that included CK Hutchison Holdings and CK Asset Holdings, the then 89-year-old already had succession in his mind for many years.

His son, Victor Li, who took over the reins, had a 33-year apprenticeship with the CK Group of companies, first starting in 1985.

Case study – Swatow Restaurant did not have a plan[3]

The Swatow Restaurant chain was at its height in 1992 with 18 restaurants and 500 staff when its owner Mr Yang died suddenly after suffering a stroke. He was the only keyman and didn't have a succession plan. After all, he was just 38 years old and he must have thought he was far too young to think about an exit plan.

His wife was unable to run the business and things came to a standstill. Suppliers got nervous, landlords like Changi Airport and Singapore Indoor Stadium cancelled their leases and the chain was sold for "a token sum, amounting to five digits".

---

2   "Rags-to-Riches 'Superman' Li Ka-Shing Stages Well-Planned Succession", 22 March 2018, www.campdenfb.com.
3   "Swatow Sale 'Hit by Hidden Creditors and Lease Disputes'", *The Straits Times*, 24 March 1992.

KEYMAN SUCCESSION – SUDDEN DEPARTURE

If a company has put in place a succession plan for its keymen, it can be expected to survive and thrive "if the CEO is suddenly run over by a bus." Just how well prepared are Singapore SMEs for such emergencies? Not very well at all.

According to a survey by UOB Bank in 2014, 72% of Singapore SMEs say they will not be able to find a successor fast enough and 88% say they will incur revenue, profit and cashflow problems.[4]

What can a company do to protect itself if there is a sudden departure of a keyman – whether or not it has a succession plan in place? One cost-effective solution is keyman insurance.

How Keyman insurance works

Keyman insurance protects a company's most important asset: its key people. Such an insurance policy provides financial compensation if a keyman becomes unable to work.

Figure 22.1 is a self-explanatory diagram to show how a basic keyman insurance pays in the event of death.

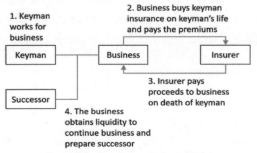

Figure 22.1 – How Keyman Insurance Works

When the business purchases keyman insurance on the keyman's life, the business is both the policy owner and the beneficiary of the policy. The insured person does not receive any benefits from the policy.

---

4   "The key to business continuity", 5 November 2014, www.todayonline.com.

Keyman insurance is usually written as either a term policy or a permanent policy. A term policy is the more affordable of the two. It applies for a specific period of time and coverage ends when the term expires or the insured person dies, whichever happens first.

Permanent keyman life insurance such as whole life insurance stays in effect for the life of the insured individual. It has other benefits:

- It can later be transferred to the insured, say at the worker's retirement, if the firm no longer needs the coverage.
- It can be used as collateral for a loan. In fact, when the business borrows money from the bank, it is normal for the bank to require that keyman insurance be in place before financing for the business is provided.

How much to insure?

No one wants to put a dollar value on a human life but this is necessary in order to determine how much insurance to purchase.

Case study – John, a keyman of Tanker Timber

Suppose John owns 30% of Tanker Timber Pte Ltd with his father (retired) and mother (office manager). As CEO, he is responsible for at least 75% of the $10 million profits of the company. It is estimated that it would take two years to replace John should he pass away. One suggestion is:[5]

Amount of keyman insurance = 75% of $10M X 2 years = $15M

One year later, John passes away. The keyman insurance policy is paid out to the company, which provides the business with sufficient funds to maintain their liquidity as well as to cover the recruitment and training costs for John's replacement.

---

5   Another way to determine the amount of insurance needed is his annual income multiplied by the number of years it will take to find and train his replacement.

> **Case Study – USD21 million Keyman Cover for Gianni Versace**[6]
>
> A USD21 million keyman insurance policy was purchased by the fashion house Gianni Versace S.p.A. on the life of designer Gianni Versace, who was gunned down in July 1997. The insurer was Lloyd's of London. The Italy-based Versace business, which produces luxury clothing, perfumes and fashion accessories, had estimated sales of USD1 billion a year. 50-year old Gianni held 45% of the shares of the family-owned business.

ARE KEYMAN INSURANCE PREMIUMS TAX DEDUCTIBLE?

Generally, for a company, an expense is deductible only if it is revenue in nature. This means that the expense must have been wholly and exclusively incurred in the production of income and is not be capital in nature.

Conditions for deductibility of key person insurance premiums

Premiums incurred on a keyman insurance policy is deductible if all of the following conditions are met:

1. The purpose of the policy is to insure the business against loss of profits arising from the death or disability of the keyman. It cannot be for the loss of capital.
2. The sum insured is directly related to the extent of the annual profits directly attributable to the services of the keyman.
3. The insurance policy remains the property of the business. It cannot belong to the keyman. Also, the proceeds of the policy cannot be used to benefit the keyman's family.
4. The insurance policy does not provide for a cash surrender or investment value. The company should not be earning a return from the policy.

---

6   "Versace Is Covered For Death Of Designer", 20 July 1997, www.businessinsurance.com.

5. The loss of the keyman does not affect the business' entire profit-making structure.

Where the premiums paid on a "keyman" insurance policy qualify for deduction, any recovery made under the policy will constitute a trading receipt and be subject to tax.

CONCLUSION

Keyman insurance provides many important benefits, such as:

- compensating the company for lost profits;
- providing recruitment and training expenses for the successor;
- assuring existing customers and key stakeholders like creditors and suppliers that the company can withstand the keyman's departure;
- payment of loans that may be called in on the keyman's death; and
- protection of the personal assets of the keyman.

Companies need keyman insurance even if they have a succession plan in place. Business fortunes can be very fickle. You do not want your company to be caught out at a bad time when your keyman suddenly passes away.

Chapter 23

Protecting the Shareholders (with Buy-Sell Agreement)

by **Michael Seow** and **Masagoes Abdul Karim**

If you own a part of a business, you should know about buy-sell agreements. Without it, your business faces an unpredictable series of financial and succession issues when any of its owners face drastic events like death, disability, divorce and others.

Here's a situation that is similar to many that we have seen.

Case study – Vicky passes away with no agreement in place

Max and Vicky are about 60 years old and they have been 40-60 shareholders in a successful toy company they started 25 years ago.

Max runs the operations while Vicky runs marketing.

Vicky has a heart attack and dies. She has a Will that she wrote 20 years ago, which gives all her assets to her husband. It was a mirror Will that she made with her husband, on the understanding that the survivor would care for their children.

On her death, the shares in the toy company passed to her husband who is an engineer and who has never worked a single day in the toy industry. Max wants to buy those shares and Vicky's family wants to sell but they cannot agree on the price. Their discussions become heated and ugly.

Without a buy-sell agreement in place, shareholders risk facing such scenarios that can disrupt the business and hurt its value. Furthermore, it can hurt the departing shareholder's family who may not get fair value for the shares as well as the remaining shareholders who want to keep the company going.

WHAT IS A BUY-SELL AGREEMENT?

When anyone first starts a company, a constitution must be adopted at the time of its incorporation. The constitution defines the scope of the company's activities, its legal name, and the procedures that govern how its shareholders interact and conduct business. By law, the company and its shareholders must act in accordance with its constitution. In spite of the importance of this document, many business owners adopt without modification one of the model constitutions provided by the Accounting and Corporate Regulatory Authority (ACRA) of Singapore.

Since model constitutions cannot fit all business situations, shareholder agreements between shareholders are used to complement the company constitution. For example, shareholder agreements may specify that:

• Only family members can become shareholders.
• Any departing shareholder must give the other shareholders first right of refusal to purchase the departing shareholder's shares.
• The value of the company is to be appraised on a regular basis.

A buy-sell agreement is a type of shareholder agreement between all or some of the shareholders. It is a legally binding contract that stipulates how a shareholder's share of a business may be reassigned if that shareholder dies or otherwise leaves the business. Most often, the agreement stipulates that the departing shareholder's shares are to be sold

Figure 23.1 – Key Decisions in a Buy-Sell Agreement

to the remaining shareholders at a pre-established price. In short, a buy-sell agreement as seen in Figure 23.1:

- is a legally binding agreement between shareholders as to what to do with a departing shareholder's shares;
- specifies that remaining shareholders want to continue the business;
- specifies that departing shareholder and his family want to be compensated for his share of the business; and
- is not prohibited by Constitution.

HOW DOES A BUY-SELL AGREEMENT WORK?

There are several methods of organising the exchange of shares and funds. We shall describe the cross-purchase method, which is the most commonly used method.

In a cross-purchase agreement, as illustrated in Figure 23.2, the remaining shareholders purchase the shares of the departing shareholder. To ensure that funds are available at the time of buyout, shareholders commonly purchase life insurance policies on one another's lives.[1] In the event of a trigger event like death, the proceeds from the policy are used towards the purchase of the deceased's shares.

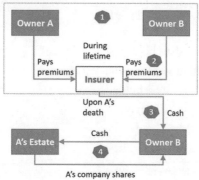

Figure 23.2 – How the Cross-Purchase Works

---

1   According to section 57 of the Insurance Act, business owners can buy on one another's lives because there is insurable interest. That is, A can effect a policy on B because A is "wholly or partly dependant" on B.

1. Shareholders A and B enter into a buy-sell agreement.
2. B buys policy on A, pays premiums, and is beneficiary to the policy. A does the same on B.
3. If A dies, insurer pays death benefits to B.
4. B uses proceeds to pay for A's shares at previously agreed upon price.

Case Study – Vicky Passes Away with a Buy-Sell Agreement in Place

Let's now suppose Max and Vicky did put in place a buy-sell agreement. They engage an accountant to provide a valuation of their company. The accountant appraised the company at $10 million. Since Max owned 40% and Vicky owned 60%, their shares are worth $4 million and $6 million, respectively. To fund the agreement, each purchased life insurance on the life of the other.

When Vicky suddenly passes away, we see that:

- there is a guaranteed market for Vicky's shares; and
- there are funds to pay Vicky's family while Max receives Vicky's shares.

THE IMPORTANCE OF FUNDING WITH INSURANCE

Suppose Max and Vicky did not purchase life insurance to fund their buy-sell agreement. Then on Vicky's death, Max would have to scramble to find $6 million worth of funds through:

- Tapping into his personal savings.
- Making instalments to Vicky's family over time, which relies on the future success of the business.
- Liquidating company assets.
- Borrowing external funds.

Each of these options is as equally unappealing as the next.

That is why "using other people's money" through life insurance is the most cost-effective way of funding a buy-sell agreement.

LIFE INSURANCE FUNDING OPTIONS

You can fund a buy-sell agreement with term or permanent life insurance. Each has its own benefits.

Term insurance is more affordable. It provides temporary coverage for a specific period of time although it has no cash value. It is an attractive option where there are cash flow and budgetary constraints. The tenure of the policy should be at least till the retirement of the shareholder or the mandatory retirement age (if any) by the company, whichever is later. We normally recommend extending the tenure till the maximum such as 99 years so that even if the shareholder retires, the policy can be transferred to the shareholder as a legacy for his family.

Permanent life insurance such as whole life insurance, on the other hand, offers protection for life. In addition to the death benefit it provides, permanent life insurance accumulates cash value. That money can be used to fund all or a portion of a buy-sell agreement. And after a period of time, the cash value can accumulate to an amount that is larger than the amount of premiums paid. At that point, it is as if you have obtained the insurance for free.

When you retire, the policy could be transferred to you and your family can further benefit from the proceeds on your death.

CROSS-PURCHASE WITH TRUST

In an insurance-funded cross-purchase agreement, the shareholders buy insurance on the lives of each of the other shareholders. For an agreement consisting of three shareholders:

Number of policies required = N X (N – 1) = 6 policies

For a buy-sell agreement of five shareholders, the number of policies climbs to 20 [5 X (5 – 1)], and the setting up of the agreement becomes quite cumbersome. There is also the worry that the surviving shareholders who receive the policy proceeds will not hand over the proceeds as required by the agreement.

We can introduce a Trust into the planning to mitigate these risks where:

- Each shareholder purchases insurance on his own life and transfers the policy to a trustee. In this way, only N policies are required.
- The trustee holds the policies and on the death of any shareholder, the proceeds are received by the trustee.
- The trustee is then able to help secure performance by exchanging the proceeds for the shares from the deceased's estate.

A trusteed, insurance-funded buy-sell agreement offer a number of advantages:

- The number of policies is reduced to N, the number of shareholders in the agreement.
- It stops the shareholder from dealing in his policy such as borrowing or even terminating the policy.
- The trustee helps to secure performance by being the central point to pay premiums, receive policy proceeds and transfer shares. This is especially important where there are very large policies of a few million dollars each.

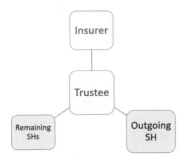

Figure 23.3 – Trustee Plays a Central Role to Hold the Policies

TRIGGER EVENTS

Death is a standard event that triggers the buyout. There are others that can be included and it depends on what the shareholders wish to include. Trigger events can be insurance-funded and non-insurance-funded.

Insurance-funded trigger events

These are self-explanatory in that the funds required to purchase the departing shareholder's shares are provided by insurance:

- death
- critical illness
- terminal illness
- total permanent disability

Care should be taken to make sure that the definitions of these trigger events as defined in the agreement are aligned with how the life insurance policies define them. Because definitions change such as for critical illness, it is prudent for the shareholders to revisit the agreement every two to three years or as needed.

Non-insurance-funded trigger events

Any event can be included as a trigger event as long as it is relevant to the company and the industry it belongs to.

Examples of such events might include any shareholder:

- Going missing for a period of time and is later declared dead
- Being declared bankrupt by a court order
- Being declared mentally incapable as defined by the Mental Capacity Act
- Going through a divorce
- Retiring
- Getting convicted of a criminal offence and is imprisoned for a time
- Acting in a way that damages the reputation of the company

When you are setting up your buy-sell agreement, never just adopt an off-the-shelf set of standard trigger events. Imagine the three partners of a music production company coming together to set up a buy-sell agreement with standard trigger events that did not include deafness. Then one day, one of the partners becomes deaf from an accident and is unable to produce music anymore. He has to leave the business but the buy-sell agreement is not triggered to effect the exchange of shares and funds.

Spending time to lay out the trigger events that are relevant to the company is a critical task. That's because there isn't a set of trigger events that apply in all situations.

VALUATION

If you suddenly leave your company, wouldn't you want your shares to fetch an amount that is fair for yourself and your family?

What is a fair amount is based on the concept of fair market value (FMV):

> Fair market value is the price at which the shares would change hands between a willing buyer and a willing seller when the former is not under any compulsion to buy and the latter is not under any compulsion to sell, both parties having reasonable knowledge of relevant facts.

Coming up with what is the FMV of your company can be tricky because it is not only quite subjective, the value can easily change when business conditions change from month to month. In the end, the shareholders have to agree among themselves what the value is as far as the buy-sell agreement is concerned.

We recommend that you engage a professional appraiser such as an accountant to perform the valuation. Also, you may consider having a clause in your buy-sell agreement along the lines of: "The company shall obtain a fresh valuation from a professional appraiser such as an accountant every 1 to 3 years or when needed."

Whenever a valuation is done, the shareholders have to review how funding is to be arranged. If the company's value has risen by a large amount, should new insurance policies be purchased or a larger amount of funds be set aside? The buy-sell agreement should leave room for adjustments.

CONCLUSION

For many business owners, a buy-sell agreement is like the last Will and testament for the family's largest asset perhaps besides the family home. It enables the remaining shareholders to decide who the next shareholder might be and to prevent the possibility of a shareholder selling his shares to unwanted parties.

Buy-sell agreements are quite technically demanding as you can tell from the discussion above. This is because of their flexibility and the countless business situations that are possible. We have thus covered a rather limited series of situations. In reality, the circumstances of each company are unique and buy-sell agreements would have to be customised each time. As a result, it is a good idea to work with a lawyer, accountant and financial planner who are experienced with such agreements rather than rely on agreements that are template-based.

Chapter 24

Protecting the Family Business (with Family Governance)

by **Joe Teng**

Family owned businesses form the backbone of most economies. In Singapore, as well as all over Southeast Asia, the majority of businesses, whether SMEs or large listed companies, are family businesses, meaning that they are still managed and often majority owned by their founders or founding families. Think of companies like the Kuok Group, Far East, UOB, CP in Thailand and the SM group in the Philippines as examples of listed companies where the founder and founding family are still very much in control.

The cliché is that a family business does not survive beyond three generations and the challenge for business families is to prove the cliché wrong.

In this chapter, we discuss some of the key issues faced by families who wish to preserve and grow their family business and pass their business on to the next generations. We will look at a typical business family – the Widjaja family – whose patriarch started the company and still holds tightly to the reins despite having grown up children who can start to take over. In my experience with family businesses, such family dynamics are commonplace and are, unfortunately, detrimental to business succession. Finally, I will explain how putting in place a formal corporate governance programme can help a family business to not only transition but also thrive for more than three generations.

THE FORCES BEHIND A FAMILY BUSINESS

A family business is a business that is mostly owned by one

family. This family plays a key role in the day to day running of that business or the family plays a supervisory role and provides the direction of the business. Family members usually hold the most important executive roles in operations, finance and business development.

The interaction between family and business is an intricate matter. A useful tool to describe and understand the dynamics behind a family business is the Three Circle Model, as seen in Figure 24.1, which was developed by Renato Taguiri and John Davis in 1978.

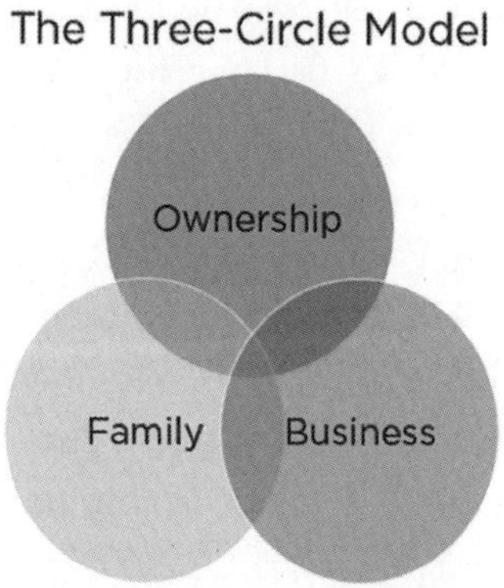

The Three-Circle Model

Figure 24.1 – Three-Circle Model of the Family Business System[1]

Taguiri and Davis illustrated the family business universe as three partly overlapping circles in a single diagram – the business itself, the family and the ownership of the business (shareholders).

A person connected to a family business would fit in one of the seven groups below:

1. Family members not involved in the business, but who are descendants or spouses/partners of owners.
2. Family owners not employed in the business.
3. Non-family owners who do not work in the business.
4. Non-family owners who work in the business.
5. Non-family employees.

---

1   "The Three-Circle Model celebrated 40 years in 2018", https://johndavis.com/three-circle-model-family-business-system/.

6. Family members who work in the business but are not owners.
7. Family owners who work in the business.

By placing each individual in any of the seven areas formed by the three overlapping circles, one can get a better understanding of the role, perspective, concerns and expectations that each individual in the Three Circle Model would experience or be exposed to.

CASE STUDY – THE WIDJAJA FAMILY

Agus is married to Fanny and they have four children.

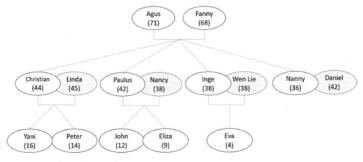

Figure 24.2 – The Widjaja Family

The Widjaja family owns a substantial family business in Indonesia with three major subsidiaries contributing about 50-30-20 to total revenue. Agus started the pharmaceutical company in 1983 when the Indonesian economy took off in a big way. During the Asian financial crisis, Agus bought a prominent Indonesian manufacturer of biscuits and confectionary. The food company experienced exponential growth supported by its affiliated distribution company.

Agus is the CEO and controlling shareholder of the businesses, as well as the patriarch of the family. Fanny has no formal role in the operating businesses. Agus is a traditional Chinese Indonesian businessman, who relies on quick decision making. He focuses on getting sales done, making money and does not worry too much about risk. Fanny is used to juggling her time between taking care

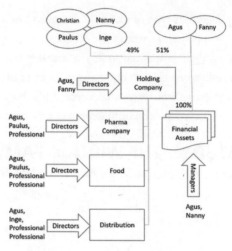

Figure 24.3 – The Widjaja Family Business

of the children and the household, as well as assisting her husband in the business.

Eldest son Christian

Christian has a PhD in Pharmacy and works in Singapore. His American wife, Linda, studied pharmacy and marketing. While Christian enjoys his senior position in Singapore, his dream is to join the family business and apply his technical know-how to produce new products, rather than rely on the mass-produced painkillers that made the company big.

However, he finds it difficult to discuss new ideas with Agus. For Christian, maintaining harmony within the family is also very important.

Second son Paulus

Paulus obtained an MBA from UC Berkeley and upon his return to Jakarta, he became a director in the pharmaceutical company and in the food company. Paulus is married to Nancy, who is the Financial Controller of the pharmaceutical company and the distribution company. Nancy is always worried about the high debt position of the companies and the generous credit terms the company extends to its clients, in order to gain market share.

Paulus is a shareholder and a director in the business. The close relationship with his father has made him talk, think and act like his father. His wife Nancy doesn't own a share in the business and is employed as a professional in the business. As a professional, Nancy has been raising her concerns about the business, but to no avail.

Eldest daughter Inge

Inge has a business degree from UC Berkeley and prior to her return to Jakarta, she worked a few years in a US business consulting firm. Inge is a director in the distribution company. Her husband, Wen Lie, is a mechanical engineer and heads the production in the pharmaceutical company. Inge and Wen Lie are often worried about the quality standards of the pharmaceuticals. Most of the machinery is getting old and they are increasingly observing a rise in sub-standard batches.

As a shareholder and director in the business, Inge is in a similar position as Paulus, but her educational background and work experience in the US has changed her views on the business significantly from her brother Paulus and she feels closer to her eldest brother, Christian.

Youngest daughter Nanny

Nanny is a law graduate from NUS in Singapore. After working a few years in a leading Singapore law firm, she started a successful consulting business. Nanny is very keen to acquire a competitor. The acquisition would allow her to quadruple her business in two years. She is planning to ask her father for a USD 8 million loan to finance the acquisition.

Nanny administers several private banking accounts on behalf of her father, Agus. Although she always signs off on every transaction, including loans and margin financing, her father in Jakarta makes the investment decisions. Nanny often worries about the risks taken in the bank accounts and the speculative nature of her father's investment decisions. Nanny is engaged to Daniel, an equity partner in the law firm where she used to work. She is planning to stay in Singapore and take up Singapore citizenship.

Non-family directors

Five non-family directors make most of the executive decisions in the three companies. They all have a reasonable degree of authority, although Agus and Paulus make the strategic decisions.

The two non-family directors who own some shares feel that they could contribute much more if they knew more about the family's expectations with respect to the business. The three directors who don't own any shares are not sure about their long-term career prospects. These feelings play up especially when Fanny interferes in their work or when the wheeling and dealing of Agus and Paulus frustrate them.

THE FAMILY IS KEEN ON BUSINESS SUCCESSION

The Widjaja family is a typical example of a family where all is fine from the outside. However, each of the children has concerns about the future of the business and with the way the business is being run. They realise that if they don't manage their different views as family members, shareholders and directors in the business in a proactive manner, their family business could run into the ground.

The four children took the initiative to start a discussion with other family members, in-laws included to discuss the issues faced by each individual member of the family. During the discussions, each member of the family was given some time to explain their positive feelings towards the business, their concerns and a "wish-list", spelling out what changes they would like to see.

Agus was hesitant to participate at first because he was not used to open discussions and having others ask questions about his way of doing business. He felt as if he was being criticised. For his children who are used to open discussions, this was not a problem but they understood that such discussions were difficult for their father.

After a few rounds of discussion, Agus began to realise that his objectives and the objectives of his children were the same, but due to differences in educational background, age and experience, his way of doing business would now have to be blended in with the way his children would run the business. After all, his days at the helm are numbered.

High-level decisions on business strategies, the markets to target, the products and services to offer and how the family's long-term interests are maintained while accepting non-family members as valuable stakeholders – these all required a team to work together, and a corporate structure and governance that everyone could align themselves with. Gone were the days when the inputs and force of one hard driving founder was enough to bring success and wealth for the family.

The family realised that each member had common goals – to keep the family together, to grow the business in a sustainable manner and to pass the business to beyond the third generation, when the family members who are working in the business would be cousins rather than just siblings!

FAMILY BUSINESS GOVERNANCE

The family decided to engage a consultant who specialises in family businesses, to design and implement a plan for the family that will help the family achieve their objectives, which now also includes a plan to ensure better communication between business, family and shareholders and a clear career path for non-family members who are working in the business and may be a shareholder.

After almost one year of meetings with the family and directors and managers in the business, the consultants and the family came out with a plan.

The plan contained among others:

1. A description of the family objectives.
2. A policy with respect to paying out dividends versus re-investment of profits into the business.
3. A policy and process to choose and support the CEO's and directors.
4. Collective decision-making process by the family for certain transactions or strategic decisions.
5. A protocol for sharing information.
6. An employment policy with respect to family and in-laws.
7. Conflict of interest rules.
8. A family code of conduct.
9. A liquidity plan to build a buffer for difficult times or in case one or more family members want to be bought out.
10. An investment policy for the financial assets that are held under the family.
11. A separate bank account for Agus so that he could continue the speculative trading in shares and derivatives, which he admitted during the many meetings, was his passion and the excitement provided him joy!
12. A policy for family members to apply for financing from the family funds if they wanted to start a new business.
13. An agenda for quarterly and annual family meetings, including fixed agenda items.
14. The plan also prescribed that some of the agenda points were to be discussed with all the directors of the businesses, including the professional directors and department heads.

Besides the plan for the family, the business consultants also started work on the corporate governance for the businesses. The main challenge for the consultants was to design and implement a plan that fully recognises the position and the role that the family plays as owners of the business and as bosses or colleagues in the teams that operates the business, while at the same time giving non family members the comfort of career prospects similar to the family members who are working in the business.

The next step for the Widjaja family was to decide how they would implement the plan. The consultants gave them some options ranging from a common understanding between family members based on a Family Constitution and supplement the constitution with a shareholders agreement all the way to a more formal arrangement using a Trust structure to formalise the contents of the family constitution and legally firm up the policies that had been agreed in the Family Constitution.

The family decided to keep the arrangement flexible and informal for the time being, with the adaptation of a Family Constitution. Given the progress they had made compared to two years back, they felt this was already a huge leap forward working towards a sustainable business that they could pass on to the next generations while keeping the family in harmony. The family is aware that a constitution is just an arrangement between family members and the articles in the constitution are not legally enforceable. Nanny and Inge volunteered to be the administrators for the family, preparing the reports, calling the meetings and preparing the minutes of the meetings.

To ensure that the ownership of the assets in the family would not be disrupted by death, bankruptcy or divorce, the family members all contributed their shares in the holding company to a Singapore based Trust, with the exception of the distribution company since Indonesian law does not allow a distribution company to be owned by foreigners.

CONCLUSION

The Widjaya case study is reflective of what goes on in many Asian family businesses. The first-generation patriarch or matriarch builds a successful business and rules with an iron fist and finds it difficult to let go even as he nears retirement. The second-generation family members with new ideas from working outside the family and from their overseas studies, are eager to contribute. Family business governance is a process by which the family and non-family members can come together to build a forum for positive discussion, problem solving and decision making.

The pioneer entrepreneurs who started business roughly 30 to 40 years ago when a wave of industrialisation all over Southeast Asia sparked the Asian growth story, have generally done very well for themselves and their families. They have become very wealthy, were able to send their children abroad for tertiary education, multiplied their business revenues and have been able to invest some of their wealth in other investments, usually real estate and other businesses.

Roughly speaking, for the past 10 to 15 years, the transition of ownership and control of family business from the pioneer generation to the next generation has started, while over the next 10 to 20 years another wave of transitions of ownership and, or control to the next generation will be taking place. A lot has been spoken and written about the transition of a family business from one generation to the next and, sadly, the failure rate of succession of family businesses has been discussed even more. This is unfortunately even more true when it comes to the transition of the business from the second to the third generation, the transition we will be witnessing in the next 10 to 20 years.

I am fortunate to have seen and worked with numerous family businesses that have succeeded in putting in place good governance processes that make me confident that they would indeed prove the cliché wrong that family businesses would not last more than three generations.

Chapter 25

Family Offices

by **Joy M E Lim**

You are a citizen of an Asian country and have spent a lifetime accumulating wealth. You have operating businesses, real estate assets, several dozen employees, investment managers overseeing portfolios, multiple travel arrangements, adult children and grandchildren. Your wealth management and family members are spread across several countries.

You meet your professional advisers – lawyer, accountant, estate planner, financial planner and wealth manager – maybe once a year or when needed. Your secretary keeps your calendar and financial details, and it is up to you to communicate changes in your life and businesses among your professional advisers.

With so much going on, you should not be concerned about coordinating these details when you should be focused on what you do best – acquiring wealth through investing, assessing deals and starting new businesses.

You also face obstacles and fears in maintaining your wealth for your family and future generations. These may include high estate taxes, children squandering your wealth, expropriation of assets by governments, political instability, and operating businesses experiencing difficulties.

You set up a family office to consolidate your wealth. You are attracted to Singapore's rule of law and the government provides residence options and tax incentives.

In this chapter, I will share my overall experiences in wealth management and give you an idea how family offices work. I am the director of a single family office.

WHAT IS A FAMILY OFFICE?

A family office is a privately held company that handles the succession planning and wealth management for a wealthy family, generally one with over $100 million in investable assets. The company's financial capital is the family's own generated wealth.

The term "family office" may be used in many different contexts, with different meanings, differing from family to family.

A family office is often created for the purpose of centralising the management of a significant amount of family assets for the preservation of family wealth across generations. This is illustrated in Figure 25.1.

Figure 25.1 – Typical functions found in a family office

The family's operating companies are managed by the family itself. Their investment assets that are within their wealth management function are either

1. actively managed within the family office by the family and appointed investment professionals, and/or
2. allocated to external managers in private banks, fund managers, hedge funds, or outsourced to an independent CIO.

KEY REASONS FOR SETTING UP A FAMILY OFFICE

The key reasons for any family office to be set up can vary. Primarily, they are for:

1. Allocation & Diversification of Asset Classes – involving the consolidation and investment of primary and secondary market assets, outside the ownership of the primary family businesses. This may include establishing an offshore location for the family office in a jurisdiction which provides for tax efficiency on investment returns.

2. Succession Planning & Wealth Structuring – strategic planning related to multi and inter-generational asset protection. This includes inheritance issues, creation of trust funds, active stewardship by the next generation under the guidance of the current patriarch/matriarch and family-appointed advisors. Inter-generational communication is facilitated via a family governance structure and a formalised family constitution. Certain assets may also be structured under an umbrella Trust Fund specifically for the creation of income flow and preservation of wealth for multi-generations.

3. Philanthropic Interests of the Family – such objectives can be actively managed via a family office where the family's mission statement is to be invested for the community in which they wish to contribute. This may include the setting up of charitable foundations, for example.

4. Family Governance and Family Management issues – in situations where family members have diversified their home base globally in several geographical locations, and/or where the family patriarch/matriarch wishes to promote the family heritage and historical legacy by uniting family members and branches under one family office entity.

5. One Stop Shop Services – the family wishes to consolidate

the resources of external service providers such as lawyers, accountants, tax advisors, bankers, fund managers under the ambit of the family office.

SIZES AND TYPES OF FAMILY OFFICES

Family offices are typically focused on wealth management activities and as Figure 25.1 shows, may also provide services such as family governance, philanthropy management, management of the family's operating businesses and estate planning.

They can vary in size from $20 million to a few billion dollars. Although there is no clear demarcation of the sizes and types of family offices, Figure 25.2 depicts what I believe to be a reasonable categorisation of the main types of family offices based on size of investable assets:

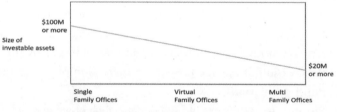

Figure 25.2 – Sizes and Types of Family Offices

Single Family Offices (SFOs)

The SFO is the classic form of the family office. It serves only one single family with all the services under one roof. It is the ultimate form as it allows full customisation. However, it is probably the most demanding in terms of management and, as a result, the most costly form of family office to run. It is thus the domain of ultra high net worth families with usually $100 million or more in investable assets.

Virtual Family Offices (VFOs)

A VFO is like an SFO except that it has a high degree of outsourced functions. It may have a very limited number of full-time staff with the rest of the required services obtained externally from a trusted group of advisors and managers on a part time or as-needed basis.

With technological advances gathering pace and allowing outsourcing to become more and more cost effective, I expect VFOs to become more popular. In fact, during the economic downturn brought on by COVID-19, SFOs are looking at VFOs in an attempt to downsize to reduce overhead costs.[1]

Multi Family Offices (MFOs)

The MFO serves more than one family to manage a substantial part of their investable assets to their entire wealth. Some MFOs may provide services that include the full suite of services shown in Figure 25.1, including tax and estate planning, philanthropy and others.

An MFO can be created in one of three main ways:

- An SFO opens its doors to additional families. This is what the Rockefeller SFO did in the late 1900s and became one of the world's first MFOs.
- By a team of advisors who have strong investment credentials and who also provide tax and legal services.
- By banks creating an MFO division – generally known as the "Family Office division" within a private bank.

WHY SINGAPORE?

In recent years, there has been a rise in the number of Family Offices being located in Singapore. The country is a choice location for various reasons:

- a strong and stable government;
- transparent financial, legal and regulatory structure;

---

1   "Rise of the 'virtual family office'", 4 May 2020, www.spearswms.com.

- ready availability of qualified multinational professionals; and
- a ready framework of incentives for funds managed by single family offices which provide tax exemption for most investment gains.

Additionally, the Singapore government has introduced tax incentive schemes to encourage the setting up of family offices in Singapore. These schemes allow funds managed by family offices to be exempted from Singapore income tax on gains on many categories of investments.

These tax incentive schemes are overseen by the Monetary Authority of Singapore (MAS), and are outlined in the following sections of the Singapore Income Tax Act:

1. Onshore Fund Tax Incentive Scheme – section 13R
2. Enhanced-Tier Fund Tax Incentive Scheme – section 13X[2]

In addition to tax exemptions:
- section 13R enables access to 1 employment pass; and
- section 13X enables access to 3 employment passes.

There is also the Global Investor Programme (GIP). The GIP is administered by Contact Singapore, a division of the Singapore Economic Development Board (EDB) which advises entrepreneurs and business owners who are interested in relocating to and investing in Singapore.[3]

SHOULD MY FAMILY SET UP A FAMILY OFFICE?

In assessing whether or not a family office should be created, a meeting of family members or branches of family members should be convened after preliminary discussions, to review the following objectives:

---

2   You can read more these tax incentives here: "Fund management in Singapore – A summary of the regulatory and tax framework", www2.deloitte.com/sg/en.html.
3   "About the Global Investor Programme", 1 April 2020, www.edb.gov.sg.

1. Is there a need to consolidate, centralise and co-ordinate various assets and needs of the family members? These will include activities such as family governance issues, investment accounts consolidation, tax filing, accounting and legal services, immigration and tax residency considerations, reporting considerations such as the Common Reporting System (CRS), FATCA.
2. Which country would best serve these needs and objectives?
3. What assets will be held by the centralised family office? Will it be investable assets mainly, operating businesses, and/or fixed assets ranging from global real estate and yachts to art and wine collections?
4. What should be the Family Office ownership structure?
5. How should the family continue to carry out its philanthropic objectives?

CONCLUSION

Singapore has fast become a global base for family offices, thanks to its pro-business environment, stable government, the availability of expertise and tax incentives among other things.

This chapter provides a guideline of objectives to consider in creating a successful family office as an ideal vehicle for high net worth families to ensure inter-generational wealth protection and succession planning.

Part 4

SPECIAL SITUATIONS: FOREIGN ELEMENT

My father took his first plane ride when he was 55 years old. I was 22 when I took my first plane ride to Illinois for my undergraduate studies. My daughter, Sarah, was five months old when she took her first plane ride, and she's been taking plane rides a few times a year ever since.

Singaporeans have become geographically mobile and culturally diverse. As a result, it is not uncommon for Singaporeans to own assets in other countries – cash in a bank account, shares in a local listed company and a home. If you do own assets in a foreign country, what should you do about your estate planning? Should you write a foreign Will or one Will to cover your worldwide assets? How will your foreign assets be transferred to your family in Singapore on your death?

We invited lawyers and estate planning specialists from these nine countries to give their views:

- Malaysia
- Indonesia
- Thailand
- The Philippines
- Vietnam
- China
- Australia
- United Kingdom
- United States

Their unanimous recommendation is that you should as a minimum make a local Will in that country. For example, if you own Thai assets, you should make a Thai Will with a Thai lawyer. The Thai lawyer can advise you on any substantive issues regarding your assets, such as whether there may be estate duties and whether the Will needs to be translated to Thai. You should also consider appointing a Thai person to act as executor in your Will so that on your passing, this local person can facilitate the subsequent transfer of your Thai assets to your beneficiaries.

At the same time, you should make a Singapore Will to deal with your Singapore assets, and you should be careful to make sure one Will does not revoke the other.

For each country that a Singaporean resident, John, owns assets in, we asked five questions:

1. What are the formalities of a Will (in that country)?
2. Who can act as executor in his Will? Are professional executors permitted under the law?
3. When John passes away, are there any duties or taxes on his estate?
4. What is the process of transferring his foreign assets to his Singaporean wife, Mary, who is his sole beneficiary?
5. Are there any forced heirship obligations to be met?

Following the country chapters, we look at the reverse situation of foreigners who own assets in Singapore. Wherever the foreigner is from, we find out if the foreigner should be writing a Singapore Will to deal with his Singapore assets.

You may have wondered whether your ownership of foreign assets might be known to the Singapore authorities. For example, if you own an Australian property and are collecting rental income in an Australian bank account, would any Singapore authority know about that? We answer this question in the last chapter of this Part on the Common Reporting Standard, which is an information exchange procedure between countries.

Chapter 26

Malaysia

by **Wong Wai Sam**

ABOUT MALAYSIA

Population	32.6 million
Religion	Muslim 61.3% Buddhist 19.8% Christian 9.2% Hindu 6.3% Others 3.4%
Median age	29.2 years
Life expectancy	75.9 years
Legal system	Mixed legal system of English common law, Islamic (sharia) law, and customary law.
GDP per capita	US$29,100
Literacy	93.7%
Labor force	agriculture: 3.6% industry: 21.1% services: 75.3%

Adapted from "The World Factbook", www.cia.gov.

Malaysia is a country in Southeast Asia. The federal constitutional monarchy consists of 13 states and three federal territories, separated by the South China Sea into two regions, Peninsular Malaysia and Borneo's East Malaysia. Peninsular Malaysia shares a land and maritime border with Thailand and maritime borders with Singapore, Vietnam, and Indonesia. East Malaysia shares land and maritime borders with Brunei and Indonesia, and a maritime border with the Philippines and Vietnam. The country is multi-ethnic and multi-cultural. About half the population is ethnically Malay, with large minorities of Chinese, Indians, and indigenous peoples. While recognising Islam as the country's established religion, the Constitution grants freedom of religion to non-Muslims. The government is closely modelled on the Westminster parliamentary system and the legal system is based on common law.[1]

CASE STUDY

John, a Singaporean non-Muslim, has the following assets in his sole name as of 1 April 2020:

- an apartment in Kuala Lumpur worth MYR1 million that he purchased for MYR800,000 on 1 June 2017;
- Genting Berhad stock worth MYR1 million that he purchased for MYR900,000 on 1 June 2017; and
- a bank account with MYR1 million with CIMB Bank that he uses for spending and making occasional trades in Malaysian securities.

He has a Singapore Will and Trust that deals with his Singapore assets but not his Malaysian assets. On his passing, he wants to give his Malaysian assets to his wife Mary in Singapore, who is also a Singaporean non-Muslim. He is non-resident in Malaysia.

John is concerned about these questions:

1. What are the formalities of a Malaysian Will?

---

1   Source: Wikipedia.

2. Who can act as an executor in his Will? Are professional executors permitted under the law?
3. Suppose John passes away on 1 June 2020. Are there any duties or taxes on John's estate?
4. What is the process of transferring his Malaysian assets to his Singaporean wife, Mary, who is his sole beneficiary?
5. Are there any forced heirship obligations to be met?

1. Formalities of a Malaysian Will

For a Malaysian Will to be valid:[2]

- the Will must be in writing;
- the Will maker must be at least 18 years old;
- the Will must be signed by the Will maker in the presence of at least two witnesses;
- the witnesses must sign in the presence of each other and the Will maker; and
- the Will maker must be of sound mind.

Beneficiaries or the spouse of beneficiaries should not be the witness; otherwise, the gifts to the beneficiaries would be void although the Will remains valid.

The Will does not have to be stamped, notarised or registered for it to be valid.

John makes a Will with a lawyer called Thomas in Kuala Lumpur on 1 April 2020.

2. Appointing executors in a Malaysian Will

The executor is the person appointed by the Will maker to bring his Will to court for validation at the time of the Will maker's death. The executor then manages and distributes the assets to the beneficiaries.

An executor can be an individual who is at least 21 years old. Up to four executors can be appointed to act jointly. A beneficiary can be an executor in the same Will.

2　Section 5 of the Wills Act 1959.

An executor can also be a licensed Trust company.

Let's suppose John appoints a Malaysian lawyer, Thomas, to be the executor of the Will.

3. Are there any duties or taxes on the estate?

There are no estate duties or tax payable on Malaysian assets where the deceased died on or after 1 November 1991.

There is no capital gains tax.

There will be nominal stamp duty of MYR10.00 for each transfer of real estate property, be it landed or high-rise building, and regardless of value.

4. Process of transferring Malaysian assets on death

Since John passed away with a Malaysian Will, Thomas the executor named in his Will would be the person to bring the Will to court to obtain a grant of probate. The grant is a court order that states that John's Will is valid and that Thomas is authorised to deal with John's assets and liabilities.

There are three steps to take during this period of administering John's estate:

- to call in the John's assets,
- to pay off John's debts and liabilities, and
- to distribute the estate in accordance with John's wishes found in his Will.

Transferring apartment to Mary

To transfer the apartment to Mary, Thomas needs to ascertain first whether the strata title to the apartment has been issued or it is being held under the master title. Strata title is the individual title to each apartment while the master title is the block title for the entire blocks of apartments registered under the name of the developer.

1. Transfer under Master Title

    For transfer of the apartment under the master title, Thomas just needs to write in officially to the developer informing them of John's death and the name, ID number and address of Mary. Thomas must enclose in his letter a copy of the grant of probate certified by the court who granted it, together with John's death certificate duly certified by Thomas as the lawyer and Mary's ID. With the details, the developer will update its developer's records that Mary is the new owner of the apartment.

2. Transfer under Strata Title

    If the strata title to the apartment has been issued and registered under John's name before he passed away, Thomas needs to submit the instrument of transfer to Inland Revenue Board for an assessment of the stamp duty payable. The good news is that in Malaysia, all property transfer under a Will and grant of probate only attract MYR10.00 nominal stamp duty, rather than the full ad valorem stamp duty for normal lifetime transfers of properties. This is another great advantage of getting a Will written.

    After the stamp duty is paid, Thomas can register the transfer of the strata title into Mary's name at the relevant land registry. The registration fee follows the scale determined by the respective land registry in the different states of Malaysia.

    Should the strata title to the apartment be issued but have not been registered under John's name, Thomas would need to liaise with the developer to have the strata title transferred to Mary's name directly. This will involve additional procedures.

    As Mary is non-Malaysian, she is required to apply for the consent of the land registry for the transfer to be registered under her name. However, Mary can apply for the waiver of the consent from the land registry.

Transferring shares to Mary

A transfer of shares is relatively simpler. Thomas just needs to present to the share remisier/security company holding John's Genting Berhad stock the grant of probate certified by the court, John's death certificate duly certified by Thomas, and Mary's bank account details together with the bank statement to prove the account number. The share remisier may sell those stocks and remit the sales proceeds to Mary, or transfer the stock into a new CDS account opened by Mary if she wishes to continue holding the stocks.

Transferring cash in bank account

To retrieve or withdraw the cash in a bank account, Thomas is required to attend at the home branch in which John opened his bank account and present to the bank the grant of probate certified by the court, John's death certificate duly certified by Thomas or any lawyer and Mary's ID. The bank will take around two to four weeks to close John's account, after which Mary can withdraw all the moneys from it. For convenience, Mary can even arrange for the money to be transferred directly into her bank account in Singapore.

5. Any forced heirship obligations to observe?

There are no forced heirship obligations on non-Muslims, and especially in this case as John is a foreigner.

Chapter 27

Indonesia

by **Kevin Omar Sidharta**

ABOUT INDONESIA

Population	267 million
Religion[1]	Muslim 87.2% Protestant 7% Roman Catholic 2.9% Hindu 1.7% Other 0.9% (includes Buddhist and Confucian) Unspecified 0.4%
Median age	31.1 years
Life expectancy	73.7 years
Legal system	Civil law system based on the Roman-Dutch model and influenced by Islamic and customary law
GDP per capita	USD12,400
Literacy	95.7%
Labor force	agriculture: 32% industry: 21% services: 47%

Adapted from: "The World Factbook", www.cia.gov.

Indonesia is a country in Southeast Asia. It consists of more than 17 thousand islands, including Sumatra, Java, Borneo, Sulawesi and New Guinea. Indonesia is the world's largest island country, the world's fourth most populous country, as well as the most populous Muslim-majority country. The country's capital, Jakarta, is the second most populous urban area in the world. Indonesia consists of hundreds of distinct native ethnic and linguistic groups, with the largest one being the Javanese. A shared identity has developed with the motto "Bhinneka Tunggal Ika" ("Unity in Diversity"), defined by a national language, ethnic diversity, religious pluralism within a Muslim-majority population, and a history of colonialism and rebellion against it.[1]

INDONESIAN INHERITANCE LAW

Indonesian inheritance law is extremely complex due to the absence of unified legislation. During the Dutch colonial era, the colonial government implemented a discriminatory[2] policy (the Policy) towards the residents of the Dutch East Indies through various Dutch legislations. This Policy differentiated the residents based on certain groups and determined the applicable legal systems to each group.

The post-independence Indonesia carried over these Dutch legislations and continued to practice the Policy when applying the inheritance law system on its citizens. However, the Policy was no longer upheld in the fields outside of family law, in which unified legislations in various sectors were enacted (equally applicable to any Indonesian citizen, regardless of the group they belong to).

As part of the Dutch colonial era legacy, three different inheritance legal systems are applicable to different groups of Indonesian citizens: (i) civil law; (ii) *adat* (customary) law; and (iii) Islamic law. Civil law is applicable to Indonesians with certain

---

1 Source: https://en.wikipedia.org/wiki/Indonesia
2 See: 4th paragraph of the general elucidation of Law Number 23 of 2006 on Residence Administration (unofficial translation):
   "… In fulfilling the residences' rights, especially in the civil registry sector, the grouping of residences based on discriminative treatment differentiating ethnic group, descents and religion as regulated by various Dutch colonial legislation products is still found. The grouping of residence and the discriminative treatment practice is not in accordance with Pancasila and the 1945 Indonesian Constitution. …"

foreign descent (for example, those of Chinese descent) who are non-Muslims or Indonesians who voluntarily and explicitly declare that they submit themselves to be governed by civil law. Various different unwritten *adat* laws exist in different regions in Indonesia and are applicable to numerous Indonesian *adat* communities living in respective regions. Islamic law is applicable to Muslim Indonesians (regardless of descent or residence). Further, each legal system is upheld by a different court: (i) civil law and *adat* law by the district court; and (ii) Islamic law by the religious court.

Due to the discriminative nature of the Policy, Law Number 23 of 2006[3] on Residence Administration was enacted to abolish the Policy by formally revoking the underlying Dutch legislations. Unfortunately, the absence of a unified inheritance legal system until today in practice continues to preserve the application of the Policy and the complexities in determining the inheritance legal system applicable to an Indonesian citizen. In fact, it can be even more complicated due to various possible modern scenarios, including:

- inter-group/religious marriage between Indonesians (which would result in the birth of an Indonesian citizen child who could belong to more than one group and could be subject to different inheritance legal systems);
- change of religion/citizenship;
- mixed marriages between Indonesians and foreigners and marriage between foreigners which result in the birth of an Indonesian citizen child as defined by the broad coverage of "Indonesian citizen" definition under Law Number 12 of 2006 on Citizenship. This includes Indonesian citizen children born in Indonesia from unknown/stateless parents;
- Indonesian citizen children born outside of marriage with a known biological father.[4]

---

3 Law Number 23 of 2006 is later amended by Law Number 24 of 2013.
4 The Constitutional Court decision Number 46/PUU-VIII/2010 dated 17 February 2012 declares that Article 43 (1) of the Law Number 1 of 1974 on Marriage: "a child born outside a marriage only has civil relationship with the mother and the mother's family" is against the 1945 Indonesian Constitution and does not have binding effect to the extent that it is interpreted as omitting the civil relationship with the man who can be proven based on science and technology and/or any other lawful evidence to have blood relationship as the father.

Finally, Law Number 1 of 1974 on Marriage separates personal assets (being obtained from inheritance and gift or acquired prior to the marriage) from joint marital estate (being established when no pre-nuptial agreement exists). This feature, together with the conditional polygamy possibility (that is only available to Muslim Indonesians), has added further complications in determining the scope/perimeter of the inheritance estate (that is, the assets to be inherited by the lawful heirs of the testator/deceased). Last but not least, Indonesian laws and legislations impose various restrictions on foreign ownership of certain assets in Indonesia. Such restrictions significantly affect the capability of non-Indonesian heirs to acquire Indonesian inheritance assets, especially when the testator/deceased is an Indonesian.

Due to the above factors, it is necessary to be very restricted in the following case study, which does not necessarily depict what is typical.

CASE STUDY

John, a Singaporean non-Muslim who is also an Indonesian resident possessing an Indonesian stay/work permit and Indonesian tax ID, has the following assets in his sole name as at 1 April 2020:

- an apartment in Jakarta worth IDR10 billion that he purchased for IDR8 billion on 1 June 2017 (assuming John holds the Certificate of Strata Title Ownership over an apartment unit in a building erected on a land with a Right to Use (*Hak Pakai*) land right);

- Astra International stock worth IDR10 billion in a securities account opened with an Indonesian securities company that he purchased for IDR9 billion on 1 June 2017 (assuming John holds a securities account containing the stocks with an Indonesian securities company); and

- A bank account with IDR10 billion deposited in it, opened with an Indonesian bank that he uses for everyday expenditure and making occasional trades in Indonesian securities.

He has a Singapore Will and Trust that deals with his Singapore assets but not his Indonesian assets. On his passing, he wants to pass his Indonesian assets to his lawful wife Mary in Singapore, who is also a Singaporean. John and Mary have no children.

In this chapter, we will answer these questions:

1. What are the formalities of an Indonesian Will?
2. Who can act as an executor in his Will? Are professional executors permitted under the law?
3. Suppose John passes away on 1 June 2020. Are any duties or taxes payable on John's estate?
4. What is the process of transferring his Indonesian assets to his Singaporean wife, Mary, who is his sole beneficiary?
5. Are there any forced heirship obligations to be met?

1. Formalities of an Indonesian Will

With respect to John's Indonesian assets, it is recommended that John writes an Indonesian Will with contents in line with his Singaporean Will. Please note that under Indonesian law, the law of the deceased's nationality will be applicable in governing the inheritance distribution. This means that in Singapore, where there is testamentary freedom, John can Will to whomever he wishes. In this case, it would be to Mary, his wife.

For John to make a valid Indonesian Will, these requirements must be met:

- it must be made in a notarial deed form;
- it should clearly declare the beneficiaries of John's Indonesian assets and must be in line with John's other Will made in another jurisdiction;
- It must be signed by John, the testator, before the notary and witnesses;

The notary will register the signed Indonesian Will with the Will Central Registry at the Ministry of Law and Human Rights in Indonesia.

John makes a Will with a notary in a Jakarta law firm.

2. Appointing executors in an Indonesian Will

It is recommended that John appoint a local Indonesian individual to be the executor of his Will. Otherwise, he can appoint one of the heirs as the executor of John's Will.

It is not common to appoint a law firm to act as the executor of one's Will.

3. Are there any duties or taxes on the estate?

In Indonesia, inheritance and assets being granted to a blood family relative within one degree lineally (from child to parent or parent to child) does not constitute a taxable object and, therefore, Indonesian income tax is not applicable. However, with respect to the registration of certain assets in the name of the heirs, certain tax/duty may be involved (for example, duty to obtain land and buildings for inheritance assets in the form of land and buildings).

4. Process of transferring Indonesian assets on death

Suppose John has passed away. The process of carrying out the wishes in the Will and administering John's estate is undertaken by the executor, who for the purpose of answering this question, is assumed to be John's wife.

In order to transfer the Jakarta apartment to Mary:

1. Mary, acting as testament executor, needs to sign a deed of grant (*Akta Hibah*) before a land conveyancer (*Pejabat Pembuat Akta Tanah* or *PPAT*) to implement the Indonesian Will so that John's apartment unit under the Certificate of Strata Title Ownership can be transferred to her.

2. Prior to the signing, Mary would be required to provide the necessary documentation (to establish that Mary is John's lawful heir, to acquire John's apartment unit, and is permitted by Indonesian law and regulations to own the apartment unit in her name), acceptable to a land conveyancer.

3. Afterwards, the land conveyancer will register the deed of grant with the relevant land office, and the Certificate of Strata Title Ownership will be updated in Mary's name.

In order to transfer the Astra International stock in the securities account opened with an Indonesian securities company to Mary:

1. Mary, as the beneficiary, needs to open a securities account in her name. For this purpose, Mary needs to comply with and fulfill the relevant securities account opening requirements.

2. Afterwards, Mary, as the testament executor, needs to provide the securities company with the following documents that are acceptable to the securities company: (a) documents to establish that Mary is John's lawful heir to acquire John's Astra International stock; and (b) the transfer instruction to her securities account to implement the Indonesian Will.

In order to transfer the cash in the bank account opened with an Indonesian bank to Mary:

- For the purpose of receiving the funds, depending upon the bank's policy, Mary, as the beneficiary, may either (a) open a bank account with an Indonesian bank (either with the same bank or a different one) in her name or (b) use her existing offshore bank account. To open a bank account with an Indonesian bank, Mary needs to comply with and fulfill the bank's account-opening requirements.

- Afterwards, Mary as testament executor needs to provide the bank with the following documents that are acceptable to the bank: (a) documents to establish that Mary is John's lawful heir to acquire John's cash deposited in the bank; and (b) the transfer instruction to her bank account (either in Indonesia or abroad, as the case may be) to implement the Indonesian Will.

5. Any Forced Heirship Obligations to observe?

Indonesia has forced heirship rules that apply to Indonesian nationals. However, these do not apply to John as a foreigner. Nevertheless, any possible forced heirship obligations applicable to John under Singapore law would need to be observed when making an Indonesian Will.

Chapter 28

Thailand

by **Julalak Phunsawat**

ABOUT THAILAND

Population	69 million
Religion	Buddhist 94.6% Muslim 4.3% Christian 1% Other 0.1%
Median age	39 years
Life expectancy	75.6 years
Legal system	Civil law system with common law influences
GDP per capita	USD17,900
Literacy	92.9%
Labor force	agriculture: 31.8% industry: 16.7% services: 51.5%

Adapted from: "The World Factbook", www.cia.gov.

Thailand (formerly known as Siam) is a country at the centre of the Southeast Asian Indochinese Peninsula. The capital and largest city is Bangkok. Thailand is a constitutional monarchy and parliamentary democracy. However, in recent history, its government has experienced multiple coups and periods of military dictatorship. Following a bloodless revolution in 1932, Siam became a constitutional monarchy and changed its official name to "Thailand". Apart from a brief period of parliamentary democracy in the mid-1970s, Thailand has periodically alternated between democracy and military rule. Since the 2000s, Thailand has been caught in a bitter political conflict between supporters and opponents of Thaksin Shinawatra, which culminated in two coups, most recently in 2014 and the establishment of its current and 20th constitution.[1]

CASE STUDY

John, a Singaporean non-Muslim, has the following assets in his sole name as of 1 April 2020:

- a condominium in Bangkok worth THB40 million that he purchased for THB35 million on 1 June 2017;

---

1   Source: Wikipedia.

- Thai Oil stock worth THB40 million that he purchased for THB30 million on 1 June 2017; and
- a bank account with THB40 million with Bangkok Bank that he uses for spending and making occasional trades in Thai securities.

He has a Singapore Will and Trust that deals with his Singapore assets but not his Thai assets. On his passing, he wants to give his Thai assets to his wife Mary in Singapore, who is also a Singaporean non-Muslim. He is non-resident in Thailand.

John is concerned about these questions:

1. What are the formalities of a Thai Will?
2. Who can act as an executor in his Will?
3. Suppose John passes away. Are there any duties or taxes on John's Estate?
4. What is the process of transferring his Thai assets to his Singaporean wife, Mary, who is his sole beneficiary?
5. Are there any forced heirship obligations to be met?

1. Formalities of a Thai Will

When a person like John invests or buy properties in Thailand, he should think about the management of his properties after passing away. Without at least a Will, he could be creating big issues for his heirs and any person who would have to handle his estate.

There are many types of Will formats that are permitted in Thailand.[2]

"Thammada" Will[3]

This is the most common type of Will made by foreigners, where the requirements are:

- it must be made in writing;
- it must be dated the time the Will is made;

---

2   According to the Civil and Commercial Code (sections 1655 to 1672).
3   Under section 1656 of the Civil and Commercial Code.

- it must be signed by the testator before at least two witnesses present at the same time who should then sign their names to certify the signature of the testator; and
- no erasure, addition or other alternation in the Will is valid unless made in the same form as prescribed.

A Thai Will can have a limited jurisdiction clause and choice of Thai law. In the case of John, such a clause can be used to say that the Will applies only to his assets located in Thailand.

"Holograph" Will[4]
In a holograph Will:
- The testator writes with his own hand the whole text of the document, affixes the date and his signature.
- No erasure, addition or other alteration in such Will is valid unless made by the testator himself and signed by him.
- A fingerprint, cross, seal or other such mark affixed to a document instead of signature is equivalent to a signature if it is certified by the signature of two witnesses.[5]

"Public Document"[6]
Where a Will is made by a public document:
- the Testator must declare, to the Kromkarn Amphur (Municipality Officer) before at least two other persons as witnesses attending at the same time, what dispositions he wishes to make in his Will;
- the Officer must write down the declaration of the Testator and read it to the latter and to the witnesses;
- the Testator and the witnesses must sign their names after ascertaining that the statement written down by the Officer corresponds with the declaration made by the Testator;
- the statement written down by the Officer shall be dated and signed by such official who shall certify under his hand and seal

---

4   Under section 1657 of the Civil and Commercial Code.
5   Under section 9-2. The provision in section 9 of the Code shall not apply to such Will.
6   Under section 1658 of the Civil and Commercial Code.

258 Planning Your **Will, Trust, LPA & More**

that the Will has been made in compliance with the foregoing three requirements; and
- no erasure, addition or other alterations in such a Will is valid unless signed by the testator, the witnesses and the Officer.

When John writes a Thai Will for his Thai assets, it simplifies the management of his assets on his death and it would remove ambiguity about his gifting intentions. The existence of John's Will under Thai Law can avoid such problematic questions from arising as:
- What is the applicable law? Answer: Thai law.
- Who will be John's beneficiaries? Answer: His wife Mary.
- Who will be John's Will administrator? Answer: One of the beneficiaries or other persons who is closest to the testator.
- What are John's properties in Thailand? Answer: His cash in bank, condominium and stocks.

2. Appointing executors in a Thai Will

It is recommended that John appoints one of his beneficiaries to be his executor or administrator of his Will as this person should be present to testify on the family relations between him and the testator to the judge. The person designated in the Will should contact a Thai lawyer who understands the process of how to execute a Thai Will and obtain Thai probate. This Thai lawyer can also assist and provide the legal counsel on how to transfer, manage and divide the properties relating to the Will.

The procedure of enforcement of a Will in Thailand is judiciary. The administrator would have to seek probate from a Thai court in order to administrate John's estate in Thailand.

3. Are there any duties or taxes on the estate?

The country's first inheritance tax law became effective on 2 February 2016.

The tax is levied on heirs who are either:

- Thai nationals;
- non-Thai nationals who are resident in Thailand according to immigration law;
- non-Thais inheriting assets located in Thailand; or
- Thai juristic persons (companies).

  This inheritance tax law will not be applied to:
- the estate of the testator who passed away before the effective date of the inheritance tax law; and
- the spouse of the testator.

  There are five categories of assets that are taxable:
- immovable properties;
- securities in the markets;
- money in bank deposits or other types of money which the deceased had the right to withdraw from the bank or the person who kept them;
- registered vehicles; and
- other assets as specified by a royal decree.

The tax rate is 10% of the value of the estate received by the heir that exceeds THB100,000,000 (USD3.1 million). If the heir is an ascendant or a descendant, the rate of inheritance tax is reduced to 5%.

In the case of Mary who is a non-resident Thai heir, the total amount of her net inheritable estate is THB119 million (assuming the cost of administering the estate is THB1 million). The condominium, stocks and cash in bank are all subject to Thai inheritance tax as this exceeds the threshold of THB100 million. Normally, the beneficiary who is not an ascendant or a descendant would have to pay inheritance tax on his Thai assets from John's estate equal to THB19 million X 10% = THB1.9 million. However, as Mary is the spouse of the deceased, Thai inheritance tax will not apply to her (as she receives the estate from her husband).

4. Process of transferring Thai assets on death

Once the administrator obtains Thai probate and the certificate of final decision from the Thai court, there are three steps to take during the administration of John's estate:

- to call in the John's assets;
- to pay off John's debts and liabilities, including any estate duty; and
- to distribute the estate in accordance with John's wishes as found in his Will.

Each beneficiary is responsible for paying taxes if the estate that he receives is more than THB100 million.

To transfer the Bangkok condominium to John's wife

The transfer of the condominium should be done at the Land office where the condominium is located. Once the administrator shows the Thai probate and the relevant documents such as the death certificate, the passport of the administrator, the Wil,l etc, the officer will change the name from the deceased to the administrator's name. The administrator then has the duty to distribute the property to the beneficiaries as designated in the Will. The transfer fee of inheritance will be applied.

To transfer the stock to his wife

The administrator should contact the company that is taking care of the stocks and show the Thai probate to them. They will require the Thai probate and any other relevant documents and in particular the Will to be verified. If there are no issues, the company will change the deceased's name to the administrator's name and the administrator can then divide the stock among the beneficiaries as specified in the Will or the administrator can request the company to change the name to the beneficiary's name directly. The transfer fee will depend on the internal regulations of each company.

To transfer the cash in the Bangkok bank account

The administrator should be presented before the officer of the bank. They will require documents mostly similar to transferring the condominium and stocks such as Thai probate and relevant documents as the death certificate, the passport of the administrator, the Will, etc. The officer will provide the bank form to be used by the administrator for the transfer. If the administrator would like to transfer the cash in the Thai bank to a Singapore bank, the account number and other required details should be handed over to the banker.

Moreover, if there is a large amount of money, the bank will verify the balance with the head office, which may take at least two weeks before the bank can validate the transfer or the withdrawal. The administrator then has the duty to divide the cash among the beneficiaries as designated in the Will. However, the administrator may also instruct the banker to transfer the money to the beneficiary's account directly. The rate of transfer fee or withdrawal fee of the bank will be applied.

5. Any forced heirship obligations to observe?

A property owner is free to Will his property. There is no concept of a reserved portion based on forced heirship in Thailand. Forced heirship means that by law, the assets must be divided up amongst immediate family members such as spouse and children. Countries such as France, Italy, Japan and Indonesia have forced heirship.

Furthermore, since John passed away a citizen of Singapore where there are no forced heirship obligations, his estate is not subject to any forced heirship obligations. He is free to give his assets to whoever he wishes.

Chapter 29

The Philippines

by **Hilario B Paredes (Larry)**

ABOUT THE PHILIPPINES

Population	109 million
Religion	Roman Catholic 80.6% Protestant 8.2% Other Christian 3.4% Muslim 5.6% Other 2.2%
Median age	24.1 years
Life expectancy	70 years
Legal system	Mixed legal system of civil, common, Islamic (sharia), and customary law
GDP per capita	US$8,400
Literacy	98.2%
Labor force	agriculture: 25.4% industry: 18.3% services: 56.3%

Adapted from: "The World Factbook", www.cia.gov.

The Philippines is a country in Southeast Asia. Situated in the western Pacific Ocean, it consists of about 7,641 islands that are broadly categorised under three main geographical divisions from north to south: Luzon, Visayas and Mindanao. The capital city of the Philippines is Manila and the most populous city is Quezon City, both within the single urban area of Metro Manila. The Philippines' location on the Pacific Ring of Fire and close to the equator makes the country prone to earthquakes and typhoons, but also endows it with abundant natural resources and some of the world's greatest biodiversity. Approximately 10 million additional Filipinos lived overseas as of 2013, comprising one of the world's largest diasporas. Multiple ethnicities and cultures are found throughout the islands.

The Philippines is a founding member of the United Nations, the World Trade Organization, the Association of Southeast Asian Nations, the Asia-Pacific Economic Cooperation forum and the East Asia Summit. It also hosts the headquarters of the Asian Development Bank.[1]

---

1   Source: Wikipedia.

CASE STUDY

John, a Singaporean non-Muslim, has the following assets in the Philippines in his sole name as of 1 April 2020:

- an apartment in Manila worth PHP30 million that he purchased for PHP25 million on 1 June 2017;
- San Miguel Corporation stock worth PHP30 million that he purchased for PHP25 milion on 1 June 2017; and
- a bank account with PHP40 million with BDO Unibank, Inc, that he uses for spending and making occasional trades in securities in the Philippines.

He has a Singapore Will and Trust that deals with his Singapore assets but not his Philippine assets. On his passing, he wants to give his Philippine assets to his wife Mary in Singapore, who is also a Singaporean non-Muslim. He is non-resident in the Philippines.

John is concerned about these questions:

- What are the formalities of a Will in the Philippines?
- Who can act as an executor in his Will? Are professional executors permitted under the law?
- Suppose John passes away. Are there any duties or taxes on John's estate?
- What is the process of transferring his assets in the Philippines to his Singaporean wife Mary, who is his sole beneficiary?
- Are there any forced heirship obligations to be met?
- What are some of the estate planning tools in the Philippines?

1. Formalities of a Will in the Philippines

The Civil Code[2] specifies the formal requirements for Wills. There are two kinds of Wills that are recognized: Notarial and Holographic Wills.

---

2   The Civil Code of the Philippines is the codified private law of the Philippines. It governs family and property relations. It was enacted in 1950 and remains in force with some significant amendments since enactment.

The formal requirements of a Notarial Will are:
- It must be in writing.
- It must be written in a language or dialect known to the testator.
- It must be signed or subscribed by the testator himself or by the testator's name written by some other person in his presence and under his express direction, at the end of the Will, in the presence of the witnesses.

It must be attested and subscribed to by at least three credible witnesses in the presence of the testator and of one another.

The testator and the witnesses must also sign each and every page of the Will, except the last, in the left margin, in the presence of one another and the testator (or the person signing for him), and
- the pages must be numbered consecutively in letters on the upper part of each page;
- it must contain an attestation clause (in a specified form) and signed by the witnesses; and
- it must be acknowledged before a notary public by the testator and the witnesses.

Holographic Wills on the other hand must be entirely handwritten, dated and signed by the testator. They do not need to be witnessed. However, in the probate of a Holographic Will (post mortem probate), it is necessary that at least one witness who knows the handwriting and signature of the testator explicitly declare that the Will and the signature are in the handwriting of the testator. At least three witnesses are required if the Will is contested. In the absence of any competent witness, expert testimony may be resorted to.[3]

---

3   Article 811 of the Civil Code. Note that in the case of *Azaola v Singson* 109 Phil 102 (1960), the court ruled that the first paragraph of Article 811 of the Civil Code (regarding the necessity of a witness) is merely directory and is not mandatory.

2. Appointing executors in a Will in the Philippines

The executor is the person appointed by the Will maker to administer his Will and estate on his death. A foreign person cannot be appointed to perform this role. The executor has to be a resident of the Philippines. If no person was appointed in the Will, the court will appoint an administrator to take charge of the estate.

An individual is considered competent to be an executor or administrator if he is of legal age, or at least 18 years old, a resident of the Philippines, and is not in the opinion of the court unfit to execute the duties of the trust by reason of drunkenness, improvidence, or want of understanding or integrity, or by reason of conviction of an offense involving moral turpitude.[4] The testator is not prohibited from nominating more than one person as his executor and the court may appoint multiple executors who may act jointly.[5]

Should there be delay in the appointment of an executor or administrator, the court may appoint a special administrator who may take charge of the estate in the meantime. Special administrators need not follow the order of preference as in determining an administrator.

An institution can be an executor.

Corporations or associations authorised to conduct the business of a trust company in the Philippines may be appointed as an executor, administrator, guardian of an estate or trustee, in like manner as an individual.[6]

3. Are there any duties or taxes on the estate?

In case of death, John, as a non-resident alien at the time of his death, is required to pay estate tax based only on the value of all his properties situated in the Philippines.

His gross estate would include the fair market value of his Manila apartment and his San Miguel stock. The cash in his BDO bank

---

4   Section 1, Rule 78 of the Rules of Court.
5   Section 5, Rule 78 of the Rules of Court.
6   Article 1060 of the New Civil Code.

account would be part of his estate for the purpose of calculating his estate tax obligation.[7] However, note that withdrawals from the bank deposit account are allowed, subject to a final withholding tax of six percent (6%).[8] This should be done within one year from the date of the depositor's death.[9]

Under the new tax reform law (TRAIN Law), which went into effect on 19 December 2017, a tax rate of 6% based on the value of the net estate is required to be paid, within one year from the decedent's death, regardless of whether he was a resident or non-resident of the Philippines.[10]

To compute his net estate, which is basis of the estate tax, the following should be deducted from the value of all his properties or gross estate within the Philippines:
• standard deduction of PHP500,000;
• claims against the estate, claims of the deceased against insolvent persons, and unpaid mortgages upon or any indebtedness in respect of property where the value of the decedent's interest is included in the gross estate;
• expenses, loses, indebtedness and taxes;
• property previously taxed; and
• properties donated for public use.

Assuming the fair market value of the apartment, stock and cash in bank total PHP100 million, and deductions equal PHP150,000, his net estate would be PHP70 million. Then:

$$\text{Estate tax} = 6\% \times \text{PHP99.85 million} = \text{PHP5.94 million or SGD166,000}$$

4. Process of transferring Philippines assets on death

There are several steps to take during this period of administering John's estate:

7   Section 85 of the National Internal Revenue Code.
8   Section 27 of Tax Reform for Acceleration and Inclusion Law (TRAIN Law) (RA 10963).
9   RMC No 62-2018.
10 TRAIN Law (RA 10963).

- probate of John's Will;
- name the executor or, if none, appoint an administrator who must be a resident of Philippines;
- executor or administrator will then collate and administer John's assets;
- pay off John's debts and liabilities, including estate taxes; and
- distribute the estate in accordance with John's wishes found in his Will.

Executors must identify, gather and value the assets of the decedent, arrange for the preparation and filing of required tax returns and the payment of estate taxes.

The executor is responsible for paying for estate taxes, which is due one year after John's death.

To transfer the Manila property to John's wife

Assuming there is a Will, a petition must be filed for the allowance/probate of the will. It must be filed by the executor, devisee, legatee or other interested person.[11] Once the court order allowing the Will or admitting it to probate is obtained, letters testamentary or administration will be issued.[12]

The executor or administrator must file a bond and an inventory of all goods, chattels, rights, credits and estate of the deceased within three months.[13] The payment of debts must be done within one year (extendible for another one year).[14] After the payment of debts and other expenses, the court will approve the final accounting and project of partition. The copies of final orders and judgments of the court relating to real estate will be recorded in the Registry of Deeds of the province where the property is situated.[15] The estate tax return must be filed within one year from the decedent's death.[16]

---

11 Sections 1 and 2, Rule 76 of the Rules of Court.
12 Section 4, Rule 78, Section 5, Rule 79 of the Rules of Court.
13 Section 1, Rule 81 of the Rules of Court.
14 Section 15, Rule 88 of the Rules of Court.
15 Rule 90 of the Rules of Court.
16 Section 25, RA 10963.

Once the taxes are paid, the title of the real estate may be transferred by presenting to the Registry of Deeds the court order and the tax clearance document.[17]

To transfer the San Miguel stock to John's wife

Assuming there is a Will, a petition must be filed for the allowance/probate of the Will. It must be filed by the executor, devisee, legatee or other interested person.[18] Once the court order allowing the Will or admitting it to probate is obtained, letters testamentary or administration will be issued.[19]

The executor or administrator must file a bond and an inventory of all goods, chattels, rights, credits and estate of the deceased within three months.[20] The payment of the debts must be done within one year (extendible for another one year).[21] After the payment of the debts and other expenses, the court will approve the final accounting and project of partition.[22] The estate tax return must be filed within one year from the decedent's death.[23] The court order and the tax clearance document (BIR CAR) must be presented to the corporation for the transfer of shares and for recording the transfer in the books of the corporation.

To transfer the cash in the BDO bank account

The executor, administrator or any of the legal heirs of a decedent may be allowed to withdraw from bank deposit accounts within one year from the date of death of the depositor but the amount withdrawn will be subject to 6% Final Withholding Tax (FWT). Prior to the withdrawal, the bank will require the executor, administrator or any of the legal heirs withdrawing from the deposit account to present a copy of the Tax Identification Number (TIN)

---

17 Tax clearance is evidenced by the Bureau of Internal Revenue (BIR) Certificate Authorizing Registration (CAR). This tax clearance document is issued by BIR relative to the transfer of certain properties. It is a mandatory requirement and the title of the property will not be transferred in the absence of such CAR.

18 Sections 1 and 2, Rule 76 of the Rules of Court.

19 Section 4, Rule 78, Section 5, Rule 79 of the Rules of Court.

20 Section 1, Rule 81 of the Rules of Court.

21 Section 15, Rule 88 of the Rules of Court.

22 Rule 90 of the Rules of Court.

23 Section 25, RA 10963.

of the estate of the decedent and BIR Form No 1904[24] of the estate.

The bank will issue the BIR Form No 2306 certifying the withholding of 6% final tax, file the prescribed quarterly return on the final tax withheld and remit the same on or before the last day of the month following the close of the quarter during which the withholding was made.[25]

5. Any forced heirship obligations to observe?

Philippines citizens are subject to forced heirship obligations, where a portion of a decedent's net estate is reserved for certain family members.

John's estate in the Philippines is subject to his national law. Since John passed away a citizen of Singapore where there are no forced heirship obligations, his estate is thus not subject to any forced heirship obligations.

6. Estate planning tools in The Philippines
1. Life insurance

The advantage of a life insurance is that it provides cash, it addresses liquidity issues and "enlarges" the estate and/or future inheritance of children. It can also be an "equaliser" of inheritance of children.[26]

2. Outright gift or transfer to a child or heir

Even if the statutory rates for both the donor's tax and estate tax are the same at a flat 6%, depending on the nature of the asset, the fair market value of a property currently will more likely than not be lower than the fair market value in the future. Therefore, the donor's current tax will more likely than not be lower than the estate tax in the future.

Gifts not exceeding PHP250,000 in each calendar year are also exempt from donor's tax.[27] If the asset donated is conjugal or absolute community property, each spouse is considered a donor

---

24 This a tax form that one-time taxpayers and people registering under Executive Order 98 use to apply for a TIN before paying any tax due, filing a tax return, or receiving a TIN.
25 RMC No 62-2018.
26 Section 85(E) of the National Internal Revenue Code includes in the gross estate the proceeds of life insurance taken out by the decedent upon his life to the extent receivable by the estate or by any beneficiary of the insurance policy, except when it is expressly stipulated that the designation of the beneficiary is irrevocable.
27 Section 28, RA 10963.

of his/her share in the property. Therefore, the annual exemption of PHP250,000 is effectively doubled if both spouses donated separately at the same time.

Donating an income-producing property to a family member who have little or no income reduces the donor's income tax liability and, ultimately, his estate tax liability because the income is shifted from the donor's higher income tax bracket to the lower income tax bracket of the donee.

Take note, however, that if the parents continue to collect the rent, pay the taxes, sign leases, discuss offers of sale and other circumstances that indicate a sham donation, this will typically cause the tax authorities to disregard the donation and include the property in the gross estate of the decedent.

3. Irrevocable Trusts

This is useful when the properties require management control. The creation of the Trust eliminates the need to institute judicial guardianship proceedings for a minor and the appointment of a guardian to manage the properties. The trustor can also choose who the trustee will be and can provide for the terms of the trust by writing these into the deed covering the trust.

Take note that the Trust must take effect during the lifetime of the trustor and must be irrevocable. The power to amend and the right to income must not be reserved in any way.

Trusts are subject to donor's tax and income tax.[28]

4. Investment in long-term deposits or investments

The Interest from these long-term deposits and/or investments is tax free, as long as the deposit/investment is not pre-terminated. The PHP250,000 annual donor's tax exemption can grow in this type of deposit and/or investments for an heir.

---

28   Section 98(B) of the National Internal Revenue Code (donor's tax) and section 60 of the National Internal Revenue Code (income tax).

5. Transfer by sale

This is useful where the heir has the financial means to pay for the sale. Like in donation, Capital Gains Tax on current sale of real property classified as capital assets will more likely than not be lower than the estate tax in the future. Capital Gains Tax on the sale of real property classified as capital assets and estate tax are the same at a flat rate of 6%.

This tool can be used, for example, in the sale of principal residence, which is exempt from Capital Gains Tax, subject to certain conditions.[29] There is also another option of PHP10 million deductible amount to the family home for estate tax purposes.[30]

The selling price should not be lower than Fair Market Value or zonal value at the time of sale. The heir buying the property must also be able to prove financial ability to pay for the property.

If the Bureau of Internal Revenue finds that the sale is a sham transaction, they will disregard the sale and throw the property back into the gross estate of the decedent.

6. Family-owned companies

This is used for:

a. Assets that the parents want to preserve and keep within the family or assets that will be used in the businesses.

b. Shielding the parents from liability arising from the businesses.

c. Splitting the income between the parents and the family company.

d. Postponing the incidence of income taxation on the shareholders until dividends are declared by the family company.

e. Income tax savings on sale of real properties which are capital assets vs sale of shares.

f. Depressing the value of the property.

No gain or loss shall be recognised if property is transferred to a corporation by a person in exchange for stock or unit of participation

29 See RR 13-1999 as amended by RR 14-2000.
30 Section 23, RA 10963.

in such a corporation of which as a result of such exchange said person, alone or together with others, not exceeding four persons, gains control of the corporation. Stocks issued for services shall not be considered as issued in return for property.[31]

While these are commonly called "tax-free exchanges", these exchanges are merely "tax-deferred exchanges" because the historical cost of the property given in exchange is carried over for tax accounting purposes.

Take note, however, that this will result in the "lock-in" of the properties in the family corporation and if the family home or principal residence is incorporated, the Capital Gains Tax exemption on sale or disposition of Principal Residence is lost.

It also forces the children to "co-own" the family home as shareholders and may result in issues of who lives in it, pays for maintenance, etc.

7. Initial Public Offering
Depending on the scale and magnitude of assets/businesses, the cost, time and effort in pre-Initial Public Offering activities and the continuing post-Initial Public Offering obligations and responsibilities of going public may be worth the tax savings.[32]

8. Family Foundation/NGO
Assets can be transferred to the Family Foundation to support the family's advocacies.

Bequests, devises, legacies or transfers to the Foundation/NGO are excluded from the decedent's gross estate.[33] Donations to the Foundation are exempt from donor's tax and are deductible from the donor's gross income for income tax purposes.[34] Income of the Foundation from donations and grants are exempt from income tax but income from property of whatever kind are subject to income tax.[35]

---

31 Section 40(C)(2) of the National Internal Revenue Code.
32 See section 39, RA 10963 for the Tax on Sale, Barter or Exchange of Shares of Stock Listed and Traded through the Local Stock Exchange or through Initial Public Offering.
33 Section 87(D) of the National Internal Revenue Code.
34 Sections 34(H) and 101(A)(3) of the National Internal Revenue Code.
35 Sections 30(E) and 30(G) of the National Internal Revenue Code.

9. Living Will and Last Will and Testament

A Living Will does not on its own generate or result in tax savings, but one of the objectives of estate planning is to achieve the decedent's personal wishes with respect to medical care when he/she is no longer able to speak for himself/herself. Those wishes can be stated in a Living Will.

The Last Will and Testament, on the other hand, is the best record of how the decedent wishes to divide the remaining assets among his/her heirs, hopefully to preserve harmony within the family.

Chapter 30

Vietnam

by **Rudy Bui Tien Long**

ABOUT VIETNAM

Population	99 million
Religion	Buddhist 7.9% Catholic 6.6% Hoa Hao 1.7% Cao Dai 0.9% None 81.8% Other 1.1%
Median age	31.9 years
Life expectancy	74.4 years
Legal system	Civil law (European style)
GDP per capita	US$6,900
Literacy	95%
Labor force	agriculture: 40.3% industry: 25.7% services: 34%

Adapted from: "The World Factbook", www.cia.gov.

Vietnam is the easternmost country on the Southeast Asian Indochinese Peninsula. It shares its land borders with China to the north, and Laos and Cambodia to the west. Its capital city is Hanoi, while its most populous city and commercial hub is Ho Chi Minh City, also known by its former name of Saigon. After North and South Vietnam were reunified as a communist state under a unitary socialist government in 1976, the country became economically and politically isolated until 1986, when the Communist Party initiated a series of economic and political reforms that facilitated Vietnamese integration into world politics and the global economy. As a result of the successful reforms, Vietnam has enjoyed a high GDP growth rate, consistently ranked among the fastest-growing countries in the world.[1]

---

1   Source: Wikipedia.

CASE STUDY

John, a Singaporean non-Muslim, has the following assets in his sole name as of 1 April 2020:

- an apartment in Ho Chi Minh City worth VND5 million that he purchased for VND4 million on 1 June 2017;
- Vinamilk stock worth VND5 million that he purchased for VND4.5 million on 1 June 2017; and
- a bank account with VND5 million with Vietinbank that he uses for spending and making occasional trades in Vietnamese securities.

He has a Singapore Will and Trust that deals with his Singapore assets but not his Vietnamese assets. On his passing, he wants to give his Vietnamese assets to his wife Mary in Singapore, who is also a Singaporean non-Muslim. He is non-resident in Vietnam.

John is concerned about these questions:

1. What are the formalities of a Will in Vietnam?
2. Who can act as an executor of his Will? Are professional executors permitted under the law?
3. Suppose John passes away. Are there any duties or taxes on John's estate?
4. What is the process of transferring his Vietnamese assets to his Singaporean wife, Mary, who is his sole beneficiary?
5. Are there any forced heirship obligations to be met?

1. Formalities of a Will in Vietnam

The Civil Code states that a Vietnamese Will must either be made in writing or dictated orally before at least two witnesses. The Will needs to indicate the following:

- the date;
- the name and address of the person making the Will; and
- the assets to be given and any conditions that need to be met.

The Will cannot contain any abbreviations, and every page must be signed by the person who made the Will. In terms of form, even though a simple and unwitnessed handwritten will is legally valid in Vietnam, it is strongly recommended that:

- John has his Will notarised by a notary public even though it is not a legal requirement. It is prudent to do so in order to minimise the risk of disputes arising when the Will maker passes away.

- John notarises his Will in the presence of at least one witness.

Note that his Will must be made in the Vietnamese language to be enforceable in Vietnam.

Vietnamese notaries generally refer a foreigner to their own consulate or embassy for notary services.

A Vietnamese Will should include only Vietnam-sited property. If the Vietnamese Will includes property outside of Vietnam, significant delays in the Vietnamese courts can be expected.

In practice, it is highly recommended that John makes a Vietnamese Will to deal with his Vietnamese assets. We are able to assist John in making a Will in English since he is not fluent in Vietnamese, then translate it into Vietnamese and authenticate such translation before further conducting the transfer procedures corresponding to each type of the inheritance.

2. Appointing executors in a Vietnamese Will

It is recommended that John appoints a local Vietnamese person to be executor or administrator of his Will even though the administrator could technically be anyone. It is also recommended that John appoints a Vietnam-based lawyer who understands the process and substance of the Will maker's Will and Vietnamese assets.

It is finally recommended that John appoints a custodian of his Will to keep it in his custody.

There are no provisions for or the concept of a professional executor or administrator under the Civil Code.

3. Are there any duties or taxes on the estate?

Generally, an inheritance above VND10 million (about SGD620) is subject to personal income tax (PIT) of 10%.

John's stock in Vinamilk is subject to PIT upon the transfer of the said stocks to his wife as inheritance. His wife will pay the PIT as follows:

PIT = [Value of stock - (VND 10m as the exemption)] x PIT tax rate of 10%[2]

John's apartment is not subject to PIT because it is an inheritance in the form of real estate directly bequeathed to his wife.[3]

John's cash in Vietinbank is not subject to PIT because under Vietnamese law, cash is not taxable.

The executor is responsible for paying the estate taxes. In the case of John's estate, the taxes levied will be paid by John's wife when she registers her ownership thereof after executing his Will.[4]

4. Process of transferring Vietnamese assets on death

There are three steps to take during the administering of John's estate:

- to call in John's assets;
- to pay off John's debts and liabilities including any estate duty; and
- to distribute the estate in accordance with John's wishes as found in his Will.

---

2   Personal Tax Income Law of Vietnam, Article 23.1, Circular 111/2013/TT-BTC.
3   Personal Tax Income Law of Vietnam, Article 3.1.d, Circular 111/2013/TT-BTC.
4   Personal Tax Income Law of Vietnam, Article 23.3.b, Circular 111/2013/TT-BTC.

To initiate the process of transferring John's assets and estate to his wife, the following steps will be taken:

1. John's Will has to be authenticated, assuming that he had written and translated his Will to Vietnamese and had it notarised prior to his death.
2. John's wife as the heir in his Will must present herself in person at a licensed notary office in Vietnam to apply for a declaration of inheritance reception. John can appoint another person to carry out this procedure specifically in his Will.
3. The responsible notary shall publicise the said declaration at the commune level of the People's Committee where the apartment or most of his assets are located or generated.
4. John's wife will then sign the said declaration and authenticate it at the same notary office.

Upon finishing the foregoing, the transfer of his inheritance can be conducted separately by his wife as follows.

John's apartment5

The transfer of the apartment to John's wife must be registered at the Land Registration Office of Ho Chi Minh City.[6] Note that John's wife must be allowed to enter Vietnam in order to be eligible to receive his apartment in Ho Chi Minh City

John's stock in Vinamilk[7]

As Vinamilk is a listed company, John's wife will have to go to the Vietnam Security Depository (VSD) to apply for transferring the ownership of John's stock in accordance with Vietnamese laws on the transfer of securities ownership.

Upon finishing the transfer, as explained in section 3 above, she will need to declare and settle her PIT at the local tax authority where she receives the said stock.

---

5   The legal basis is (a) Article 61.2.l of Decree 43/2014/NĐ-CP, (b) Article 2.40 of Decree No 01/2017/NĐ-CP and (c) Article 79 of Decree 43/2014/NĐ-CP.
6   Article 159.1.c and 160.3 of the Law on Housing 2014.
7   The legal basis is (a) Article 3.1 of Circular 123/2015/TT-BTC, and (b) Article 27 of the Regulation of registration and transfer of ownership over securities attached to Decision No 03/QĐ-VSD dated 2 January 2020.

Note that in this case, John's wife is not required to register for a security trading account (or trading code).

John's cash in Vietinbank account[8]

John's wife can present herself in person or authorise a Vietnamese individual in writing to apply for the procedure of a one-way transfer of foreign currency at the branch or transaction office of Vietinbank in Ho Chi Minh City where John opened his bank account.

The limit of transfer of foreign currency will be decided by Vietinbank in accordance with foreign currency regulations of the State Bank of Vietnam at the time of transfer.

5. Any forced heirship obligations to observe?

Vietnamese citizens are subject to forced heirship obligations where a portion of a decedent's net estate is reserved for certain family members.

John's estate in Vietnam is subject to his national law. Since John passed away a citizen of Singapore where there are no forced heirship obligations, his estate is not subject to any forced heirship obligations.

However, in the case of John's apartment in Ho Chi Minh City, the laws of Vietnam provide for forced inheritance notwithstanding the contents of his Will. This means that should John decide to transfer the apartment to only his wife when he has children who are either underage or of age but unable to work for a living, his children are respectively allowed to inherit two-thirds of the value of the apartment he has bequeathed to his wife.[9]

---

8   The legal basis is under the internal regulations of the bank.
9   Article 644 of the Civil Code 2015.

Chapter 31

China

by Jason Tian

ABOUT CHINA

Population	1.4 billion
Religion	Buddhist 18.2% Christian 5.1% Muslim 1.8% Folk religion 21.9% None 52.2% Other 0.8%
Median age	38.4 years
Life expectancy	76.1 years
Legal system	Civil law influenced by Soviet and continental European civil law systems. In May 28, 2020, China Civil Code was enacted and will come into effect on January 1, 2021.
GDP per capita	US$18,200
Literacy	96.8%
Labor force	agriculture: 27.7% industry: 28.8% services: 43.5%

Adapted from: "The World Factbook", www.cia.gov.

Located in East Asia, China is the world's most populous country. Governed by the Communist Party of China, the state exercises jurisdiction over 22 provinces, five autonomous regions, four direct-controlled municipalities (Beijing, Tianjin, Shanghai, and Chongqing) and the special administrative regions of Hong Kong and Macau. China is a unitary one-party socialist republic and is one of the few existing socialist states.

Since the introduction of economic reforms in 1978, China's economy has been one of the world's fastest-growing with annual growth rates consistently above 6 per cent. Since 2010, China has been the world's second-largest economy by nominal GDP, and since 2014, the largest economy in the world by PPP. China is also the world's largest exporter and second-largest importer of goods. China is a recognised nuclear weapons state and has the world's largest standing army, the People's Liberation Army, and the second-largest defence budget. China has been characterised as an emerging superpower, mainly because of its massive population, a large and rapidly-growing economy and a powerful military.[1]

CASE STUDY

John, a Singaporean non-Muslim, has the following assets in his sole name:

- an apartment in Shanghai worth CNY5 million that he purchased for CNY4.5 million on 1 June 2017;
- Petrochina stock worth CNY5 million that he purchased for CNY4 million on 1 June 2017; and
- a bank account with CNY5 million with Bank of China that he uses for spending and making occasional trades in Chinese securities.

He has a Singapore Will and Trust that deals with his Singapore assets but not his Chinese assets. On his passing, he wants to give

---

1   Source: Wikipedia.

his Chinese assets to his wife Mary in Singapore, who is also a Singaporean non-Muslim. He is non-resident in China.

John is concerned about these questions:

1. What are the formalities of a Will in China?
2. Who can act as an executor of his Will? Are professional executors permitted under the law?
3. Suppose John passes away on 1 June 2020. Are there any duties or taxes on John's estate?
4. What is the process of transferring his Chinese assets to his Singaporean wife, Mary, who is his sole beneficiary?
5. Are there any forced heirship obligations to be met?

1. Formalities of a Will in China

Before delving into details, it should be noted that the current China Succession Law (enacted and effective as of 1 October 1985)[2] is somewhat outdated as Chinese society has rapidly evolved the past two to three decades. This has given rise to difficulties in reconciling the old rules and new practice in today's digital era. However, the newly enacted China Civil Code will replace the aforementioned China Succession Law entirely from 1 January 2021. The following information is based on the upcoming Civil Code.

The China Succession Law provides for the following forms of Wills:

1. Notarised Will: one that is made by the testator through a notary office.
2. Holographic Will: one that is written by the testator with signature and specific year, month and date.
3. Allographic will: one that is witnessed on the spot by two or more witnesses, one of whom writes the Will, and is indicated with specific year, month and date, and is duly signed by all the witnesses and the testator.
4. Printed Will: one that is printed and witnessed on the spot by two or more witnesses; the testator and witnesses sign on

---

2   The official English translation of the legislation is Law of Succession of the People's Republic of China. We will use the term 'China Succession Law' to refer to the official law.

each page of the printed Will, and the Will is indicated with specific year, month and date.

5. Audio and video Will: one is made with at least two persons witnessing on the spot; and the testator and witnesses record their names or portraits in such audio or video format, with the specific year, month and day recorded as well.

6. Oral Will: one that is made by the testator in emergency situations with at least two on the spot witnesses. Once the emergency situation ends and the testator is able to make a Will in writing or using audio and video recording, the Oral Will becomes void.

Generally, when there are multiple Wills, the last one will prevail. However, the soon-to-be-replaced China Succession Law favours notarised Wills over all other forms by providing that a holographic, allographic, audio or oral Will will not revoke or amend a notarised Will. Under the upcoming China Civil Code, that favoritism is abandoned and the general rule of Last Will and Testament prevailing will apply.

Foreigners who are not residing in China may make their Wills for their China assets in accordance with such local laws and rules as in the place where the testators have their habitual residence or as of the country of their nationalities.

2. Appointing executors in a Chinese Will

In most mature foreign jurisdictions, there is generally an executor or executrix appointed in a Will who will be in charge of the administration of the estate. In China, however, it is still not very common for a testator to appoint an executor for his Will, due largely to the lack of operable rules regarding executorship. This may be changing soon, as the new China Civil Code has established the estate administrator framework in Articles 1145 to 1149 with regard to its appointment, court intervention, remuneration, duties and liabilities. In particular, Article 1145 provides that an executor is by default the administrator for the estate. It is expected that China's Supreme Court will issue detailed guidelines on the application of these provisions at a later time.

It is recommended that John appoints a local Chinese person to be executor and administrator of his Will and estate. It is also recommended that John appoints a China-based lawyer who understands the process and substance of the Will maker's Will and Chinese assets.

It is finally recommended that John appoints a custodian of his Will to keep it in his custody.

3. Are there any duties or taxes on the estate?

There is currently no estate duty in China.

However, it is noteworthy that heirs or beneficiaries receiving multiple estate properties may be paying more taxes (income tax, capital gains tax and VAT tax) when they sell the properties in the future since there will be no step-up in tax basis.

Here is what a step-up in basis means. In John's case, he purchased the Shanghai apartment for CNY 4.5 million and left it to his wife when the apartment was CNY5 million. If the apartment receives a step-up in basis, this makes the cost basis for the apartment to be the current market price of CNY5 million. Any capital gains tax paid in the future will be based on CNY5 million as the cost basis, not on the original purchase price of CNY4.5 million.

Hence there may be a little room for tax planning for some clients.

4. Process of transferring Chinese assets on death

There are three steps to take during this period of administering John's estate:

- to call in the John's assets;
- to pay off John's debts and liabilities; and
- to distribute the estate in accordance with John's wishes as found in his Will.

To transfer the Shanghai property to John's wife

Assuming John has a valid Will recognised by China's notary officers:

1. Present the Will to a notary office in Shanghai together with other documents to prove the family relationship such as death certificates, birth certificates, marriage certificates, etc.
2. Once the notary office issues the notarisation document affirming his wife's right to inherit the estate, the next step is to present the notarisation document and the wife's identity to the real estate registration authority in charge of the property for title transfer.
3. The real estate authority will issue a new title deed in the name of the wife.

As a matter of law and practice in China, those documents originating outside of China such as the death certificate and family documents are to be notarised in Singapore and legalised at the China consulate in Singapore.

Clients can carry out the process themselves and can appoint an attorney in China to act on their behalf throughout the whole process.

To transfer the Petrochina stock to John's wife

Assuming John has a valid Will recognised by China's notary officers:

1. The wife must first open a security account in China, which is allowed only for disposal of the inherited estate stock and cannot be used for general stock trading.

2. Present probated Will and family relationship documents to a notary office proving the wife's right to inherit the estate stock; the requirement is much the same as in the case of inheriting real estate.

3. Once the notary office issues the notarisation document proving her right to inherit the estate, the next step is to present the notarisation document to the security company or stock registration authority for the title transfer.

To transfer the cash in the Bank of China account to John's wife

Assuming John has a valid Will recognised by China's notary officers:

1. The wife must first open a bank account with a bank in China.

2. Present the probated Will and family relationship documents to a notary office proving the wife's right to inherit the estate stock; the requirement is much the same as in the case of inheriting listed stock.

3. Once the notary office issues the notarisation document proving her right to inherit the estate, then present the notarisation document to the bank to wire the funds into the wife's bank account.

In practice, if a China notary office cannot or refuses to work on an inheritance case for reasons of disputes among heirs/beneficiaries or missing documents, the inheritance will have to be resolved in court proceedings in China.

To foreign recipients of estates in China, title transfer to the name(s) of heirs or beneficiaries is not the end of the inheritance journey. It is more important to understand how those clients can cash in on those assets and take the money out of China, which is another topic related to China foreign exchange rules.

5. Any forced feirship obligations to observe?

China does not have forced heirship rules.

However, the China Succession Law has a provision that requires a Will to reserve a necessary share for an heir who does not have labour capacity and does not have a source of income. However, the law is silent on what constitutes a necessary share, leaving the matter to the discretion of judges.

Chapter 32

Australia

by **Lynda Babister**

ABOUT AUSTRALIA

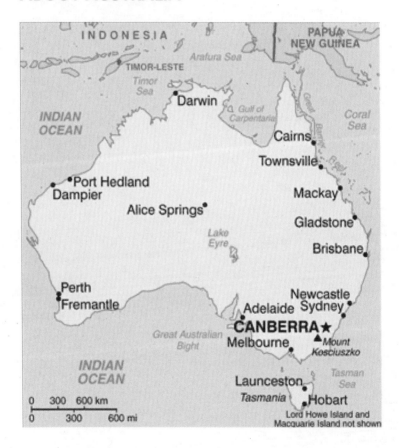

Population	25.7
Religion	Protestant 23.1% Roman Catholic 22.6% Other Christian 4.2% Muslim 2.6% Buddhist 2.4% Orthodox 2.3% Other 12.7% None 30.1%
Median age	37.5 years
Life expectancy	82.7 years
Legal system	Common law system based on the English model
GDP per capita	USD50,400
Literacy	99%[1]
Labor force	agriculture: 3.6% industry: 21.1% services: 75.3%

Adapted from: "The World Factbook", www.cia.gov.

Australia is an island continent, made up of six States, and two Territories. The overarching Australian Government is a federation which has English style, legal and parliamentary systems, similar to Singapore. Each State and Territory has its own legal jurisdiction – New South Wales, Victoria, Queensland, Western Australia, South Australia, Tasmania, Northern Territory and Australian Capital Territory. For convenience, we will refer to each of the States and Territories as "States" – although there are legal differences, this is the way most Australians think of the Territories anyway. The final jurisdiction is the Australian Commonwealth Government. Australia has jurisdictional separation between the legal and parliamentary systems. In legal matters, the Australian High Court is the principal legal authority.

CASE STUDY

John, a Singaporean non-Muslim, has the following assets in his sole name as of 1 April 2020:

- an apartment in NSW worth AUD1 million that he purchased for AUD800,000 on 1 June 2017;
- BHP stock worth AUD1 million that he purchased for AUD900,000 on 1 June 2017; and
- a bank account with AUD1 milion with Westpac Bank that he uses for spending and making occasional trades in Australian securities.

He has a Singapore Will and Trust that deals with his Singapore assets but not his Australian assets. On his passing, he wants to give his Australian assets to his wife Mary in Singapore, who is also a Singaporean non-Muslim. He is non-resident in Australia.

John is concerned about these questions:

1. What are the formalities of an Australian Will?
2. Who can act as an executor in his Will? Are professional executors permitted under the law?
3. Suppose John passes away on 1 June 2020. Are there any duties or taxes on John's estate?
4. What is the process of transferring his Australian assets to his Singaporean wife, Mary, who is his sole beneficiary?
5. Are there any forced heirship obligations to be met?

1. Formalities of an Australian Will

Each State jurisdiction has its own formal requirements for Wills. Whilst a person makes his Will according to the requirements of the State in which he lives or holds property, the Will is valid in all States across Australia. There is no need to have a Will for each State, even if you hold property in different States. In certain circumstances, an International Will may validly apply to a testator's Australian property, however, it is recommended that the testator makes an Australian Will to deal with his Australian assets.

The basic requirements for a Will In Australia are:

- The Will is in writing, although the definition of writing is broad, and may include video in some States.
- The testator is at least 18 years of age, unless the testator is married then he may make a Will as a minor.
- The testator must have legal testamentary capacity – that is, he must be aware he is signing a Will, he must be aware of the extent of his assets and who he ought to be giving his assets to.
- The Will must be signed by the testator (or if he is incapable of signing, someone else in the presence of and at the direction of the testator), also in the presence of two independent adult witnesses who are present at the same time and who each attest and sign the Will in the presence of the testator. The witnesses must not be executors or beneficiaries of the Will.

Once the Will is made, it is not legally ratified until the time of the testator's passing. The Will must be presented for a grant of probate at the Supreme Court. Once the court grants probate, that would be conclusive evidence of the formal validity of the Will.

Due to the complicated requirements, it is advisable to obtain professional legal assistance when writing a Will. There can be challenges to the validity of the Will, and alternatively, challenges to the nature of the gifts. It is not mandatory to instruct a lawyer to prepare the Will and, in fact, a person can make a valid Will by himself or herself. However, the risks involved if one makes a mistake in a "do it yourself" Will may be very costly to the estate and beneficiaries.

Wills can also be made by the Public Trustees who operate under government authority. Their fees are government regulated. The Public Trustee can also apply for probate on behalf of the estate and charge a fee for that process.

---

1   World Data Atlas, www.knoema.com.

John's apartment is in Sydney. He makes a Will with a lawyer in New South Wales on 1 April 2020.

2. Appointing executors in an Australian Will

In Australia, an executor is the person or entity that applies to the court for a grant of probate. The position involves the identification of the assets and liabilities, gathering in the assets, paying the liabilities and also distribution to the nominated beneficiaries. Another name for the executor is the Legal Personal Representative.

It is recommended that John appoints a local Australian individual to be the executor of his Will. The executor could technically be anyone over the age of 18, including an individual from Singapore, however, if an overseas executor is appointed, he will need to arrange for the use of an address in the State where the property is held. If John decides to appoint a local Australian executor, it is suggested that he appoints a lawyer who understands the process and substance of his Will and his Australian assets.

Australia allows a Will maker to nominate the Public Trustee, or a trustee company as executor. A corporate executor can offer a neutral and independent service. A corporate executor, being an institution, can also be expected to be longer lasting as compared to an individual.

An executor is entitled to make an application to the court to be paid a commission from the estate. Alternatively, the Will may provide for payment to the executor, either by a nominated sum, or an hourly rate for their time involved in administering the estate.

John decided to appoint the New South Wales lawyer who wrote his Will as his executor.

3. Are there any duties or taxes on the estate?

Although Australia does not have any inheritance tax or death duties, there may be taxes involved in transferring property from the estate to the beneficiaries.

The executor is responsible for arranging the final tax return and to ensure that any estate taxes are paid. After John passes away, his estate can continue to gather income, for example, rental from the property, interest on bank accounts, share dividends and capital gains from the sale of assets.

Mary, who is the sole beneficiary of John's estate, would be subject to Capital Gains Tax (CGT) as a non-resident. The transfer of assets is considered to have occurred on the day the person died; in John's case on 1 June 2020. Assets which were acquired before 20 September 1985 are exempt from CGT, as these acquisitions pre-date the introduction of CGT.

In the case of Mary who is a non-resident, she would be liable to pay CGT before the transfer of the assets can take place. If John had been an Australian resident at the time of his death, Mary may have had the benefit of CGT losses to balance some of the tax payable and may have had the benefit of capital gain discounts. Calculation of capital gains tax is complicated, as acquisition costs, depreciation, asset income and asset losses must all be taken into account. It is recommended that an Australian accountant be engaged to ensure that all the calculations are properly made.

- Capital gain on John's Sydney property = $200,000.00.
- Capital gain on John's BHP shares = $100,000.00
- There is no CGT on John's Westpac Bank account.

Capital Gains Tax is paid on the income overall, rather than on each asset.

Therefore, assuming that the above capital gains are the only income, the tax payable on the capital gains made by Mary would be $116,550 ($62,550 + .45 X $120,000).

Foreign resident tax rates 2019–2020	
Taxable income	Tax on this income
0–$90,000	32.5c for each $1

| $90,001–$180,000 | $29,250 plus 37c for each $1 over $90,000 |
| $180,001 and over | $62,550 plus 45c for each $1 over $180,000 |

Source: ato.gov.au

4. Process of transferring Australian assets on death

Following the grant of probate, there are three steps to take during this period of administering John's estate:

- to call in John's assets;
- to pay off John's debts and liabilities including estate duty; and
- to distribute the estate in accordance with John's wishes as contained in his Will.

The primary function of a legal personal representative is to collect the estate of the deceased (real and personal) and to administer the estate according to the provisions in the Will, and subsequently, the grant of probate.

Additionally, there are detailed statutory rules for each State that govern the transfer of assets from the deceased's estate to the beneficiary.

Call in John's assets

The dealings with the estate begin with obtaining searches of title. That is, to ensure that the asset is held in the name that the testator believed they were held. It is perhaps not surprising how many asset owners are described in different terms to that which they recollect. This may include variations in spelling of the owner's name, different order of names, or even, on occasion, completely different names to what the owner thought was used. If there is a discrepancy, this must be addressed both in the application for probate and when the transfer is being performed.

Pay off John's debts and duties

The second step for the executor is to ensure all debts and liabilities are paid. Depending on what the debts are, they may need to be paid at the same time as the transfer, for example, if there was a mortgage over the Sydney apartment, the executor may choose to use part of the money in the Westpac Bank account to repay the loan.

Distribute and transfer tssets

In order to transfer the Sydney apartment to Mary, the executor must complete a Transmission to Beneficiary application at the Land Registry Service. Each State has their own Registry, which controls the transfer of real estate property between parties. In New South Wales, stamp duty must be paid on the Transmission Application. This is a nominal sum of $AUD50.00, provided the transmission is in accordance with the terms of the Will. The Transmission Application must be accompanied by a certified copy of probate, and the paper certificate of title. If there is a mortgage on the property, there may not be a paper certificate and the title may pass electronically. Australia is moving towards electronic transfer of real estate property, and most States already conduct these transactions via an online platform.

Transfer of shares which are registered on the Australian Stock Exchange may be done via an "off-market" transfer. That is, without the use of a stockbroker. This is the method which is used for transfers between family members or from an estate to a beneficiary.

Each company which is listed on the Australian Stock Exchange nominates a share registry company which holds the register of shareholders of that company. BHP is a publicly listed company, on the Australian Stock Exchange.

In order to transfer the BHP stock to Mary, the executor must prepare a Transfer of Shares form, arrange for it to be signed by Mary, and forward it to the share registry company. There is no stamp duty on the transfer of shares in New South Wales. The share registry company will make the transfer, and forward a letter to both the executor and Mary as confirmation.

There are two ways to transfer the cash in the Westpac Bank account to Mary. Westpac Bank will close John's account when the estate is distributed to Mary. They will not just change the name on the account to Mary's name. The first is for the executor to obtain Mary's bank account details. This can be either an Australian bank account or her overseas bank account. There are no limits to the amount of money Mary can transfer to her overseas bank account, but she should consider the exchange rate and the bank's fees, which can be sizeable. The second method is for the executor to transfer the money into the lawyer's trust account first, ensure all of the debts and liabilities are paid, including his own legal fees or commission, and then transfer the remainder to Mary's nominated bank account.

5. Any forced heirship obligations to observe?

An Australian testator may give his assets to whoever he wishes, including to charity.

There are no forced heirship obligations, however, if an eligible family member feels that they have not been provided for sufficiently for their maintenance, education and advancement, they may make an application to the court for a part of the estate. There are rigorous evidentiary requirements to satisfy the court that the Will should be changed to benefit the applicant. Such an application is costly and time consuming.

Chapter 33

United Kingdom

by **Christian RM Brown**

ABOUT THE UNITED KINGDOM (UK)

Population	65.8 million
Religion	Christian 59.5% Muslim 4.4% Hindu 1.3% Other 9.1% None 25.7% (2011 est.)
Median age	40.6 years
Life expectancy	81.1 years
Legal system	Common law system
GDP per capita	USD44,300
Literacy	99%[1]
Labor force	agriculture: 1.3% industry: 15.2% services: 83.5%

Adapted from: "The World Factbook", www.cia.gov.

The UK is a sovereign country located off the northwestern coast of the European mainland. It is a unitary parliamentary democracy and constitutional monarchy. The current monarch is Queen Elizabeth II, who has reigned since 1952, making her the world's longest-serving current head of state. The capital is London, a global city and financial centre. The UK consists of four countries: England, Scotland, Wales and Northern Ireland. Apart from England, the countries have their own devolved governments, each with varying powers, but such power is delegated by the Parliament of the UK.

The UK has the world's sixth-largest economy by nominal gross domestic product (GDP), and the ninth-largest by purchasing power parity (PPP). It was the world's first industrialised country and the world's foremost power during the 19th and early 20th centuries. The UK remains a great power, with considerable economic, cultural, military, scientific and political influence internationally.[1]

CASE STUDY

John, a non-Muslim Singaporean citizen, domiciled in Singapore, has the following assets in his sole name as of 1 April 2020:

1   World Data Atlas, www.knoema.com.

- an apartment in London worth GBP1 million that he purchased for GBP800,000 on 1 June 2017;
- Glencore stock worth GBP1 million that he purchased for GBP900,000 on 1 June 2017; and
- a bank account with GBP1 million with Lloyds Bank that he uses for spending and making occasional trades in UK securities.

He has a Singapore Will and Trust that deals with his Singapore assets but not his UK assets. On his passing, John would like to give his UK property and Glencore stock to his wife Mary in Singapore, who is also a non-Muslim Singaporean and his GBP1 million cash to his son Peter. John, Mary and their son, Peter, are all residents of Singapore.

John is concerned about these questions:

1. What are the formalities of a UK Will?
2. Who can act as an executor in a UK Will?
3. Are professional executors permitted under the law?
4. Suppose John passes away on 1 June 2020. Are there any duties or taxes on John's estate?
5. What is the process of transferring his UK assets to his Singaporean wife, Mary, who is his sole beneficiary?
6. Are there any forced heirship obligations to be met?

1. Formalities of a UK Will

John is a Singaporean national, living in Singapore. He owns a London property, Glencore stock and has a Lloyds UK bank account which receives rental income from the property, all of which is in his sole name.

John wishes to give all his assets to his wife, Mary, on his death. He chooses to write a UK Will under one of the UK laws (England & Wales or Scotland) to deal with his UK estate only.

In order to write a legally valid UK will, John must:

- be age 18 or over;
- be of sound mind;
- make the Will voluntarily and under no duress;
- make the Will in writing, revoking earlier Wills;
- sign the Will in the presence of two witnesses who are both over the age of 18 and do not benefit from the Will; and
- have the Will signed by his two witnesses, in his presence, who each witness the other signing as witness.

If all of the above have been adhered to, the Will would be validly executed. If John makes any changes to his Will, he would have to meet the same requirements with a new Will or a Codicil, which acts as an addendum to the original Will.

John decides to engage a UK solicitor and wrote his Will on 1 April 2020.

2. Appointing executors in a UK Will

John needs to appoint an executor to be responsible for administering his estate, applying for probate in the UK and then distributing the assets of the estate in accordance with his wishes as set out in his Will.

The executor of John's UK Will may be an individual friend, family member or lawyer, or it can be a trust company. If a single individual, it is advisable for John to nominate a backup executor in his Will to act in the event the first executor is unable to act, for instance having predeceased John. The executor appointed would have the power under the Will to apply to the local court in the UK for the grant of probate.

The court would then grant the power to the executor to take ownership of John's UK assets as executor of the estate and then distribute to Mary as the beneficiary.

It is recommended that John appoints a UK person to be wxecutor of his Will such as a UK-based lawyer who understands the process and substance of John's Will and his UK assets.

John decided to appoint the UK lawyer who wrote his Will to be the executor of his Will, with another partner of the law firm as his backup.

3. Are there any duties or taxes on the estate?

UK Inheritance Tax (IHT) is a tax on the estate (the property, money and possessions) of someone who has died.

On his death, John's UK assets of GBP3 million would be within the scope of IHT. The value of the estate after exemptions and reliefs and the tax-free allowance (nil rate band) of GBP325,000 is charged to tax at the rate of 40%. As John is not domiciled within the UK (he is domiciled in Singapore), only his UK-situs assets fall within the scope of the UK's IHT net.

John's executor is responsible for determining the estate and settling any liabilities, one of which is any IHT due to Her Majesty's Revenue & Customs (HMRC). Only when that has been done can the net estate be distributed to the beneficiaries, in this case to his wife, Mary, and son, Peter.

For Mary, there is an unlimited Spouse Exemption available which exempts the value of UK assets passing under John's Will to Mary on his death. For Peter, there is no such exemption other than the nil rate band. This means that the GBP2 million in value (the property and shares) are exempt from IHT, leaving the cash of GBP1 million subject to IHT after the deduction of the £325,000 nil rate band, leaving £675,000 subject to IHT at 40%, with a tax of £270,000 which must be paid to HMRC before the executor is granted the power by the courts to distribute the assets to Mary and Peter.

This liability could be higher if John left more assets to Peter in his Will or none if he left everything to Mary.

To mitigate the eventual IHT bill, John might consider:

- Leaving everything to Mary so the Spouse Exemption applies to everything.

- Moving the cash destined for Peter to Singapore so it is outside of the scope of the IHT.
- Giving the shares to Peter before his passing and survive seven years after the gift, or the estate pays a tapered IHT reduced by 20% for each year he survives the gift past two years.
- Moving the assets into a trust, although generally that results in entry tax of 20% where the value exceeds the nil rate band and prohibitive annual taxes on the trustees.
- Selling the property and shares, and moving everything out of the UK.
- Purchasing life insurance sufficient enough to settle the IHT liability in the event of his death and assign the policy to a trust for the benefit of Mary and/or Peter.

Each of these strategies require expertise which is beyond the scope of this chapter to discuss. Furthermore, UK tax laws are constantly evolving. It is best to consult a UK chartered tax adviser or lawyer to advise you on the best strategies for your situation.

4. Process of transferring UK assets on death

There are three steps to take during the period of administering John's estate:
- to call in or collect John's assets;
- to pay off John's debts and liabilities, including funeral expenses and inheritance tax; and
- to distribute the estate in accordance with John's wishes laid down in his Will.

In order for the executor to transfer John's London apartment to Mary, a legal transfer of the property must be undertaken which would involve the assignment of any leases to the ownership of Mary and the completion and submission of form TR1 to the UK Property Registry in order to register Mary as the new legal title holder of the property, annexing a court copy of the grant of probate with the Will annexed in support of the transfer and Mary's identification documents and proof of residential address There would be no Stamp Duty or Land Tax due on the transfer because a transfer on death is exempt from tax.

In order for the executor to transfer the Glencore stock to Mary, he will need to complete and sign a Stock Transfer Form confirming Mary's details as the new owner or to make an application to the share registrar to transfer ownership electronically to Mary. The Registrar would require sight of a court copy of the grant of probate with the Will annexed, and Mary's identification documents and proof of residential address, in support of the transfer.

In order for the executor to transfer the cash in the Lloyd's Bank account to Peter, he will need to write to the bank with a court copy of the grant of probate with Will annexed, requesting that the money be transferred to Peter's account, setting out Peter's bank details and enclosing Peter's identification documents and proof of residential address.

5. Any forced heirship obligations to observe?

The UK has no forced heirship rules.

Chapter 34

United States

by **Geoffrey Lee**

ABOUT THE UNITED STATES (US)

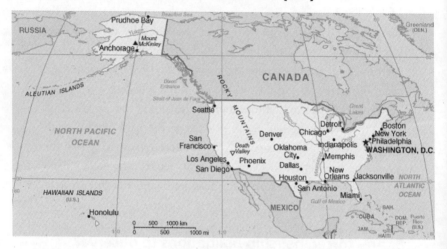

Population	333 million
Religion	Protestant 46.5% Roman Catholic 20.8% Jewish 1.9% Mormon 1.6% Other Christian 0.9% Muslim 0.9% Other 4% None 23.4%
Median age	38.5 years
Life expectancy	80.3 years
Legal system	Common law system at federal level; state legal systems based on common law, except Louisiana, where state law is based on Napoleonic civil code
GDP per capita	USD59,800

Literacy	99%[1]
Labor force	agriculture: 0.7% industry: 20.3% services: 79.0%

Adapted from: "The World Factbook", www.cia.gov.

The US is a country consisting of 50 states, a federal district, five major self-governing territories, and various possessions. At 3.8 million square miles, it is the world's fourth-largest country by total area. With an estimated population of over 332 million, the US is the third most populous country in the world (after China and India). The capital is Washington, DC, and the most populous city is New York City. A highly developed country, the US is the world's largest economy by nominal GDP, and accounts for approximately a quarter of global GDP. Although its population is 4% of the world total, it holds 29.4% of the total wealth in the world.[1]

CASE STUDY

John, a Singaporean non-Muslim, has the following US assets in his sole name as of 1 April 2020:

- an apartment in California worth USD1 million that he purchased for USD800,000 on 1 June 2017;
- Microsoft stock worth USD1 million that he purchased for USD800,000 on 1 June 2017; and
- a bank account with USD1 million with Chase Bank that he uses for spending and making trades in US stock.

He has a Singapore Will and Trust that deals with his Singapore assets but not his U.S. assets. On his passing, he wants to give his US assets to his wife Mary in Singapore, who is also a Singaporean non-Muslim.

John is concerned about these questions:

1. What are the formalities of a US Will?

---

1   World Data Atlas, www.knoema.com.

2. Who can act as an executor in his Will? Are professional executors permitted under the law?
3. Suppose John passes away. Are there any duties or taxes on John's estate?
4. What is the process of transferring his US assets to his Singaporean wife, Mary ,who is his sole beneficiary?
5. Are there any forced heirship obligations to be met?

1. Formalities of a US Will

Each US state has its specific probate code requirements for what constitutes a legally enforceable Will. The common requirements include:

- Your age: You must typically be over the age of 18 to make a Will.
- You must be of sound mind: This normally means that you have an understanding of what a Will does, what you own and your moral obligation towards your family members. You may be suffering some mental illness, but if you're lucid and aware of these things on the day you make your Will, it's usually considered that you had a sound mind when you made your Will.
- Your signature: You should sign your Will. The signature typically appears at the very end of the document.
- Witnesses: There should usually be at least two persons who must witness you signing your will and they must sign it themselves. Your witnesses should not be beneficiaries under the terms of your Will.

In California where I practice, the basic requirements for a Will include the following:[2]

- The testator must be at least 18 years old.
- The testator must be of sound mind.
- The Will must be signed by the testator.

2   California Probate Code 6100 -6113.

- The Will must be signed by at least two witnesses who are present at the same time.
- The Will must be in writing.

California also recognises holographic Wills. Such a Will is handwritten and signed by the testator, but witnesses are not required.

2. Appointing Executors in a US Will

The executor is the person appointed by the Will maker to petition his Will to be admitted by court for validation. The executor then manages and distributes the assets to the beneficiaries.

An executor can be an individual who is at least 18 years old.

An institution can be appointed executor. However, there is a risk that the institution may not act in the future for whatever reason. I suggest that an institution or professional fiduciary or attorney can be the backup executor after the spouse and children.

3. Are there any duties or taxes on the estate?

A US permanent resident residing in the US and US citizen are subject to US estate tax on his worldwide assets on death after reaching the estate tax exemption. Current exemption as of 2020 is USD11.58 million per person. However, the amount will be reduced to USD5 million (adjusted for inflation) per person in 2026. John is not a US resident; however, his estate would be subject to US estate tax only on property located in the US on the date of his death.

What is considered US situs assets for the purpose of calculating estate tax include any real estate interest in the US and ownership holdings in US incorporated or non-incorporated companies such as Microsoft or any US Limited Liability Company (LLC).

Certain assets are exempt from US estate taxes and these include securities that generate portfolio interest such as unit trusts, bank accounts not used in connection with a trade or business in the US such as his Chase bank account and insurance proceeds. However, cash in a brokerage account is not exempted.

In John's case, his US situs estate for the purpose of estate duty is USD2 million value based on his apartment and Microsoft stock; the cash in his Chase bank account is not included; but the bank account is subject to probate proceedings.

As a non-US person, John's estate is provided an exemption of USD60,000. The net amount of USD1,940,000 is then subject to 40% US estate duty. In other words, the estate duty bill to be paid on his estate is equal to USD776,000 or about SGD1.1 million!

4. Process of transferring US assets on death

There are three steps to take during this period of administering John's estate:

- to call in the John's assets;
- to pay off John's debts and liabilities, including estate duty; and
- to distribute the estate in accordance with John's wishes as found in his Will.

The role and power of executors is determined according to state law. The beneficiaries are vested with the beneficial interest in the estate, although the personal representative holds legal title during administration.

Executors must identify, gather and value the assets of the decedent, arrange for the preparation and filing of required tax returns and the payment of federal and state estate taxes, for which they are generally personally liable if failed to pay but distribute to beneficiaries of the estate.

An executor is responsible for filing the federal estate tax return, which is due nine months after the deceased person's death or an extension granted for another six months for filing. However, payment has to be made within the first nine months.

In order to transfer the California property to John's wife, the executor would have to go through California probate proceedings, which includes:

- File petition to admit the Will of the decedent.
- Publish newspaper notice.
- Mail Notice of Hearing.
- Court hearing confirms the validity of the Will and appoints the executor of the Will.
- Court issues Letters Testamentary.
- Executor will use the court letters to administer the estate, including marshalling the estate assets and pay applicable taxes.
- Notice to creditors.
- Prepare Inventory and Appraisal for all decedent estate; real property, Microsoft shares and bank account.
- File Federal Estate Tax and income taxes for the estate.
- Executor may sell the properties if beneficiary prefers.
- File First and Final Accounting and Order for Distribution.
- Mail Notice of Hearing.

The court hears the case and the order is granted to distribute his assets pursuant to the Will. Attorney fees in probate are statutory, based on USD3 million probate estate gross value; regardless of tax or mortgage, estimated attorney fees are USD43,000 and the executor is entitled to the same statutory fee. This excludes cost for court filing and charges; approximately another USD3,000.

In order to transfer the Microsoft stock and the cash in the JP Morgan bank account to John's wife, the same procedure as for transferring the California property would apply.

5. Any forced heirship obligations to observe?

There are no forced heirship obligations that John has to observe.

Chapter 35

Foreigner in Singapore

by **Patrick Tan** and **Andrew Wong**

In the previous nine chapters, we learned that if you are Singaporean and you own foreign assets, then you should write a Will in that country to deal with those assets.

Would the reverse be true? That is, if a foreigner owns assets in Singapore, should he be writing a Singapore Will to deal with his Singapore assets? It turns out that the answer is yes.

When a foreigner passes away in Singapore with a Singapore Will, probate can be done on his estate in Singapore separate from everywhere else that he may have assets. This is the most efficient way to deal with his international estate – which is to have probate performed simultaneously in each country.

We at Fortis Law have written many Wills for foreigners who own assets in Singapore. We have also dealt with their estates when they passed away. Let's look at a simple case study to show how foreigners can get their estate planning done in Singapore.

CASE STUDY

Rolando is a Filipino and Catholic from the Philippines. He is a permanent resident of Singapore.

He is married to Wanda who is also a Filipino and Catholic. They have two teenage children who attend a Singapore international school. He has a DBS bank account, listed Singapore shares and a fully paid up condo in Orchard Road – all solely owned by him.

He wants to give all his Singapore assets to his wife Wanda on his death.

WRITING A SINGAPORE WILL

Rolando should write a Singapore Will to deal with his Singapore assets.

He is subject to the Philippines national law which has elements that are different from Singapore's. For example, Rolando is subject to forced heirship where a portion of his estate is reserved for members of his family. There is estate duty and a strong conjugal property regime where properties, whether acquired before or during marriage by one partner, are considered owned by his spouse upon marriage. Whether Rolando is from the Philippines or from any other country, it is clear that as a Singapore lawyer, we cannot advise on matters of foreign law.

Therefore, to assist Rolando with his estate planning:

- We recommend that he writes a standalone Singapore Will that deals only with his Singapore assets. His Singapore Will would have to have a revocation clause that revokes any previous Singapore Wills that deal only with his Singapore assets. If he has written a Philippines Will, he would have to review it with his Philippines lawyer to make sure its revocation clause does not revoke his Singapore Will.

- We ask that he signs a declaration on our Letter of Engagement that he accepts that the distribution of his estate may be subject to the laws of his nationality and domicile, and that we cannot and did not advise him of his national law.

- We recommend that he appoints an executor who is based in Singapore even though there is no requirement for executors to be Singaporean, or even be based in Singapore. By appointing a lawyer or a licensed Trust company as executor, his estate can be probated and distributed more speedily than if he were to appoint someone who is overseas.

- If he has minor children in Singapore, he should appoint a guardian in his Will in the event he and Wanda pass away together. Such a guardian who is appointed in the Will is called a testamentary guardian. His testamentary guardian is likely to be a relative who lives in the Philippines. Rolando can also consider appointing a temporary guardian who is typically a person resident in Singapore who can temporarily look after his children until the testamentary guardian arrives to take over the permanent guardianship of his children.

ON ROLANDO'S PASSING

Assuming that Rolando is resident in Singapore at the time of his death:

- The executor would apply for a grant of probate in the Singapore courts, on the basis of the Singapore Will.
- Once the grant has been obtained, the executor can proceed to follow the Will to distribute Rolando's assets to Wanda.

CONCLUSION

There is a significant number of foreign persons in Singapore who are likely to own enough Singapore assets to be concerned about estate planning. If one were to add the number of permanent residents[1] and the number of employment pass holders,[2] the total is close to 750,000.

For them, especially for those with young children, the need to plan is pressing given that they tend to travel frequently and their permanent families may be far away from Singapore.

---

1   "Population and Population Structure", Singapore Department of Statistics, www.singstat.gov.sg.
2   "Foreign workforce numbers", Ministry of Manpower, www.mom.gov.sg.

Chapter 36

Common Reporting Standard

by **Dominique Burnett**

The tax information reporting landscape has changed substantially in recent years as governments are increasingly cooperating to deal with money laundering and tax evasion across borders.

FATCA is a US legislation which was enacted in 2010 with the aim of combating tax evasion by US persons. Following FATCA, the Organization for Economic Cooperation and Development (OECD) formed an initiative for global tax transparency known as the Common Reporting Standard (CRS) in 2014. CRS is a broad reporting regime that draws extensively on the intergovernmental approach to the implementation of FATCA.

How do these tax regulations affect you? It depends on whether as a Singaporean, you own reportable assets outside of Singapore or perhaps all that you own are located in Singapore.

WHAT IS CRS AND WHY IS IT RELEVANT?

CRS is the Common Reporting Standard, a system whereby countries can share information between tax authorities regarding their tax payers. It was introduced as a concept by the OECD to help protect the integrity of tax systems by fighting tax evasion. As a result, governments around the world are introducing new reporting and information-gathering requirements for financial institutions (FIs).

Under the CRS, all reporting FIs (such as banks, investment managers and Trust service providers) are required to determine each of their account holders' tax residency and may be legally obliged to share financial information with the relevant tax authorities. An account holder under CRS may be an individual or a company and the category includes all settlors, protectors and beneficiaries of a Singapore Trust.

As of now, CRS legislation implemented by countries taking part in the information exchange requires and empowers all reporting Financial Institutions to collect and retain CRS information for all non-local tax residents. The CRS information may be provided to the FI in the form of a self-certification by the account holder.

For example, in the case of a bank, the CRS information reportable include your name, address, jurisdictions of tax residence, Tax Identification Numbers (TINs), date and place of birth (for individuals), account number, account balance and certain payments made into the account.

Singapore implemented CRS in January 2017. Information collection is now in force and FIs reporting CRS information for 2017 must make reports to IRAS starting on 31 May 2018.[1]

ALL MY ASSETS ARE IN SINGAPORE. DOES CRS AFFECT ME?

CRS deals with reporting on individuals holding assets outside their jurisdiction of tax residence. If you are tax resident in Singapore and all your assets are held in Singapore, there will be no reporting obligations under CRS, as all your assets will be taxed domestically. However, when dealing with financial institutions (for example, banks, investment managers, etc) you will have to provide them with a self-certification of your tax residence in Singapore along with details of your tax identification number (commonly called your NRIC Number in the case of Singaporeans). Under CRS, each country is entitled to impose penalties on account holders that do not provide these to the FI requesting the details.

---

1   "The Income Tax (International Tax Compliance Agreements) (Common Reporting Standard) Regulations 2016 ("CRS Regulations") incorporate the requirements of the CRS into Singapore's domestic legislative framework. The CRS Regulations has entered into force on 1 January 2017." –https://www.iras.gov.sg/irashome/CRS/#CRSFilingRequirements

REPORTING OBLIGATIONS

Tom has assets outside Singapore. What reporting obligations does he have?

Suppose Tom is from Singapore and he has a bank account and property in the Philippines.

The Philippines bank may request Tom's TIN and personal details (address, date of birth) as the account holder of the bank account. Tom will be obliged to provide these to the bank; if he does not, the bank may close the account. The bank will have the obligation under CRS to report to the tax authorities on any income and assets held in Tom's account.

Property is not generally included in CRS reporting if it is owned by an individual. However, if the property is rented out and the rental income goes into the Philippines bank account, then this will be included in the bank's CRS report on Tom.

I've written a Will. What reporting obligations do I have?

A Will does not affect an individual's obligations under CRS. Property that passes via a Will must be reported by a financial institution once transferred, if the recipient is a reportable person under CRS.

I have set up a Trust. What reporting obligations do I have?

As the settlor of a Trust, you will have the same obligation to provide the Trust service provider with a self-certification in respect of your tax residence and personal details as with a bank.

Whether the Trust has reporting obligations depends on the nature of the Trust. Under CRS, a Trust is treated as an entity (just like companies) and so it can be either a Financial Institution (FI), or a Non-Financial Entity (NFE). If it falls under the category of

Non-Financial Institution, it could be either an Active NFE or a Passive NFE.

The Active NFE category is limited to certain types of institutions, so it is most likely that your Trust will be either a FI or a Passive NFE.

A FI Trust will have its own reporting obligations. In this case, the Trust (via its trustees) will be obliged to report on its account holders. For a Trust, most CRS jurisdictions consider the account holders to be: settlor, protector, beneficiaries with a vested interest or discretionary beneficiaries who have received a distribution during the reporting period.

A passive NFE Trust does not report for itself. Reporting will be made by a bank or other FI with which it has accounts in respect of the controlling persons of the Trust. For a Trust, most CRS jurisdictions consider the controlling persons to be the same as the account holders of a FI Trust.

CONCLUSION

Chapter 37

Finding the Right Estate Planner: 10 Questions to Ask

by **Keon Chee**

Estate planning can be difficult to think about because of the variety of concerns you may have, including the following:

- Is the gifting in my Will fair to my family?
- Should I have a trust to stagger money to my children?
- Can my spouse who is my LPA donee manage my affairs?
- How do I safeguard the condo I leave to my son in the event he divorces?
- Who can manage my investments when I am gone?
- Can my partners take over my position in our business?
- How do I transfer my Beijing property to my daughter?

I can safely say that no estate planner can competently answer all of these questions that span across such a diverse set of concerns. You can, however, find an estate planner who has a good sense of your concerns and is able to coordinate the advice of other specialists to give you a holistic and well-balanced estate plan.

10 QUESTIONS TO ASK

You are ready to take action and you are going to meet an estate planner. Here is a list of 10 questions you can consider asking the estate planner.

1. What qualifications do you have?

He should have a basic degree such as in law, accounting or finance, or a professional qualification such as the CFP and ChFC. Persons with these academic backgrounds would have received a basic grounding in some areas of estate planning in their studies.

Some estate planners have specialist knowledge and may have some of these additional qualifications or knowledge in their background:

- An Advanced Diploma qualification or Advanced Certificates from STEP.
- A lawyer in private wealth practice in a law firm.
- A trust advisor in a licensed trust company.
- A financial adviser whose practice revolves around estate planning.

2. What estate planning have you done for yourself?

It gives me greater comfort to know the estate planner has done his own planning. How would you feel if the estate planner asking you to do a Will or LPA has not done any planning for his own family?

3. What estate planning have you done for people like me?

Replace the "like me" with your unique needs, such as a private business owner, a caregiver of a person with special needs, a divorced mother with young children, a foreigner with assets in Singapore.

Look for experience that they have planned for people like you.

4. Can you help me create a comprehensive estate plan?

Most people need at least a Will, Trust and LPA. It is important that your estate planner is knowledgeable in these basic areas. Very likely, you would also need advice on your insurance policies and the homes you own. You may also need help with your private business and foreign investments.

As mentioned, no estate planner can be expected to be competent in so many areas but the estate planner you choose should be able to coordinate the advice of other specialists for you.

5. Do you conduct periodic reviews?

Some estate planners will review your plans every 12 months or when necessary. You will go through life events or a change in your finances, and adjustments to your plan are necessary to keep it from becoming outdated.

Periodic reviews are thus important. Be prepared to pay a reasonable professional fee for the review.

6. How good is your firm's admin support?

You want to know if your documents will be handled efficiently and confidentially. How are your documents filed away and retrieved? Who is the administrator you can follow up with in case the estate planner is not available?

7. Who will take over your work when you leave the company or retire?

You may prefer a larger company that has been around for many years, knowing that if your estate planner leaves for whatever reason, there is someone else there to take over. This is especially true if the estate planner is a few decades older than you are.

8. Suppose I pass away tomorrow. Can you tell me how my plan will be implemented?

Your estate planner should know how your Will and Trust are activated, how assets are called in and managed. He should give you an idea what fees are chargeable based on your situation today.

9. Can you give me a fee estimate?

"How much do you charge?" should never be the first question you ask an estate planner.

The amount you will spend depends on the complexity of your needs, the location of your assets and your estate planner's experience level. It also depends on how your estate planner charges.

Some may offer a free consultation for the first visit while others will charge you.

Some estate planners charge only when you obtain a service from them. Some charge fees for their time especially when you have a non-standard situation or one that requires research and coordination. The fee may range between $200 and $800 an hour. If you plan to use one who charges this way, ask approximately how long the process will take, so you have an idea of the total cost from the start.

Estate planning is a professional service and paying a fee obligates the estate planner to give you advice specific to your situation, rather than general advice that may not directly address your concerns.

10. Can you provide references?

Good estate planners usually have clients willing to vouch for them.

CONCLUSION

Your estate plan is one of the most important plans in your life. The estate planner you work with will help you ensure that your plan is well set up, updated and executed.

Having a technically competent estate planner is a must but that alone may not be enough. Think of your relationship with your estate planner as an ongoing, long-term relationship. Then ask yourself these questions:

- Do I have rapport with him?
- Do I feel comfortable sharing personal details about my life with him?
- Do I understand what he is saying?
- Do I agree with his general values about family and people?
- Does he listen carefully to what my concerns are?

Use your instincts to determine if a particular estate planner is right for you.

Contributors

Chapters 1, 2, 7 & 17
Samuel Tan
Director, First Light Estate Planning Pte Ltd
Email: samuel.tan@firstlight.com.sg
Contact: +65 9168 8264

Samuel runs an estate planning company that aims to provide estate planning, wealth protection, and business succession solutions rooted in strong values.

Prior to his current position, Sam has crafted more than 4,000 Wills and was the deputy head of the legal department in a licensed trust company with more than 700 estate planners.

He is committed to helping families understand that the foundation of estate planning is not just about getting your final intentions documented, but also appreciating the value of proper planning for you and your loved ones.

"Helping families pass their values to future generations is what I do best."

Chapter 1
Patrick Chang
Founding Director, SimplyWills Pte Ltd
Email: patrick@simplywills.com.sg
Contact: +65 9698 4444

Patrick is the Founding Director of SimplyWills Pte Ltd, an organisation specialising in writing Wills.

He started his career as a bank manager in 1984 and moved on to become an insurance practitioner in 1988. He helped some of his colleagues achieve the prestigious Million Dollar Round Table (MDRT) award during his stay in the insurance industry.

He started to practise Will writing in 2001 and founded his own Will writing company in 2006 and has a team of more than 1,000 trained Will Planners. His team has written more than 18,000 Wills and helped more than 1,200 families in applying for the grant of probate/letters of administration.

Chapters 3 & 4
Shen Kiat TAN BBA/LLB/TEP
Managing Director & Lawyer, Kith & Kin Law Corporation
Email: shenkiat.tan@kithkinlaw.com
Contact: +65 8688 4783

Shen Kiat ("SK") is a Singapore-qualified private-client solicitor in the area of Succession, Trusts, Estates & Mental Capacity (STEM Law). He is also a registered professional donee and deputy, and is currently one of the emerging figures in the mental capacity law and practice space, is passionate about raising legal literacy and teaches law at the Singapore University of Social Sciences and the Singapore Association of Social Workers.

He believes in keeping healthy families strong and purpose-driven. In his spare time, he helps out at Kizuna cafe bakery, his family's business started in 1983.

Chapters 6 & 35
Patrick Tan
Founder & CEO, Fortis Law Corporation
Email: patrick.tan@fortislaw.com.sg
Contact: +65 6535 8100

Patrick's areas of practice include general litigation and arbitration, private client matters and real estate. He is a Notary Public, Commissioner for Oaths, a Fellow of the Singapore Institute of Arbitrators, as well as an accredited Associate Mediator with the Singapore Mediation Centre. He also currently serves as a Volunteer Mediator with the State Courts of Singapore.

Patrick obtained his LLB (Hons) at the Nottingham University, where he received top honours in several subjects, clinching academic awards in land law, company law and partnership law. In 2017, he was awarded the Singapore Skillfuture Study Award and successfully completed the SAL-INSEAD Law Firm Leadership Programme.

In 2007, Patrick steered the firm into becoming the first law firm in Singapore to be accredited with the PrimeLaw Practice Management Excellence Standard awarded by the Law Society of Singapore.

Chapter 10
Ronald Wong
Managing Director, Financial Perspectives Pte Ltd
Email: ronald@fp-edu.com
Contact: +65 8233 0259

Ronald is the Managing Director of Financial Perspectives Pte Ltd. With close to 20 years of consulting and teaching experience, he has consulted and coordinated planning for business owners and high net worth individuals in the region. His experience ranges from personal financial planning to coordination of private placements and family wealth and legacy planning. Teaching is his passion, and he has developed many professional courses and regularly taught in various financial institutions and universities, specialising in business and finance subjects.

Ronald has a "3-E Mission" in the Marketplace: to Educate the public about financial planning, to Empower them to take personal ownership and make the right choices and Encourage them to take practical action towards achieving their financial aspirations.

Chapter 11
Eric Seah
Senior Financial Services Manager, Prudential Assurance Company Singapore
Email: eric.seahsm@gmail.com
Contact: +65 9387 7385

Eric has over 25 years' experience in financial services. He joined Prudential as soon as he completed his National Service as a platoon commander and plans to remain in the same industry until the day he retires. In 2019, he was Winner of Financial Planning Awards 2019 – Insurance Open Category organised by the Financial Planning Association of Singapore. He won an Outstanding and Dedicated Moderator award in 2018 for his work in the industry-wide Agency Management Training Course (AMTC). His lifelong passion is helping families and businesses with their financial and estate planning needs.

Chapter 12
Louise Gan
Director, finexis advisory Pte Ltd
Email: louise.gan@finexis.com.sg
Contact: +65 9062 6922

Louise Gan has two decades of experience in the financial services industry. In her corporate capacity, she has held roles in training, product development and spearheaded the High Net Worth business for onr of the largest insurers in Singapore. She has coached more than 1,000 advisers on High Net Worth concepts and solutions.

She now runs her own advisory team, working with clients in the region on their estate and legacy planning. She is also grooming the next generation of advisers and collaborating with other financial practitioners to deliver comprehensive solutions for their clients. Louise believes in engaging clients beyond their financial concerns and has an affable and practical style.

Chapter 12
Thomas Lim
Director, finexis advisory Pte Ltd
Email: thomas.lim@finexis.com.sg
Contact: +65 9061 9422

Thomas Lim has over 24 years' experience in the financial services business, where he specialises in the HNW market in Singapore and the Asia Pacific region.

His success comes from his fundamental principle of genuinely having a liking for people, treating them as friends rather than as business transactions.

He believes in forming strong and meaningful relationships with clients based on integrity and trust, and is equipped with confident technical knowledge and a capacity to deliver value-added service in areas of business insurance, wealth management and estate planning, which has been the foundation to his stellar career.

Chapter 13
Adam Wang CFA

Chief Executive Officer, Kredens Capital Management Pte Ltd
Email: adam.wang@kredenscapital.com
Contact: +65 6291 0297

Adam specialises in multi-strategy investing including global credit, equities and special situations, and has previously managed Assets Under Management (AUM) in excess of USD500 million. Prior to that, Adam was a research analyst who conducted bottom-up analysis to identify new public and private direct investments in investment grade, high yield and distressed and special situations in Asia. He assisted the portfolio manager to oversee USD800 million in AUM.

He obtained a Master's degree in Financial Engineering from Tepper Business School (Carnegie Mellon University) and Nanyang Business School, Singapore. He graduated with First Class Honors in Electrical and Electronics Engineering from Nanyang Technological University, Singapore.

Chapter 14
Victor Tang

Personal Wealth Manager/Estate Planner
Email: victortangkh@gmail.com
Contact: +65 9662 4675

Victor has more than 20 years in the estate planning profession, with a dedication that extends to his life experience with his four boys and three girls.

A regular guest speaker on TV and radio stations, he is consulted on management, both in the financial aspect of wealth accumulation, preservation and succession, as well as managing the challenges of parenting.

Victor's expertise lies in financial management of high net worth individuals, entrepreneurs and parents with deep aspirations for their children, ensuring their wealth is distributed to maximise growth, allowing them to spend their time on what they truly care about in life.

His clientele spreads over Singapore, Malaysia, Indonesia, Thailand, Taiwan, China, Japan, Australia, Germany, UK and USA.

Chapter 15
Angelina Hing

Managing Director, Integro Law Chambers LLC
Email: angelina@integrolaw.com.sg
Contact: +65 6909 0045

In the early years of her career, Angelina was an established litigator, handling high-value corporate disputes. She is also an Attorney and Counsellor at Law in the New York State courts.

She was a district judge of the Family Justice Courts from 2009 to 2016, and accumulated a wealth of experience adjudicating and mediating complex issues relating to child custody, including difficult issues of international relocation and allegations of child abduction, as well as all financial issues relating to divorce.

She is an accredited Principal Mediator with the Singapore Mediation Centre (SMC). She is also a Certified Mediator with the Singapore International Mediation Institute (SIMI) and the Centre for Effective Dispute Resolution (CEDR).

Chapter 16
Chong Yue-En
Managing Director, Bethel Chambers LLC
Email: cye@bethelchambers.com
Contact: +65 6980 0230
Website: www.bethelchambers.com

Chong Yue-En is the Founder of Bethel Chambers LLC, a full-suite boutique family practice firm that provides enabling and empowering solutions to its clients. As a specialist in family law, he specialises in complex domestic and international work relating to divorce, guardianship, adoption, mental capacity, elder law, estate planning, trust and probate law. As the Vice-Chairman of Singapore Law Society's Probate Practice and Succession Planning committee, he frequently engages the courts and the government in the development of mental capacity, probate and family practice in Singapore.

His international family practice has led him to work with legal counsel from different jurisdictions including, Canada, Australia, Japan, Malaysia, China and the Netherlands. Besides English, he speaks Mandarin and works well with clients from diverse backgrounds.

Chapter 18
Masagoes Abdul Karim
Managing Director, Aureus Law Corporation
Email: mas@aureuslaw.com.sg
Contact: +65 9060 6023

Masagoes (or Mas) was admitted as a barrister of Lincoln's Inn in July 1985 and as an Advocate & Solicitor of Singapore in May 1986. In the last 17 years, he has focused his work in the areas of estate planning, administration of estates, wills and trusts. He enjoys spending time doing advisory work on estate planning for individuals and business succession for corporate clients. He has worked with both local and foreign clients in organising their estates. He is very familiar with the financial services industry, having sat for various examinations, including the ChFC, CLU and AFIIBI. He is an associate fellow of the Islamic Institute of Banking and Insurance (UK) with significant legal and industry experience in Islamic insurance and banking.

Chapters 21 & 22
Yang Hezhou
Director, First Business Consultants Pte Ltd
Email: yang@askfirstbiz.com
Contact: +65 8233-3228

Yang started First Business Consultants to provide a full suite of accounting and corporate secretarial services to local SMEs. The company serves several well-known local brands across a wide number of industries. In the past two years, the firm has expanded its offerings overseas and today has associate accounting firms in Hong Kong, Malaysia, China and Cambodia.

Prior to this, he oversaw the accounting department of one of largest estate planning companies in Southeast Asia that provided services in Wills, Trusts, estate administration and company incorporations.

Chapters 22 & 23
Michael Seow
Senior Financial Services Director, Prudential Assurance Co Singapore Pte Ltd
Email: michaelseow@pruadviser.com
Contact: +65 9627 5821

Michael is a veteran in the financial planning industry, having started his practice in 1986. He is a highly experienced practitioner in estate planning, especially for business owners and their families in the area of business succession planning.

He is a member of the Society of Trust and Estate Practitioners (STEP) as well as being a Chartered Financial Consultant (ChFC).

He is a sought-after speaker and trainer in Singapore and in the region. Michael is past President of the Financial Services Managers Association (FSMA), which is the only voluntary organisation within the Financial Services & Insurance Industry in Singapore that is dedicated to serving the needs of agency field leaders and managers in their pursuit of excellence and professionalism.

Chapter 24
Joe Teng
Regional Head of Sales – South East Asia, Amicorp Singapore Pte Ltd
Email: j.teng@amicorp.com
Contact: +65 6532 2902

Joe is a Dutch national and permanent resident of Singapore. Joe has a degree in tax law from the University of Amsterdam. He worked in Jakarta from 1992 to 1998, joining PT DBS Securities Indonesia in 1993.

In 1998, Joe moved to Singapore to join Dresdner Private Banking as team head, covering the Indonesian and Malaysian markets. He later moved to Commerzbank and subsequently was Vice President at DBS Private Banking. He joined Amicorp in March 2005 as Managing Director for Amicorp's Singapore office.

Joe has extensive experience with structures for Indonesian families and has in-depth knowledge of the Indonesian economy, business environment and culture.

Joe speaks Dutch and English, and has knowledge of German, French and Indonesian.

Chapter 25
Joy ME Lim
Director of a Singapore Single Family Office
Email: joymelim@gmail.com
Contact: +65 9238 2337

Joy has practical work experience in the legal and financial services sector. She has worked in London, New York, Hong Kong, Shanghai and Singapore.

She started her legal career in London, practicing as a barrister-at-law and Crown Prosecutor. On returning to Singapore, Joy worked for US investment banks, including JP Morgan, Morgan Stanley, Citigroup Smith Barney and UBS. Her expertise is in asset allocation, trusts, inter-generational wealth and asset protection, estate planning, family office set-up and investment advisory services.

Joy is a graduate of the London School of Economics (LLM), and the University of Kent (BA (Hons)).

Chapter 26
Wong Wai Sam
Founder and CEO, WS Wong & Co
Email: wong.wai.sam@wswong.com.my
Contact: +60 3-8075 5189

Wai Sam specialises in property and conveyancing, banking and finance, corporate practices, litigation and estate planning.

She was admitted as an Advocate and Solicitor of the High Court of Malaya in 2002. She has vast experience in Islamic banking, including advising on the RM720 million Sukuk Musyarakah issued by KL Sentral.

Her corporate commercial expertise includes joint ventures, mergers and acquisitions, debt restructuring, share sale transactions, and listing exercises on Bursa Malaysia. Her commercial litigation work total more than RM1,000 million in aggregate claims.

Chapter 27
Kevin Omar Sidharta
Partner, ABNR Counsellors at Law
Email: ksidharta@abnrlaw.com
Contact: +62 21 250 5125

Kevin has extensive expertise across a wide range of practice areas, including restructuring & insolvency, TMT, banking & finance, real estate & construction,

M&A, foreign investment and cross-border inheritance, and probate & estate planning.

He is listed as a "Next Generation Partner" for Restructuring & Insolvency by Legal 500 Asia Pacific, making him one of only five Indonesian lawyers ranked for this practice area, and is recommended for Real Estate and IT & Telecoms. He is also listed as a "Name to Know in Indonesia" for Restructuring & Insolvency by Global Restructuring Review (GRR).

He majored in Business Law at the University of Indonesia, and earned his LLM degree in International Business Law from Leiden University.

Chapter 28
Julalak Phunsawat
Attorney-at-Law
Head of Family Law Department, Vovan & Associes Co Ltd
Email: julalak.phunsawat@vovan-bangkok.com
Contact: +66(0)2 261 3138

Julalak obtained certification by the Thai Bar under the Royal Patronage of Thailand. Her expertise is in international family law for both international and Thai clients, especially in the areas of marriage, pre-nuptial contracts, parental power, separation, international divorce, Wills and inheritance.

She has a Master of Laws with honours from Paul Cezanne Aix-Marseille III University, Aix-en-Provence in France, where she studied under the Eiffel Scholarship, the top scholarship offered by the French government. She obtained a Bachelor of Law in Public Laws from Thammasart University, Bangkok, Thailand. She speaks fluent Thai, French and English.

Chapter 29
Hilario B Paredes (Larry)
Partner, Paredes and Paredes Law Offices
Email: larryparedes@paredeslaw.com.ph
Contact: +632 634.8967

Hilario B Paredes is a Filipino lawyer practicing in estate planning, succession, real property, banking, infrastructure, telecommunications, corporate, commercial and immigration laws. After becoming the youngest partner in a major law firm in 2003, he founded his own firm in 2006, Paredes Lopez & Garcia Law Office (now Paredes and Paredes Law Offices), a full service law firm catering to local and multinational clients, which has established itself as one of the reputable law firms in the Philippines. When he is not at work, Larry, as he is fondly called, rides motorcycles around and outside the country, or plays golf with friends and colleagues.

Chapter 30
Bui Tien Long (Rudy Bui)
Founder, Vietnamlaw and Practice
Email: rudybui@vietnamlawandpractice.com
Contact: +84 909 069 332

Bui Tien Long earned a Master of Law (LLM) at Transnational Law and Business University in Seoul, Korea (TLBU), and a Master of Business Administration (MBA) at Shidler College of Business, University of Hawaii at Manoa. As a law practitioner, Bui Tien Long is a qualified lawyer with more than 12 years' experience in handling inbound and outbound investment, corporate and M&A, construction and real estate business, arbitration and mediation, and international family practice. Bui Tien Long was honorably granted bar scholarships by International Bar Association (IBA) and Inter-Pacific Bar Association (IPBA) as Young Lawyers of Developing Countries.

Chapter 31
Jason Tian
Founding partner, Landing Law Offices
Email: jie.tian@landinglawyer.com
Contact: +86 13816548421

Jason Tian is a senior partner at Landing Law Offices, which is the first Chinese-led global law firm headquartered in Shanghai with branch offices in most major Chinese cities and more than a dozen in foreign countries. Before joining Landing, Jason has worked at Clifford Chance, Zhonglun, Zhongyin and Dentons Shanghai.

His main areas of practice cover cross-border family law matters such as estate planning, divorces, and inbound and outbound investments, real estate, and arbitration and litigation. Most of the time, he represents foreign clients in dealing with inheritance and divorces involving real properties and corporate shares, and over the recent years, his team has been focusing on advising Chinese HNWIs in creating offshore estate plan employing offshore trusts.

Chapter 32
Lynda Babister
Principal, Babister Legal
Email: lynda@babisterlegal.com.au
Contact: +61 0418 604 098

Lynda Babister is an experienced Australian estate planning lawyer. Following a decade of working in the Sydney CBD, just over ten years ago she opened her own firm in the Wollongong area of New South Wales. She spends the majority of her time helping clients to organise their estates. Lynda has worked with clients all around the world, from simple estates to those needing complex trust and estate planning advice. Lynda has a down to earth, practical style, ensuring her clients understand her advice.

Chapter 33
Christian RM Brown CTA, ATT, TEP
Managing Director, Lutea Advisory Services Pte Ltd
Email: cbrown@lutea.sg
Contact: +65 6256 8146

Christian is a Chartered Tax Adviser, Trust & Estate Practitioner and member of the Association of Taxation Technicians with over 25 years' experience in UK taxation and 15 years as a trustee. He spent five years with HMRC, three years with Ernst & Young, before joining Lutea in the UK on 1 July 2002, moving to Jersey in 2006 and then to Hong Kong to set up the office on 1 February 2009. Christian has been working with clients in Asia since joining Lutea and opened the Singapore office on 1 April 2019.

Chapter 34
Geoffrey Lee
Principal Attorney, Legato Law
Email: Geoffrey@LegatoLawFirm.com
Contact: +1 408-645-0100

Geoffrey Lee is the founder of Legato Law, which he established in 2015. He enhances the firm's offerings with several definitive areas of expertise. As a certified specialist in estate planning, trust and probate law, his work is widely commended by clients who find comfort in his ability to bring clarity to a complex process.

He has vast international business experience and has worked in Singapore, Hong Kong, San Francisco and New York. Besides English, he is fluent in Mandarin, Cantonese and Shanghainese, with a strong knowledge of cultures to deal with ethnically diverse clients.

Chapter 35
Andrew Wong
Associate, Fortis Law Corporation
Email: andrew.wong@fortislaw.com.sg
Contact: +65 6645 4505

Andrew is an Advocate & Solicitor of the Supreme Court of Singapore. At present, he serves as an Associate in Fortis Law Corporation and a Legal Advisor to FortisWills Pte Ltd. His main legal interests revolve around private client practice and personal law, including Wills, Probate & Letters of Administration, Elder Law, Family Law and Criminal Law.

Andrew is also active in the firm's community outreach and regularly conducts legal talks at various private events, public libraries, and Lifepoint, a voluntary welfare organisation.

Prior to being called to the Singapore Bar, Andrew graduated with a Bachelor of Laws Magna Cum Laude from the Singapore Management University, where he also served as President of the SMU Law Society.

Chapter 36
Dominique Burnett

Former director of international trust & fiduciary services provider
Email: dominique.gough@gmail.com

Dominique Burnett is a member of the Society of Trust and Estate Practitioners and a Fellow of the Chartered Governance Institute. She holds an MSc in Corporate Governance from Bournemouth University and a PhD in Cultural Studies from the University of London. Dominique entered the private client services industry in 2000 and has since gained considerable international private client, trust and company management experience in her native Jersey, as well as London, Geneva, Singapore and Auckland. She was most recently a director of an international trust and fiduciary services company in Europe.

About the Author

Keon Chee is an estate planner with many years' experience in advising families and businesses on their succession and wealth management needs. He has the ability to relate to people and give insightful advice that is backed by experience, sound technical knowledge and a matchless ability to simplify.

Keon has degrees in Mathematics and Computer Science from Southern Illinois University and obtained an MBA from Columbia University. After working in finance for many years, he went on to obtain a Law degree from the University of London.

Keon is a sought-after estate planner and trainer, and commentator on estate and financial matters. He is also co-author of a few best-selling books published by Marshall Cavendish, including books on Islamic finance and financial literacy for kids.

Keon works at Kensington Trust Singapore Limited as a Trust & Estate Planning Consultant. He is also the founder and director of Legasy Planners Pte Ltd, a training company focusing on estate planning and life skill courses.

Keon Chee
Email: keonchee@legasyplanners.com *or*
       keon.chee@kensington-trust.com